Gillian Darley is a writer, journalist and broad-caster, biographer of Octavia Hill, Joan Soane and John Evelyn. She has written widely on architecture and landscape in publications ranging from the *Financial Times* and the *Observer* to the *London Review of Books* and the *Times Literary Supplement*.

Villages of Vision

For R.D. — an enthusiast

Villages of Vision

Gillian Darley

Five Leaves Publications
www.fiveleaves.co.uk

Villages of Vision
(revised and updated edition)
by Gillian Darley

Published in 2007 by Five Leaves Publications
PO Box 8786, Nottingham NG1 9AW
info@fiveleaves.co.uk
www.fiveleaves.co.uk

ISBN: 978 0907123507

First edition published by
The Architectural Press (1975)
and Paladin (1978)

Five Leaves acknowledges financial support
from Arts Council England

Typesetting and design:
Four Sheets Design and Print
Printed in Great Britain

Five Leaves is a member of Inpress
(www.inpressbooks.co.uk),
representing independent publishers

Contents

Acknowledgements

Those who helped with the original edition of this book were thanked more fully then. They included George Cooke, Maurice Craig, Alan Crawford, Fenella Crichton, A.S. Gray, Stephen Heath, Peter Howell, Edward Hubbard, David Lloyd, Eddie McParland, Dorothy Stroud and David Walker.

Improving the detail and scope of the gazetteer, which has been the main object of this revision, means that I have more names to add. Editors of *The Buildings of England*, including some still under preparation, have been exceptionally helpful; Nicholas Antram, James Bettley, Susan and David Neave and the series editor Simon Bradley. The revised volumes of that series, together with those of Scotland, Wales and Ireland, have provided much of my new information. Others who have helped me with specific queries include Susan Palmer at the Soane Museum, David King, Sara Sullivan, Pem Goldschmidt, Kevin Webb, Ben Tindall and Sue Rowlands. Chris Coates' *Utopia Britannica* has also been really useful — a circular process since his gazetteer also drew on mine. Now I am able to repay the favour. Colin Ward and Ken Worpole steered me towards Ross Bradshaw of Five Leaves Publications, and in him I have found an obliging, patient and sympathetic editor and publisher. The jacket has been designed by a master, Richard Hollis.

In the intervening years, some of the cheerful oddities and disarming eccentrics who pepper this book have been celebrated in other media. Jonathan Meades especially turned quite a few into televisual delights. But one person above all deserves my particular thanks and he is, except on the page, a stranger to me. David McKie — McElsewhere — has tirelessly promoted the republication of my book in his column. He even suggested that cars be fitted with special bookshelves "where one could keep a copy of Darley alongside Betjeman and whichever Shell Guides and Pevsners are appropriate for the direction one's taking". David has been my *Guardian* angel and I am absolutely delighted that he has agreed to write a foreword.

2

Photographic Acknowledgements

Foreword

"Whenever you buy a book" said my old history master, "write in it, not just your name, but when you bought it, and where." So thanks to him I know exactly when *Villages of Vision* came into my life; in the Charing Cross Road, London, in August 1982, just before we left for a holiday in Northumberland and the Scottish borders; a holiday which, but for Gillian Darley, would not have brought us to Ford, the creation of benevolent Lady Waterford (of whose frescoes, Gillian Darley tells us, the visiting Ruskin so disapproved, and of whom she prints an enchanting picture) or its near neighbour Etal, or wholly delightful Dirleton in East Lothian. Since when, the number of journeys enriched by this book, the deviations from tedious trunk roads it has occasioned, and the number of notions for inclusion in books or columns it has provoked, are beyond any counting.

It must have travelled thousands of miles in the glove pockets of a succession of cars or clutched in hot hands when walking, and gradually over the years my good old Granada edition reached the autumn of its life and, tree-like, started to shed its leaves. The section which begins with the creation of Nuneham Courtenay by Lord Harcourt ("described tartly by Walpole as 'civil and sheepish', he died that most British of all deaths, falling into a well by rescuing his dog") and concludes with pictures of George Dance's cottages at East Stratton and sagging rooflines of "unique and completely eccentric" houses at Marford, Flintshire, were the first to part company with the rest, and gradually the book has divided itself into five or six separate chunks, having to go on their travels encased in a rubber band. The book has been thumbed too often, re-read too assiduously, loved too well; and now, Ross Bradshaw and Five Leaves having repaired the neglect of previous publishers, here, just in time to celebrate my 25-year association with it, is a *Villages of Vision* in a perfect state of repair and eager to get on the road.

And, better still, with a richer gazetteer than before, as well as new creations to be explored: Lightmoor at Telford for instance, and the Joseph Rowntree Trust's village for the elderly at New Earswick. That means more places now where as you read you can make a note to go there some time soon; and more names to lodge in your memory, as the name Blaise Hamlet did when I first read Gillian Darley, ("without doubt the prime example of the Picturesque village pure" she calls it: how could one resist a sign-post pointing to that?) enabling me to redeem a dull day in Bristol by discovering yet another dream brought to reality. Of course it rather betrays the purpose of *Villages of Vision* to look at it merely as a book to travel with. Essentially it's the story, written with wonderfully easy scholarship, of attempts by the bright and the not-so-bright, the rich and the not-so-rich, the inspired and here and there the woefully uninspired, to create model communities, communities designed (Talbot Village near Bournemouth, for instance: the work of two rich, philanthropic, and more than a little bossy, Victorian sisters) to redeem the moral and spiritual as well as the physical lot of the poor, or communities which simply aimed to be different from everywhere else. Sometimes the motives of the creators were at root religious; sometimes, as with Whiteley Village, the legacy of the great department store tycoon and tyrant, William Whiteley, philanthropy was inter-woven with self-aggrandisement; sometimes, as with Robert Owen's mixed bag of creations, or the mostly doomed enterprises of the Chartists, or that source of so much early 20th century out-rage, Whiteway in Gloucestershire, the impetus was political-cum-ideological.

Perhaps, as my old history master did not say, one should after a number of years make a note in favourite books about what they've done for you. This book introduced me not just to Ford and Blaise Hamlet and Whiteley Village and the Talbot sisters, but also to extraordinary Lowther in Cumbria, which began to open up the history of one of England's most powerful, most fas-cinating and least scrupulous families; to William Madocks' visionary, never-completed, Tremadog (Tremadoc) on the Caernarfonshire coast; and to the industrial village, less famous because more modest than Titus Salt's Saltaire, which Colonel Akroyd MP built on the fringes of Halifax and modestly named Akroydon. One day I hope it will take me to such other Darleyesque destinations as Somerleyton and Thorpeness,

Suffolk, and Heronsgate near Rickmansworth, which was once O'Connorville, named after the most charismatic and craziest of the Chartist leaders; or even Tyrellspass, in Westmeath, created by a woman whose memorial in the church, Gillian Darley tells us, contains what I suppose was then regarded as the highest tribute anyone could have paid her: "gifted with a masculine understanding" it says. Darley has an unfailing eye for such details. What a pleasure her book has been all these years! And can now continue to be.

David McKie

Introduction to the New Edition

I can't quite believe how much I have enjoyed returning to this subject. The original text was written over thirty years ago and I have left it as it was published in paperback in 1978, with just a handful of factual corrections. If I was writing *Villages of Vision* now, it would be different but not necessarily better.

Most of my effort has, therefore, gone into revising and updating the gazetteer. In doing so I have unearthed dozens more schemes ranging from neat little places which were built to give self-respect and decent living conditions to working men and women to tentative experimental settlements where visionary, or even moonstruck, folk gathered with the hope and intention of setting new and inspiring models for society to follow.

I cannot include the many high quality local authority housing schemes, in particular those small cottage groups that were built across the country in the interwar and post-war years. Standing behind them, more often than not, were the Garden Cities; before them, the New and Expanded Towns. Since *Villages of Vision* was first published the march of the volume house builders, always obedient to a perceived "market" and driven by government demographic forecasts, has gathered pace. Their bucolic vision goes no further than the choice of place and road names. Good design, that rare outcome, only follows if "at least one agency — landowner, local authority, social landlord or developer — has strong aspirations... and the resources to deliver it."[1]

The best of the villages discussed in these pages can now, more than ever, be seen as exemplary. Many have been designated Conservation Areas and their buildings listed, which provides, in theory at least, a measure of statutory protection. With the rapid spread of owner occupation, these are essential controls on people's understandable wish to personalise their cottage or house — by doing so destroying its special features, to the detriment of the wider whole. Other measures too have played their part in preserving the character of the planned village. Port Sunlight would be no model

7

without its landscape setting; as housing there passed out of the hands of (the former) Unilever, the successor company agreed to be responsible for maintenance throughout the village, in perpetuity. The regeneration of Creswell colliery village, taking six years and the expenditure of many million pounds — including Heritage Lottery Fund grant aid — means that it is once again a model settlement, though mining ceased in 1991. There are dozens of other examples. Villages can speak for themselves, expressing pride in their past as in their present; the internet gives them a new voice, and brings them closer, regardless of the remoteness of their physical location.

Looking ahead, the imperatives both remain the same and differ wildly. To design innovatory small settlements which are physically and socially coherent remains a challenge; there have been all too many failures or curtailed schemes.[2] Where architectural and environmental quality is concerned, design coding and assessment (before and after the event) can play their part.[3] Yet it always falls to individuals, tenacious people with a sense of purpose, to set the pace and the objectives for themselves — just as they have always done. As a result currently there are developments being built to ambitious ecological and green standards, some which embrace the possibilities offered by wireless networking, others aiming to plough soaring development values back into the community itself (just as the Garden Cities planned to do) or designed for a given group, such as the disabled, the elderly or those seeking spiritual support.

In 1785 the Moravians at Fairfield established a successful self-sufficient settlement and in the early twentieth-century some of their land provided an ideal site for one of the earliest co-partnership housing schemes. Having seen what Samuel Greg provided for his workpeople at Styal, one of his sons was inspired, half a century later, to plan an idealistic industrial village of his own, Bollington. The original models often suggested a further step or adaptation. It is notable that contemporary initiatives for a thoughtful return to the design, sustainability and social mix of new communities are being led by several bodies with more than a century of experience, such as the Joseph Rowntree Housing Trust (part of the Joseph Rowntree Foundation) and the Bournville Village Trust, and largely in more urban areas, the Peabody and Guinness Trusts.

Quaker industrialists put their principles, their "excess of moral energy" as Andrew Martin neatly terms it, into solid practice. Their vision demonstrably changed the way we live. Since 2001 the Bournville Village Trust has been involved in planning (and more importantly still, in managing) a new "urban village" now under construction at Lightmoor, Telford. The development is pledged to follow guidelines for "lifetime living" which have been set by the Joseph Rowntree Foundation. The objective is to "push the boundaries"; to exceed energy saving specifications, to introduce sustainable drainage, flexible tenure and new standards, of specification, layout and social integration. For its part the Joseph Rowntree Housing Trust has built the first of an intended series of communities for the elderly (at New Earswick) and now plans a substantial model village, Derwenthorpe, outside York. Thirty years after the first edition of this book, the exemplary nature of the best model villages is, if anything, clearer still.

Yet from the rest, a delicious stew of crankiness, utopian thinking, architectural purity, philanthropic impulse and enlightened expediency, came a wild variety of outcomes. The only certain conclusion is that there will be more.

GD
London,
September 2007

Notes

1. CABE Housing Audit 2007, p. 51.
2. For example, in the late 1980s and 1990s, Tircoed Forest Village outside Swansea; Lightmoor, guided by the Town and Country Planning Association, a self built hamlet outside Telford; Crickhowell televillage. The neo-classical estate village designed by John Simpson for the owner of Upper Donnington, near Andover, failed to get planning permission.
3. The Prince of Wales's Poundbury in Dorset, which emphasises vernacular forms and materials, is to be followed by a second scheme. The "Scottish Poundbury" is planned on a 71 acre site close to Cumnock in Ayrshire and was part of the 2007 rescue package for Dumfries House.

Introduction to Original Edition

The more we retreat into homebound self-sufficiency and isolation, the more we hear of "the community". Cities are being increasingly broken down into manageable village-type units while, ironically, many villages disintegrate into extended housing estates as the small market town becomes the overspill town, and its neighbouring villages become absorbed. But the truly rural village retains an aura of attainable community, still representing a combination of rural escapism and human significance, an oasis into which the city people crawl thereby contributing to its disintegration.

Many thousands of villages have evolved out of traditional patterns, but, virtually ignored, many hundreds more bear virtually no relation to this development. These are the planned settlements in Britain, estate villages, industrial, religious or political communities especially, which are the subject-matter of this book. The builders of all these villages took as a basic assumption the feasibility of building and creating an immediate community and it is these model villages which have instigated, and been the testing ground, for the appearance and planning of much of the small domestic architecture good or bad which surrounds us wherever we go, in this country, in America, Europe or the developed countries of the world: an architecture we hardly know. The fact that housing estates in Britain, built in the 1920s and 1930s, consist of acres of latticed windows and half-timbered gables, that the most recent new towns are planned on the unit of the "village", that community, communes and community politics are all terms of the moment, all points to the crucial importance of the village; be it in visual, social or political terms.

Many different forms of planned community are discussed here, both those that remained on paper and those that did ultimately materialise. The common denominator is the definition "village" — though I have expanded it to include hamlets and

10

places with several thousand inhabitants — the arbitrary quality of my choice is underlined by the woolly dictionary definition of the term. All those I have chosen are the product of a particular vision, social or architectural, occasionally both, and all attempt to resolve the anomaly of the artificial creation of a community, which replaces the subtly interwoven strands and patterns of a traditional settlement with an "instant" alternative.

Village life has represented the fulfilment of an ideal on many levels over a long period. Whether it has been the positive picture of a self-sufficient community, the semi-utopian vision of country life or merely the visual charm of a cottage group — village green and church spire — the pervasiveness of this picture has affected writers, painters, politicians and reformers who have contrasted these values against the inverted standards commonly attributed to city life. Country villages in the traditional mould served as a convenient pipedream and were seldom exposed to closer scrutiny by those subscribing to the vision.

Model villages were originally almost entirely the creation of the landowning classes; usually they were "closed" villages, under the sole ownership of one man. An ancient collection of disintegrating hovels would be removed from the parkland and replaced by a pristine new line of cottages. This was contemporary with the era of the great "improvements" of park and estate in the eighteenth century, when the building of garden architecture, temples, grottoes and hermitages was at its height. Under changing aesthetic conditions this continued into the nineteenth century, as the hermitage became the *cottage orné* and the *cottage orné* became the Picturesque village. The attitudes were constant if the buildings changed and the village remained just another decorative appendage. The Picturesque, the term which became associated with the conscious prettification of villages, meant, by implication, the overriding importance of style and associations. The cottage might still be a hovel with earth floors, a single room and mud walls but disguised under thick thatch, its windows darkened by the heavy mullions and latticework and the walls masked by luxuriant creepers — the text books even ordained which variety — its owner could proudly designate himself a man of "Picturesque Sensibility".

These extremes provoked reaction towards the mid-century in the form of practical building manuals — emphasising construction not style — and, most important, in the surveys and reports

11

on conditions in villages, which had not seen positive innovations in living conditions for generations. Where estates were administered by conscientious landowners they began to turn their attention to bettering standards and many prosperous Victorians accompanied their new mansions with a village, underlining the fact that they had "arrived" in style.

Beside the movement to improve the conditions for country people, and the occasional attempts by political or religious groups to provide communities founded on idealism, there was a parallel awareness in industrial areas. Here equal poverty was accentuated by the rigours of working conditions under relatively new circumstances, those of the industrial slum. Here too the production of reports and recommendations by hygiene reformers and others induced change and prompted legislation, although often long after the event.

To produce a facsimile of a traditional pattern, such as the village, is a gamble and a very doubtful one. The theorists whose writings abounded with schemes veering from the hare-brained to the potentially workable fell foul of many obstacles and the higher the aims of the community builder, the further they might fall. The energies of these utopian thinkers, Robert Owen chief among them, were hardly justified by the immediate results — yet many of the ideas lay dormant and in a more advanced social climate could be readopted. Advance was very slow — the eighteenth-century model village could hardly fail to be an improvement on its antecedent, but it was still far short of the minimum standards recognised in the nineteenth century. Similarly, industrial experiments were often merely marginal improvements, concentrating in early days on better education and facilities than the norm. Inevitably each step advanced the standards and gradually the aspirations of the social reformers were realised.

Allied to the comparatively simple aims of improved housing and conditions came the far more complex theories of environmental community reform which the village builders of the late nineteenth century, and early twentieth, attempted to voice through their creations. Here, by effecting revolution in environment, was one way to influence future living conditions. All idealists of varying persuasions, they set precedents and provided practical examples of workable communities which had immense influence abroad and in this country.

Occasionally time has served to blur the motives of those who set up model communities — they were sometimes less crystalline than we might imagine and expediency often hovered nearby. In industry reasonable housing was the best insurance of a constant workforce.

Planned villages, and more important still, the concept of village community, became even more important in the early years of this century. The Garden City movement was based on both visual and social elements of the village and the genesis of the 1930s speculative detached villa is the best proof of the way in which so many innovations of the early model villages, themselves based on the vernacular, insinuated themselves into design vocabulary. Ribbon development — unplanned, cheaply constructed housing — is the outcome of a long historical sequence and at the same time is the absolute negation of all hopes; the loss of community finalised.

"At Rievaulx Abbey, Yorkshire" by Roger Fenton. This early photograph, taken during the 1850s, captures in its natural state much of the imagery that the Picturesque movement had previously tried to recreate

13

The tendency to adopt architectural styles of extreme irrelevancy — the epitome of which must be the Jacobethan railway station — is a reflection of escapist tendencies which range from mock Gothic through to Tudor eaves in suburbia. All are evasions of reality, conformity and rationality which express, in fact, the same tendencies as the creation of fake villages and the recreation of rural life out of context. Their importance lies in the symbolism and associative qualities they imply. If the sense of community can be induced as readily as the authentic touch of age, the model village builders will have succeeded in their aims.

Stifling paternalism, the charge levelled at many of the most ambitious philanthropic creations, is the quality that strikes us most unfavourably today and which, with its irrelevancy to the welfare state, seems most archaic. It is, however, important to view these villages in the spirit in which they were built, through contemporary comment and reaction, and not in the light of hindsight. Without this perspective, distortion is inevitable.

Apart from the many communities built over the last two and a half centuries on the basis of the ideas already outlined, architects today retain a very strong interest in the small community — whether in the neighbourhood units of the new towns or in a constant attempt to elevate the housing estate into a more worthy environment for an advanced age.

Running through the recent story of villages of vision is an enduring thread of idiosyncratic settlements, tipis and woodland huts in far corners of the country, whose tenacious founders have fought to convince the planning system of their rights to continue their unconventional existance.

Villages of Vision is an attempt to link the practical and the ideal. By describing the way in which villages have been created, from widely differing motives, and their form, and setting this against the ideal and the popular visions of community life, it is clear how interconnected the various threads are. Little attention has been paid to the evolution of the environment we are so blindingly familiar with — many well informed eyes seem blinkered, even shut, in this field — and this is an attempt at a remedy.

Chapter 1

The Park
Overtakes the Village

Gathered at the gates of many of the great eighteenth-century mansions, shut out from the vast acres of parkland, are small groups of identical cottages. They are the result of "emparking", a word the period made its own, and the presence of such villages is one pointer to the existence of the great wealth that was shielded behind the walls and fences of the new estates.

Emparking often involved the removal of entire communities and, therefore, their rehousing elsewhere or in a planned settlement nearby. The additional embellishments to the newly built mansions of the Whig supremacy were being treated with increased architectural sophistication in their design, and so the village itself became an object of interest and gave a foretaste of the magnificence of the mansion beyond. Sometimes the areas taken over — aided by the law in the form of the enclosures — had been scattered with cottages before they became the pleasing vistas of the park or the serpentine form of an artificial lake. As the eighteenth century progressed, more and more of these were torn down and their occupants rehoused (in the more fortunate cases) in a "model" village well out of sight of the windows of the great house; for it was not yet deemed suitable to encourage groups of villagers to wander decoratively over the greensward.

The signs today of such devastation are clear enough; an isolated church, marooned in the park or close by the house, and a line of uniform cottages by the gates or on a nearby road. Instead of the signs of a community which has gradually evolved in an organic fashion, unplanned and made up of random elements, the cottages are immediately obvious, built from the same materials and placed symmetrically.

In the early part of the century rehousing the villagers posed no great problem; cottages could be placed side by side in parallel lines but as taste assumed an ever-increasing importance for the landed classes, so the job of rebuilding a village was more frequently passed to an architect, as opposed to a master builder, who would then bring the further reaches of urban sophistication to bear on remote rural communities.

The inner sanctum of the elevated and moneyed of the period was the Society of Dilettanti, founded in 1733. It gave rise to a widespread artistic sophistication and meant that many of the

Plan by George London, c1699, for Henderskelfe village (Castle Howard) showing it, bottom left, as a formal group, sixteen cottages and a central church. Never built

landed aristocracy, the men who held sway in every sphere — commerce, finance and government — were well aware of developments in architecture. When constructing the great mansions which demonstrated their position and wealth they encouraged those twin figures of prominence, the architect and the landscape gardener, to indulge their every whim in the interests of fashion, stylishness and taste. Humanitarian considerations came low on the list of priorities.

From the mid-century onwards the villages built ceased, on the whole, to be the mundane solutions to a housing problem that they had previously been, but took on a new importance in the aesthetic sense. Several leading architects turned their hands to planning a village or two, and before long the architectural amateur was at work himself.

The motives of the village builders of the eighteenth century went little beyond aesthetic dabbling and, perhaps, a faint suspicion of expediency. Philanthropy was not merely unfashionable, it was eccentric. Philanthropists then tended to be men risen from the lower classes — merchants who repaid their debts by endowing schools and almshouses. From the upper end of the social scale the labouring classes were viewed as an amorphous presence; not yet even an embarrassment.

In any case the villagers could only improve their situation if they were rehoused; at this period living conditions had stagnated and bad housing became worse. It must be emphasised that even the least imaginative and traditional of the new villages was a departure which took practical building and planning into a new field — that of the small rural community. Previously, planned towns had been those of particular commercial or ecclesiastical importance, but planning had never been extended to the minor country settlement. From this point onwards, the village could assume new importance and the cottage a new significance in the history of building and architecture.

To appreciate the innovation that these villages represented it is important to consider the quality of building that the newly constructed, improved cottages replaced. Clear regional distinctions can be drawn between the poorest, least-developed areas, mostly in the north, and the relatively advanced and agriculturally rich Midland and south. In the north, economic factors had often meant that innovations in building, as in many other fields, were introduced up to a century later.

Until the eighteenth century the chief distinctions to be seen in vernacular architecture were regional; the various materials and adaptations in the buildings were local. Leaving aside the church, which was often the sole survivor of an earlier period, the notable buildings in each village were, obviously, the almshouses and the school, which were the contribution of the gentry. Cottages, on the other hand, were provided either by the parish for its poor, or by the inhabitants themselves — in either case they were cheaply and simply constructed and not likely to last indefinitely.

Taking the beginning of the eighteenth century as a rough watershed, social changes and political upheavals, above all the enclosures which were gathering momentum, occasioned various alterations in the traditional pattern of settlement. In "open" villages, that is, those not belonging to a single landowner, the few cottages built by an individual for himself, and not owned by a middleman as was usually the case, stood on his own land, or, in the case of squatters, on common land. On agricultural land farmers built cottages for their own labourers, an alternative to the earlier system whereby the single man would be given a room in the farmhouse. The replacement, the tied cottage, in some senses contributed to a new independence for the employee, no longer living under the same roof as his employer, yet also signalled the way to the many abuses inherent in such a situation of obligation and insecurity of tenure.

In addition to newly built cottages, the eighteenth century saw the conversion of outbuildings, stabling or storage sheds into housing — a movement which has now come full circle. Also at this period the first terraces of cottages were constructed, their form based on these farm buildings.

The materials a builder used obviously would depend upon his income. Housing for the vicar and farmer tended to be in brick, with a tiled roof, long before cottages could be built from such materials. Mud and stud building was gradually replaced by brick as the century progressed and at the same time, the arrangement of the rooms became more developed, with more space. Single-storey houses were enlarged by the addition of another room, made possible by flattening the pitch of the roof and lightening the construction, while two-storey houses made use of the roof space by introducing dormer windows. Two social developments helped to cement the community; these were the introduction of the inn and the shop, both of which seem to have come into being in the late seventeenth century.

It was not in terms of architecture that the first model villages broke new ground, but in terms of planning. Vernacular architecture had effectively ceased to evolve by the early eighteenth century, and in many cases the new villages merely echoed the traditional building of their areas, using local materials and providing little or no additional space. But instead of the original diffuse and irregular village, houses were built and laid out symmetrically in systematic rows along the roadside. Their plans echoed the formalism of seventeenth-century gardens, based on Dutch and French prototypes. The advances made by Kent or Bridgeman only came to affect the planning of the village many years later: as always, it remained the poor relation of the park and great house. The earliest plan for a formal village shows clearly how little importance the village had compared to the overall landscaping of the park. George London's plans of c. 1699 for the replacement for Henderskelfe, the Castle Howard estate village, show two alternatives each consisting of sixteen cottages grouped in a circle round the church. Each cottage had a small garden. It is quite a sophisticated design despite the fact that London "might not always come up to the highest pitch of design, yet that might be attributed to the haste he was generally in". Yet although the park was magnificently landscaped, the village was never built. The existing Castle Howard estate villages are much later.

At Milton Abbas only the landscaping and siting indicated more sophisticated planning. Its decade, the 1770s, marks the midway stage between the formal and the Picturesque. Lord Dorchester's cottages themselves are detached and symmetrical and not notably innovatory, although placed to emphasise the contours of the valley in which they lie.

Elsewhere the situation was usually much the same; spanking new model villages left the root problems of accommodation for the rural poor virtually untouched. The country labourer was regarded as being impervious to the stresses of tremendous overcrowding. Families were usually large and in the north the animals were still sharing the living space long after they had been banished to the outbuildings further south.

With the spread of pattern books, from the 1770s onwards, vernacular traditions became suppressed by standardisation of

1712 map of Chippenham

building via the printed page. Advances in building techniques and the use of new materials also led to a more generalised approach. A little later, country people also began to feel the effects of architectural sophistication and they ran the risk of finding themselves confined to a Swiss cottage of phenomenal extravagance or a rustic hut of fetching simplicity.

The imposition of academic theory on the necessities of the rural poor is dealt with later, in connection with discussion of the Picturesque, but the gulf which stretched between everyday cottage building in Britain as a whole and the extraordinary excesses of some of the "improvers" cannot be over-emphasised. It was symptomatic of the inverted values which astounded onlookers overseas and with which the nineteenth-century philanthropists and reformers later had to wrestle.

Returning to the early decades of the eighteenth century, in order to observe specifically the first examples of the model village, one finds that several of the earliest planned settlements were in East Anglia, where a large labour force from the land had to be housed and which, because of its advanced and prosperous agricultural economy, reflected the earliest and clearest changes in land settlement of the period.

At Chippenham in Cambridgeshire, Edward Russell, first Lord of the Admiralty and later Lord Orford, was one of the first to begin emparking.[2] In 1696 he began the work and by 1712 had produced a map to illustrate the resultant changes. The park and artificial lake had swallowed up half the village high street and another road which intersected it, and a licence to block these roads had been granted by 1702. Only two cottages remained isolated, at the furthest point of the park, which by now comprised most of the available land, Russell having bought 500 acres from five men and having taken over the common land. He made restitution by giving grazing rights for the villagers' cattle — but he carefully specified that this did not extend to sheep — on fenlands which had been common land in the sixteenth century. About fifty houses, a few new built, the church and a fine charity school of red brick with great windows along its length, constituted the village of 1712. It was about one half of its previous size.

Lord Orford's elegant school, converted from an earlier house at Chippenham c. 1708

New Houghton in Norfolk, built c. 1729, typical double cottages

This process was happening all over the country — although the same regard was not necessarily paid to the welfare of the villagers. At New Houghton in Norfolk, the first model village to be built, Sir Robert Walpole constructed a couple of lines of sturdy cottages at the gates of his mansion, Houghton Hall, one of the greatest of the Whig palaces. The church standing isolated in the park signified the disappearance of an earlier village and the spot is marked by a stone memorial.

The approach to the house is formed by a long avenue which, as it nears the gates, is broken to reveal a number of well-built whitewashed cottages standing either side of the road. They are two-storeyed buildings with black pantiled roofs, widely spaced and with particularly large gardens behind. Furthest from the house are some single-storeyed almshouses which, together with two larger farmhouses, complete the village. It is known from the parish register that foundations for the first two houses were being dug in 1729: Walpole had evidently moved fast to ensure that the elegant aspect of the hall would not suffer from the unsightly clutter of poor shacks which would have surrounded it.

Despite the peremptory fashion in which such removals were carried out, better housing did definitely result, perhaps more often by accident than by design. New Houghton seems to have been one such early example of a genuine advance in conditions. The tenants there were housed in excellent cottages, with ample space and a reasonable amount of land of their own to cultivate. Norfolk, owing to its several crusading agricultural reformers, notably Thomas Coke of Holkham, soon became noted for its superior housing conditions compared to the neighbouring counties.[3] Landowners could afford to provide their employees with reasonable accommodation on the returns from their profitable farming methods.

At Well Vale, Lincolnshire, the site of another rebuilt village, a new current can be seen to emerge. This is the first case where undisguised aesthetics come into play: the cottages were placed outside the new park, but the church, though rebuilt, was left inside, to function as a garden ornament, visible from the windows of James Bateman's mansion.[4] It was reconstructed as a classical temple, to be viewed over the long vistas of grass as a pleasing decorative feature. Carried out about 1725, this was an extremely early indication of things to come and presaged the time when cottages would be thatched follies and their inhabitants little more than an exotic species. Here, the villagers, having tramped to church, found themselves in a stark neoclassical temple rather than the fusty well-worn interior of their old village church. They must have felt very ill-disposed to listen to the sermon.

The status achieved through conscientious attention to aesthetic mores in building was enough to spur landowners on to immense efforts, often including legal battles and vast expenditure. It was never an easy task to raze a village to the ground. Leases had to expire and many voices be silenced. Milton Abbas had an obstinate solicitor, Nuneham Courtenay a disgruntled vicar, to question the passing of feudal decisions affecting the fate of several hundred people.

The wholesale shuffling around of communities by landowners was treated very much as a matter of course in circles not directly affected. One typical traveller, Bray, described the process leading up to the rebuilding of Kedleston village, in terms betraying no surprise or disapproval:

"In the front stood a village with a small inn for the accommodation of those who came to drink of a medicinal well... the village is removed (not destroyed as is too often done), the road is thrown to a considerable distance, out of sight of the house, the scanty stream is increased into a large piece of water and the ground disposed in the finest order."[5]

He is, of course, making a reasonable point; many villagers displaced by emparking had to gather up their possessions and move elsewhere. The assurance with which this, and similar operations, were carried out was supreme and in no way exceptional — nobody had the power to stand in the landowner's way, and at most the scheme could be deferred a year or two.

The surroundings of the great seats were being laid out in readiness for dynasties, not for one generation of rich and successful men, and if the full results could not be seen in their lifetime, while the parks matured and the landscape assumed its new form, that was of little concern. It took a foreign observer, such as Prince Pueckler-Muskau, to observe the oddities of this nation who thought nothing of attaching a newly built feudal village to their front gates as just another possession among countless others.

The only surprise is that the hand of the architect is not felt earlier in village building. The architect, and his collaborator the landscape gardener, were respected professional men kept constantly busy with building and emparking. The construction of the new villages, however, was left in the hands of capable master builders, for as yet the village was not considered sufficiently visually important to warrant the time and effort of the architect. From the moment the architect's contribution was felt, cottage building and small-scale planning schemes had been designated aesthetically significant, and it is essential to realise how crucial was this awakening. It is less the precise contribution to village building of the early architect-designed settlements that is important, than the elevation of such work into a class with the great houses and public buildings.

There was no architect concerned in the rebuilding at Nuneham Courtenay; the style is the local vernacular, in no way particularly exceptional, and yet the hand proves to be the client's own.* It is very similar in the essentials of the cottage

---

*See Airs, in bibliography.

24

Pairs of identical cottages along the Henley-Oxford road at Nuneham Courtenay, Goldsmith's Deserted Village, built during the early 1760s

design to a pattern drawn up by Nathaniel Kent in one of the very earliest of practical building manuals.[6] Now the local builder could furnish himself with the designs and expertise on the page and carry out the latest passing whim without looking further for advice or instruction.

Nuneham Courtenay is one of the best known model villages; its two lines of red-brick and timbered cottages stand behind their grass verges on the road from London to Oxford. Also, owing to some exhaustive detective work,[7] it has been proved without doubt to be the original for Goldsmith's poem *The Deserted Village* — the most outspoken protest in literature against the high-handed reorganisation of village life around the great estates. A rejoinder to Goldsmith's attack came from William Whitehead, Poet Laureate, with *The Removal of the Village at Nuneham Courtenay*,[8] so that, together with the ample evidence on the ground of the disposition of the earlier village, the affair has been recorded blow by blow.

Lord Harcourt, the builder of Nuneham Courtenay, was holder of various offices of state and had been given the privilege of becoming the proxy husband of Queen Charlotte on behalf of George III while he was Ambassador to Mecklenburg Strelitz. He was reputed to have an advanced social conscience for the period, particularly in his attitude to the Irish matters with which he had to deal, and was a member of an elite artistic circle. Described tartly by Walpole as "civil and sheepish", he died that most British of all deaths, falling into a well while rescuing his dog.

It was in 1761 that Lord Harcourt embarked on the landscaping of his garden in the style befitting a man of taste, and the previous year he had begun the removal of the old village of Newnham Courtenay (the name was changed on the rebuilding) which was situated on the hill-top behind the newly built Palladian mansion. The village street became the path along which visitors could stroll to observe the valley below, and the church, "the decent church that topt the neighbouring hill" of Goldsmith's poem, was soon to be metamorphosed into a classical temple which was built near the site of the medieval village church. The graveyard was flattened and the congregation, still responsible for the upkeep of the church, now had to walk a mile and a half to the comfortless and stark classical temple in which they were expected to worship.

However, Lord Harcourt was certainly not the monster his detractors, Goldsmith particularly, painted him. Rumours that he built a grotto from the bones of the dispossessed villagers that he had massacred were unfounded, and Goldsmith's stand is closer to an allegory on a more general issue. One old lady who features in the poem at length was allowed to stay in her cottage, in the midst of the newly constructed landscape garden with its Claudean pines and carefully manipulated vistas. Amidst so much artifice she was inevitably used as a convenient epitome of rural virtues, and in the time of the second Lord Harcourt, a friend of Rousseau (who had spent some time at Nuneham), she was commemorated by a poem fixed to the tree by the site of her cottage. The treatment accorded the memory of the old lady, a sort of cultivated relic of the old way of life — despite the abrupt removal of her neighbours — is in keeping with an appreciation of the poetic essence of pastoral life.

Meanwhile, as the refinements of landscaping became apparent in Harcourt's park, his new village on the turnpike was taking shape. By autumn of 1761 the two parallel lines of cottages with their inn (the Harcourt Arms, not surprisingly) were completed.

Before long Nuneham Courtenay was a regular port of call for travellers on their way to Oxford and the West, showing a standard of neatness and advanced planning which occasioned considerable interest. In 1788 Stebbing Shaw wrote of the village in the following terms:

> "[it]... consists of about 20 neat houses, at equal distances on the road; these are divided into two separate dwellings so that 40 families may here, by the liberal assistance of his lordship enjoy the comforts of industry under a wholesome roof who otherwise might have been doomed to linger out their days in the filthy hut of poverty."

He carries on to Abingdon where by contrast he "received a most terrible impression... a narrow lane, unworthy of the name of a street, made too almost impassable by the confines of dirt and water". This contrast underlines the universal impression Nuneham seems to have made at the time of its creation — dirt and poverty replaced by order and cleanliness, though whether the old Newnham had been as foul as Abingdon seems unlikely.

Pastor Moritz, passing a few years before, described the "two rows of low neat houses built close to each other and as regular and uniform as a London street". However, he had already been impressed by the order of Kentish villages "where an uncommon neatness in the structure of the houses which in general are built with red bricks and flat roofs, struck me with a pleasing surprise especially when I compared them with the long, rambling, inconvenient and singularly mean cottages of our peasants". The German visitor did not, apart from noting the regularity of the village, have a particularly good reception at Nuneham; "all the doors seemed to be shut and even a light was to be seen only in a few of them. Harcourt Inn was inhospitable" — they could offer him no food or bed, and then slammed the door in his face. He hurried on to Oxford.

The cottages at Nuneham were built in pairs from a mellow red brick, one and a half storeyed, the attic lit by dormer windows. On the gable ends timbering was used which probably came from the earlier cottages, and the odd-shaped lintels also point to this origin. The old cottages which had been adapted for the occupations of the inhabitants were replaced by apparently identical cottages, but provision was made at the back for bakehouses and other necessary outbuildings and workshops without the uniformity of façade being broken.

27

Perhaps the most obvious miscalculation in the village rebuilding was the inflexibility of accommodation; each cottage was divided into two small halves containing four rooms which meant that it was sufficient for a labourer but not for anyone in the professional classes; this left the village particularly dependent on the whims of the landowner and meant that it lacked the social cross-section present in any comparable small country community. This has remained a problem, together with its siting on an increasingly busy road which resulted eventually in the doors being moved to the sides of the cottages.

Nuneham Courtenay later became the scapegoat for a lengthy controversy on the subject of such planned villages. William Gilpin, early theoretician of the Picturesque movement and whose travels consisted principally of journeys to chosen situations which showed enough of the necessary Picturesque elements to merit a visit by the cognoscenti, wrote:

"The village of Nuneham was built... with that regularity which perhaps gives the most convenience to the dwellings of men. For this we readily relinquish the picturesque idea. Indeed I question whether it were possible for a single hand to build a picturesque village. Nothing contributes to it more than the various styles in building. When all these little habitations happen to unite harmoniously and to be connected with the proper appendages of a village the winding road, a number of spreading trees, a rivulet and a bridge and a spire to bring the whole to an apex — the village is complete."[9]

Nuneham has none of these and Uvedale Price followed Gilpin with a fierce criticism of the village which, as he saw it, had neither irregularity, surprise elements, evocative landscape or any other of the traditional ingredients which the Picturesque thinkers took to be essential to beauty in the village. "An obvious and easy method of rebuilding a village," Price wrote,

"(and one which unfortunately has been put in practice) is to place the houses on two parallel lines, to make them of the same size and shape, and at equal distance from each other. Such a methodical arrangement saves all further thought and invention: but it is hardly necessary to say that nothing can be more formal and insipid... it seems to me, that symmetry... is less suited to humbler scenes and buildings."[10]

The final word comes from John Claudius Loudon (noted equally as gardener, architect and theorist) — "cottages crowded together in a continued row have too much of the appearance, and have in fact, many of the inconveniences and nuisances, of a dirty back street in a country town", again "in villages the houses ought never to be put down in rows, even though detached, unless the ground and other circumstances are favourable for a strictly regular or symmetrical congregation of dwellings. There is not a greater error in forming artificial villages... than always having one side of the buildings parallel with the road." It is no surprise when further on he singles out Nuneham Courtenay as a village built "too like rows of street houses".[11]

The aesthetic arguments are less peripheral than they might seem, for they single out precisely those elements against which the Picturesque village was to react.

From the late eighteenth century onwards the Picturesque village was considered the perfect antithesis to this type of logic and symmetry, which was expressive of a rational age and constituted anathema to one more interested in the emotions and the response of the sensations to a situation; in short, the Romantic era.

As the landscaped park moved, under the direction of Humphry Repton and his sons, towards a closer dependence on its natural sources, so the village, in the words of Price and Gilpin, veered back to a traditional model — the pattern of village green, scattered thatched and overgrown cottages, watched over by the church spire. This evocative pastoral scene appealed to the Picturesque theorists of the eighteenth century, just as it continued to enslave the architects of the Garden City movement and their successors.

However, before tracing the progress of the ideas of the Picturesque village designers and builders, it is important to consider how the architects already referred to, more practised in grandiose town planning schemes or the construction of mansions, approached the problem and, in addition, how that ever-increasing body, the architectural amateurs, turned their hands to building their own estate villages.

Notes

1. See *English Cottages and Farmhouses*, The Arts Council, London, 1975.
2. A. Spufford, *A Cambridgeshire Community from Settlement to Enclosure:* Leicester University, Department of English Local History, Occasional Paper 20, 1965.
3. J.C. Loudon, *An Encyclopaedia of Agriculture,* 1831. Includes a county by county survey of housing conditions.
4. Gervase Jackson-Stops, "Well Vale", *Country Life*, 14, 21 December 1972.
5. W. Bray, *Tour through some of the Midland Counties into Derbyshire and Yorkshire,* 1777.
6. Nathaniel Kent, *Hints to Gentlemen of Landed Property,* 1775. This was not the first practical pattern book, but the first specifically to give plans for labourers' cottages.
7. Mavis Batey, *Nuneham Courtenay*, reprinted from *Oxoniensia*, 33, 1968.
8. Written c. 177I; final words in the controversy were those written by Arthur Parsey in *The Deserted Village Restored,* 1815, referring to the good works of the 2nd Earl Harcourt, the friend of Rousseau and arch-Romantic.
9. William Gilpin — one of his Picturesque tours, 1770s. It is interesting to note that in the time of the 2nd Earl, W.S. Gilpin was brought in to build Picturesque cottages near the original village pond.
10. Uvedale Price, *Essay on the Picturesque*, 1794.
11. John Claudius Loudon, *Encyclopaedia of Cottage, Farm and Villa Architecture and Furniture*, 1836, edition with supplement, 1842. Loudon's wife, Jane, wrote in her memoirs that "I never saw Mr Loudon more pleased than when a highly respectable gardener once told him that he was living in a new and most comfortable cottage which his master had built for him."

Chapter 2

Architects of the Artificial Village: Professional and Amateur

In the later half of the eighteenth century the effects of the Agrarian Revolution were being felt to the full; previously independent freeholders were forced, after the enclosures, to look for work on the land and in cottage and rural industries. The new villages, such as those discussed in the previous chapter, were absorbing some of these landless families and held out the prospect of secure accommodation, the best available, under an unswervingly feudal system.

The foundation of small-scale rural industry was an attractive proposition for the landowner, and the building of several villages was commenced with this object. Housing was provided for the sake of expediency and those villagers not involved in the particular manufacture could be absorbed by employment on the estate itself. Harewood, the first of the model villages discussed in this chapter, was one such example; as well as its advantageous position as a coaching stop *en route* for Leeds, it was centred on a newly established ribbon factory which would provide employment and prosperity (although in fact it did not flourish for very long).

It was now also that architects, from *c.* 1760, were required to turn their minds to the design and planning of small-scale rural communities and the type of housing previously considered as totally insignificant, the cottage. But when established and fashionable eighteenth-century architects were approached by landowners to plan and build a village on their estates, their solutions were not inevitably as well tailored to the situation as might

31

have been hoped. They tended to overstep the mark, by ensuring that the complete conception was too grandiose or inappropriate to its situation to be carried out in full. In this chapter various alternative responses to the command "build me a village" are presented, and, in addition, the way in which the architectural amateur, following in the distinguished steps of Lord Burlington, found his own way through the maze of fashion to carry out his own rebuilding.

The unifying thread in the villages constructed by the professional architect at this period was the rational approach they represented; the Picturesque landscape had already been imposed upon the park, but so far the permissible eccentricities of Picturesque architecture were confined to the far corners of the estate. William Kent built some cottages at Castle Hill, but he did not even attempt to make them habitable — from the beginning they were constructed as ruins, an alternative to the interminable sham Gothic heaps of stone littering other landscape gardens. Later, ironically, they were reconditioned as housing — in a period when the cottage and the folly were becoming interchangeable.

The architects with whom this chapter deals drew up grand plans and built with the precepts of Vitruvius and Palladio always before them; they succeeded in imposing brazen incongruity upon the countryside which cleared the way for the far more flamboyant excesses of the next century, at the height of the Picturesque.

Harewood was one case where the owner of the great mansion wished to flank his new house with a village in fitting style; none of the familiar timid lines of neat identical cottages appeared here but a great flourish of sophisticated urban-style architecture on classical lines.

Edwin Lascelles, 1st Earl of Harewood, was a sugar magnate with massive West Indian properties and was using part of his great wealth to set himself up as a landowner on the grandest scale. He commissioned John Carr of York to rebuild both his house and his village — the latter being reconstructed on part of the site of the original village. As at Nuneham Courtenay, the local materials were used, here a dark grey stone with tiled roofs. The houses, which line a T-junction, the downstroke of which continues the avenue out of the park, are built in terraces, with distinctive larger residences for the doctor and agent and arcaded buildings for the ribbon factory on which the economic success of the village depended. Later this was converted back into cottages.

Contemporary with Nuneham, the work being carried out around 1760, the concept could hardly be more different. The scheme shows every sign of a leading architect's hand and in its suave elegance provides a complete contrast to the earlier vernacular estate villages. Carr produced an entirely urban effect, using Palladian detail and linking the housing by giant blank arches — hardly a familiar detail in West Yorkshire cottage building of the period. Yet Harewood is not incongruous, its wide streets fronting the lodge gates are complementary to the scale of the buildings and later planting has also contributed to soften the effect.

The village soon became a noted port of call on tourist routes in that part of the country, and *Jewell's Guide to Leeds*[1] devotes a considerable amount of space to describing Harewood. "The whole of the town is built with fine stone procured from the neighbouring quarries and even the cottages possess a look of neatness bordering upon elegance, while the principal houses assume an air of superiority." He tells of the landscaping carried out at the beginning of the nineteenth century when the streets were lowered and gardens laid out in front of the houses, and mentions that the number of public houses was reduced from six to one (probably owing to depopulation rather than abstinence).

Jewell also recounts the visit of the Grand Duke Nicholas of Russia in 1816 — the same man who made the journey to New Lanark to observe Owen's experiments — who arrived with a party of eighteen. The party dined off gold plate, listened to a concert, and then the Earl of Harewood

> "conducted the whole assemblage through the beautiful village and pleasure grounds to the ancient Castle and Church; at which his Imperial Highness expressed his most unqualified approbation and delight, but particularly so, on seeing every cottager busily engaged in some work of usefulness or improvement on his Lordship's estate. Not less than 200 are regularly employed in this manner..."

We may be sure the villagers had prior warning of the visit.

In his effort to give a small estate village the elegance of a town terrace Carr also modulated the height from block to block, alternating between two and two-and-a-half storeys and two-and-a- half to three. The inn was particularly grand, being on the main route to Leeds, and a school was built in 1768, but the church remained close to the house in its original form. Carr built other estate cottages for Lascelles, and, unique among eighteenth-century architects, designed two terraces of miners' cottages on the Wentworth Woodhouse estate.[2]

Much more incongruously situated and conceived, however, was the great scheme of Lowther village in Westmorland (now Cumbria), the second attempt of the Lowther family to set up a model community on their estates. The first attempt, Lowther New Town, built between 1683 and 1684, was aimed at establishing a successful carpet manufacturing centre. Although it failed in this object, it did at least have the effect of producing some solid housing. Another Lowther project was the Cumberland port of Whitehaven, which was a larger-scale industrial enterprise.

A century later, 1765–73, Sir James Lowther commissioned Robert Adam to draw up plans for his village.[3] Drawings at the Soane Museum show a grandiose plan, twice the size of that

The village built by Carr of York in 1760, lining the approach to the gates of Harewood House. Some cottages are built in the local West Riding of Yorkshire vernacular, others are more sophisticated with flat arches and variations in height to break up the terracing

34

carried out, based on a Greek cross. Had the scheme been completed, a circus would have been formed, but in fact only two closes were built — strangely esoteric architecture in a spot even now inaccessible, but in the eighteenth century a particularly distant corner of Britain. In 1802 Richard Warner wrote in tones of wonder:

"stopped near new village of Lowther to smile at the fantastic incongruity of its plan which exhibits the grandest features of city architecture, the Circus, the Crescent and the Square upon the mean scale of a peasant's cottage. These groups of houses were built for the labourers of Lord Lowther but from their desolate deserted appearance it should seem that no sufficient encouragement has been held out to their inhabitants to continue in them."[4]

The country people of Westmorland must have been surprised by their new village, although the accommodation was reasonable and gardens and communal grass areas were provided. Lowther was Adam's only rural planning exercise to be built.[5]

The rebuilding of Milton Abbas[6] in Dorset was a more complex affair, for it involved the destruction of a sizeable market town with its own grammar school, almshouses, shops, four inns and a brewery. When Joseph Damer MP, later Earl of Dorchester, employed William Chambers to carry out extensive alterations to Milton Abbey, and Lancelot (Capability) Brown to work on the embellishment of its surroundings, he found the straggling village over the garden wall more than he could stand. He suffered constant irritation from pillaging schoolboys and, by the time the removal of the village was in progress, he seemed to have been in a state of mind bordering on persecution mania, which he exhibited not only by flooding the house of an obstinate householder but by even removing the church bells, which he imagined were being rung in defiance of himself. The site of the new village of Milton Abbas, in a deep cleft between the downs, seems to have been the inspired choice of Capability Brown. Exactly which were the respective parts played by Brown and Chambers in the design of the village has not been ascertained, but in a letter[7] written in 1773 by Chambers to his patron he described the village very much in the form in which it was built, thus suggesting that he was at least responsible for the outline of the plan, if not for its execution. Possibly Brown designed the uniform cottage pattern which consisted of attractive whitewashed cottages with thatched roofs in the local Dorset vernacular. The forty cottages are set on either side of a wide main street which slopes down to the valley bottom, bounded by wide grass verges. Formerly each cottage was sheltered by a chestnut tree but these have now been removed as their overhang became excessive and made the cottages dark and damp.

The interiors of the cottages belied the modernity of their careful siting and planning. Most are semi-detached, with four small rooms to each, entered through a common front door. In spite of the original demarcation of these into two halves, at one stage the houses contained four families which meant that perhaps between thirty and forty people inhabited a single cottage. The material of the cottages was traditional "Dorset cob", a combination of chalk, straw, earth and lime plastered on the outside, and the foundations consisted merely of a flat floor of flints. Thus the "model village" and architectural showpiece which was such a scenic attraction was providing very little actual advance on existing conditions, and aesthetic considerations took priority rather than the conscientious bettering of conditions, which in the West Country were particularly poor.

But, however high-handed Damer might have been, he had to abide by the law, and so the rehousing of his tenants had to wait

Lowther Village: a plan drawn up by Robert Adam in the 1760s for a new village to remove housing further from the site of the Castle. Only the left half was built in modified form

the expiry of his tenants' leases and it took until 1786 to effect the removal and complete the effect with a new church and the reconstructed Jacobean almshouses.

In 1791 Fanny Burney visited the village and considered the inhabitants unworthy of their housing and the village as such extremely artificial. She wrote that they "appear rather to be reduced from better days than flourishing in a primitive or natural state" — a comment indicative of the fashionable cult of the primitive, the same that had enshrined old Babs Wyatt the Nuneham shepherdess as an exhibit until she died. Another visitor, Greville, who visited the village with the King in 1794 pronounced it "snugly situated" but reserved most of his attention for the almswomen in their odd pointed hats.

Fanny Burney's comment on the artificiality of Milton Abbas raised the most valid criticism of such villages. The haphazard development of the traditional village leads to a variety and individuality with which no row of starkly identical cottages, however attractive and carefully situated, can compare. Gardens banished to regions behind the houses achieve their neatness at the expense of individuality. Milton Abbas, however, has the restraint of an eighteenth-century town street and, as such, has a particular charm which has never been unappreciated, despite the strictures from the Picturesque theorists and periods when the cottages were allowed to become decrepit and ill-kempt.

Milton Abbas, Dorset, begun in 1773 and completed in 1786, viewed down the main street. The church, also rebuilt, can be seen on the left

Yet Milton Abbas was by no means the last of the formal model villages, and in one case a notable architect carefully drew up plans for such a vernacular village.[8] George Dance's work at East Stratton was highly conventional. He drew up plans for Francis Baring MP for nine pairs of cottages together with additions to the nearby church at Micheldever, as well as that at East Stratton. He based his cottages (dating from 1806) closely on the local vernacular, consisting of brick, timber framing and thatch, and placed them in a line along one side of the road. The plan is entirely symmetrical and it is only the formalism that clearly marks his cottages out from the other traditionally designed houses in the village. Externally there is little which would mark them apart, despite the fact that he drew up careful plans and elevations for each cottage, even sketching in watercolour the exact layout of the garden, cabbage by cabbage. The gardens are ample and the houses semi-detached with a well between every two. Entry to the houses is from the side, through a lean-to porch, and the plans show his careful attention to the practical details of where the coppers and ovens should be placed. The general effect is strictly utilitarian with no alien Picturesque effects, though such touches as sliding wooden window casements are more sophisticated than anything the general run of local builders

Lowther village, housing on a cross plan using two-storeyed vernacular style cottages with projecting bays to break the monotony

might have thought up. It is astonishing to remember that Repton and Nash were building Blaise Hamlet only three years later.

Yet the views of the Picturesque writers were on the way to becoming common currency and the strict linear roadside village was being phased out in favour of the informal grouping around a village green. As well as sentimental connotations the central open area provided a natural focal point for an oval or circular plan, besides offering obvious advantages for recreation and safe playing areas for small children. According to the gospel preached by Price, the village green should stand in front of the church tower, with a winding stream nearby and ancient trees completing the picture; the traditional village was recreated, this time a conscious manipulation of the elements according to newly formulated principles. Not for long could those who fancied themselves to be in step with architectural fashion resist such an onslaught.

Two figures have been noticed as being of importance in eighteenth-century village building — the local builder following vernacular traditions and perhaps the outline suggestions of his client, and the fashionable architect, often imposing urban irrelevancies in remote rural situations. A third, increasingly prominent in the nineteenth century, was the rich amateur who took up both the function of patron and architect. The architectural amateur had a distinguished niche of his own, but with the advent of pattern books on small-scale architecture any local nabob with an interest and familiarity with local traditional building could build himself a village adding his own personal stamp of eccentricity and indulging himself just as he wished.

The product of one such personal interpretation of architecture, here a roadside village in Flintshire (now Clwyd), Marford, has aroused the curiosity of endless passers-by without giving more than the scantest clues to its origins. Between 1805 and 1816 George Boscawen rebuilt the cottages which lined the road to Chester in a unique and completely eccentric form. Replacing the original thatched and mud-walled hovels with stone-tiled housing he remodelled them, each one distinct from the next, achieving a most bizarre effect. The plastered walls are alternately concave or convex, punctuated by windows of every conceivable shape and follow no precedent even in the category of

39

The line of cottages carefully planned by George Dance the younger at East Stratton are dated 1806

One of a pair of identical cottages at Marford built c. 1810. The sagging roof line, curving outer walls and unusual window frames are particularly notable

Gothick oddities. There is no explanation for the bayonets which ornament some of the windows or the wilful curiosities which cover the smithy, the inn and the numerous cottages. The accounts for the building[9] list such items as "iron windows", "circular windows", "Gothic tops" and "pinnacle ornaments" together with more conventional items, but strangest of all is the use of curved roof timbers in order to give a sagging outline which complements the inward and outward curves of the verticals. The curves are taken up again in the ovals, crescent shapes and numerous other variations in window frames, to which are added crosses which are indented on the plaster surfaces, again without explanation, but which are a well-used motif in Gothick follies and sham castles — the phony arrow slit.

Less unconventional perhaps, but in terms of its situation and function somewhat odd, is the stark, neo-classical line of cottages at Belsay, an odd attempt at architectural sophistication in the Northumberland countryside. Belsay Castle is a bleak monument to Greek Revivalism, entirely square without any extraneous detail, and was created by Sir Charles Monck (born Middleton),

View along the terrace of neo-classical cottages which constitutes most of Belsay village

41

owner of the estate, together with William Gell, a topographer and dilettante figure, and the leading local architect John Dobson. It is reasonable to suppose their joint involvement in the village too, during the period 1807–17, for it is the perfect complement to the house. Two blocks of arcaded cottages built of sandstone, whose second storey projects over a covered walkway, are broken by a conventional group of gabled housing, possibly an earlier survival.

"Go to the little town of Ripley and Lodge there. Here is a feat of Sir John Ingilby whose family has resided in this place for ages." This was advice proffered by the traveller Bray, and the "feat" to which he refers is an immaculate stone village near Knaresborough which bears witness to the ideas of another amateur architect-cum-landowner. In this case the work continued from one generation to the next, extending about eighty years until 1860.

The Ingilby family had owned Ripley Castle since c. 1350, but the work of rebuilding took place in 1827–28, the estimates dating from the previous year, while William Amcotts Ingilby (a considerable character) was Lord of the Manor. Well before his death Ingilby wrote to his cousin, having reconsidered his earlier decision to make one of his nephews heir to the property. He had discovered the nephew to be "a mixture of Popery and Chilean bucaneering blood" and wrote, "I hope I am not doing wrong in making you my heir — I do so because I don't believe you are any longer the canting hypocrite I took you for... give away what money you can afford but never lend any, neither ever borrow any." This candid figure was followed by his cousin, the Rev. Henry Ingilby, who received a rhyme[10] composed by a friend on taking over the property:

"Let's be jolly — dance we — tipple we
Old Sir William's left us Ripley.
Blessings on his honoured head!
Good alive and better dead!!"

The subject of this unceremonious rhyme, William Ingilby, built at right angles to the main square a line of stout two-storey cottages either side of the road and set off by trees and broad grass verges. The cottages have Tudor details over the windows and doors and Gothic window frames but are otherwise conventional terraced blocks. It has been suggested, due to Ingilby's love of travel and particularly of Germany, that the village is modelled on continental lines — a great enthusiast for all things foreign, he referred to his castle as "the Schloss" and had inscribed above the gatehouse *parlez au Suisse*. Ingilby travelled with a notebook, scribbling down plans and architectural details as he went, so that the village was presumably the outcome of a common sense vernacular tradition,

The Hôtel de Ville Ripley, as it stands, very overpowering among the unassuming terraces on either side in the village street

East Stratton, Hants. George Dance's plans for model cottages on the Baring estate showing the garden areas. To right, a more substantial estate house in plan and elevation

as practised by the local builders,[11] with additional detailing from Ingilby's own observations. However, the neat cottage rows pale into insignificance beside the *pièce de resistance*, the "Hôtel de Ville" (as it is inscribed portentously). Soaring over them is a flamboyant Gothic creation, complete with battlements, great mullioned windows, and its date, 1854. This is where the creator of the rebuilt village made his personality felt to greatest effect, though he died before the completion of the Town Hall and it was carried through by his wife, a much misused woman. There could have been no need for such a building in a small West Riding village, and it seems to stand as an architectural expression of a particularly original character who was not content merely to commemorate himself by mundane lines of workmen's cottages.

Notes

1. John Jewell, *The Tourists' Companion*, 1822.
2. Exhibition held by the Yorkshire Georgian Society at Hull, 1973: catalogue, *John Carr of York*.
3. Drawings at the Soane Museum, Lincolns Inn Fields, London.
4. Richard Warner, *Tour through the Northern Counties*, 1802.
5. Drawings at the Soane Museum show a scheme, for John Robinson, MP for Harwich, consisting of "tenements" on his property, and another at Mistley for cottages in the form of a pedimented town house. Neither were executed, though Mistley is a planned village.
6. Maurice Beresford, *History on the Ground*, London, 1957.
7. John Harris, *William Chambers*, London, 1970.
8. Dorothy Stroud, *George Dance*, London, 1971. See plates 68a and 68b; also catalogue of Dance (father and son) exhibition at the Geffrye Museum, London, Summer 1972.
9. Marford Accounts; deposited at Flintshire County Record Office.
10. Ingilby Papers; deposited at Leeds Public Library.
11. Among the Ingilby Papers is a drawing for a plain cottage with a large Palladian window by George Elliot, the local builder.

Hulcote (Easton Neston); hamlet built c. 1815 for the 3rd Earl of Pomfret

Chapter 3

"Planning Picturesqueness"

When landowners set about rebuilding their villages in the early nineteenth century, they were obliged to entertain a specific conception of the village — the Picturesque village. The writings of William Gilpin and, a little earlier, of Uvedale Price had dictated the setting of the country house, its positioning within the grounds and, as a corollary, the appearance of the estate village. Every detail should conform to the formula, from the minutest external detail of a single cottage to the disposition of the houses in the landscape. Price presented the opportunity of building a village in two lights — the chance it gave the landowner to prove himself a man of taste and fashion and, rather incidentally, the satisfaction of carrying out a philanthropic act.

The precise requirements for the Picturesque village — the village that looked as if it emanated from a Dutch or Flemish painting — were many.

> "There is, indeed, no scene where such a variety of forms and embellishments may be introduced at so small an expense, and without anything fantastic or unnatural, as that of a village; none where the lover of painting, and the lover of humanity, may find so many sources of amusement and interest."[1]

The wording of Price's theories of architecture may read as fantastic and far fetched as he waxes lyrical on the virtues of thatch for instance but it is essential to realise how immensely influential these theories were to patron and architect alike, and it was an unsophisticated and eccentric man who dared to build his village without reference to the prevailing winds of the Picturesque.

In general, Price notes, "the characteristic beauties of a village, as distinct from a city, are intricacy, variety and play of outline".

These may be achieved by the actual disposition of the buildings, which must be anything but symmetric, by the use of additional colour washes, by the addition of overhanging eaves, porches and recessed windows to give shadow, and particularly by the chimneys which must be large and intricate. Great emphasis is given to vegetation, the choice of trees and shrubs, and above all the planting of creepers to cover the cottages. The church takes prominence as the natural focal point of the village, and in its ideal form it has a battlemented tower for "battlements are not liable to the same objection as pinnacles, for their effect, though simple, is never meagre". Other appendages to the scene are listed, such as the stream, "a brook seems to be that which most perfectly accords with the scale and character of a village", and by it, flat stones for the washing women. From all this will arise a scene imitative of Gainsborough's cottage scenes, of Greuze's "interesting pictures" or the paintings of the Dutch masters: in short, the Picturesque village.

When John Claudius Loudon, in the 1830s, continued the polemics in his *Encyclopaedia*,[2] he described what in his view constituted a Picturesque village, and it was an unchanged view. He did not draw any distinctions between the traditional village improved, Great Tew for example, or one recreated in its image. Rebuilding, or mere restoration, was one way of producing the desired effect, but where the traditional elements were suitable, then he was able to judge the effect Picturesque and approve it. The reality, however, was that most villages in this period needed drastic renovation and reconstruction, and many ancient cottages were deliberately being left to disintegrate by the landowners and tenant farmers in order to remove the pauper burden from the parish. The poor construction of these cottages gave them little life once the rot had set in.

The essential difference between the writings of Price and Loudon was that while Price sat in his house in the Welsh border country theorising, Loudon was active in exactly this field, the embellishment of extant villages. Little specific is known of his work, but Great Tew is thought to be an example of his planting and improvements long before he was writing on the subject, and because of his friendship with de Ligne Gregory of Harlaxton and his detailed analysis of the village in the *Encyclopaedia*, it seems likely that he had been busy there too. The planting of graveyards and cemeteries was one of his specialities, and though most of his

Picturesque double cottage from John Plaw's Ferme Ornée *published in 1795. The two chairs are suggestive of rural peace*

energy went into the production of influential publications such as the *Gardener's Magazine*,[3] he seems to have backed his ideas with continuous practical experience.

In this way the Picturesque village, originally regarded as only an element in the landscape giving an air of mystery with its smoking stacks behind the trees, became a more specific creation, and in Loudon's writings an exact delineation was given, with examples. The search for Picturesque landscape that had sent travellers and the cognoscenti bumping round the Lake District and North Wales clutching sketch books and umbrellas was coming closer to home. If a village could be found to exhibit taste — Blaise Hamlet being the obvious example — then the carriage would be directed to the spot and a much less strenuous tour undertaken. One indication of the popularity of certain types of scenery or buildings was the number of water-colours and engravings produced of a specific place, for the Picturesque traveller, whether observing the Alps, a group of thatched cottages or a ruined castle, was usually sketching down his impressions — just as the instamatics click around Windermere today. Subscribers to the *Virtuoso*, a drawing magazine of 1814, were sent out to draw old cottages with chalk and a milk wash, and the more sophisticated were then encouraged to travel on in search of a Gothic lodge to illustrate.

The pedantry of the theorists filtered through to a great general consciousness of certain qualities in landscape, an appreciation of some elements above others and an instinctive scale of preferences which still holds good today. The Picturesque was an attempt to define certain natural characteristics via elaborate aesthetics — to expand the distinction of Burke's "Sublime" and "Beautiful" into wider categories and to give a new pictorial vocabulary which depended on the vision of certain painters.

The contradiction lies in the precise and studied definition of elements which basically depend on informality, disorder and naturalness. As the studied artificiality of a newly built Picturesque cottage emulated the traditions on which it is so flimsily based, so the traveller to the Lake District was merely looking through newly opened eyes at scenery, familiar enough, but now seen in a new perspective and presented in a different light; it was a highly elaborate process of education but its lessons were long-lasting and in no sphere more so than in cottage and village building.

The Picturesque in fact encouraged a nostalgia which was already present but which became all the more forceful once the Industrial Revolution made itself felt. The description of Price accompanying Gainsborough into the country from Bath underlines what this nostalgia consisted of: "when we came to cottage or village scenes, to groups of children, or to any objects of that kind which struck his fancy, I have often remarked in his countenance an expression of particular gentleness and complacency." The architecture chosen to emphasise this sentiment, the romantic return to primitive virtues and innocence, was that of the Picturesque cottage. One was built in the 1770s in Kew Gardens, another, in the Gothick (a more free and ornamental version of the Gothic) style, at Stourhead c. 1806. The cottage was becoming a novel form of garden ornament.

Following the era of improvement in the mid-eighteenth century when Capability Brown had had no scruples about sweeping away housing which he saw as interfering with the grand pattern of landscaping he envisaged, a revision of attitudes took place in the next generation, and it was Repton who heralded this new move towards integrating extant cottages within his schemes. He wrote to his patrons the Foleys in 1790; "I have on several occasions ventured to condemn as false taste that fatal rage for depopulating a country under the idea of its being necessary to the importance of the mansion... there is hardly anything more picturesque and pleasing than smoke curling amongst the trees." This was the early expression of the sentiment which led to the ornamentation of existing cottages in preference to their destruction.

In addition to the actual appearance of the cottages another factor was regarded as important in purely pictorial terms, the inhabitants. Writers at the time often commented on the clothing of the villagers, and there seems no doubt that in some cases the grand design was extended this far. Just as the text books began to introduce the idea of housing being illustrative of the occupation of the inhabitant, to the point where in the mid-nineteenth century the smithy was often announced by a doorway in the form of a horseshoe, so too the clothing should be traditionally indicative of status but, more important, it should accord with the architecture. One guide book[4] commented on the red clothing that the cottagers of Old Warden wore to match the paintwork. Where there were almshouses the costumes played a great part in the scene, and the odd pointed hats worn at Milton Abbas by the almswomen attracted notice from travellers. At Selworthy Green the folk gathered under the walnut trees on the village green merited quite as much attention as the scenery. The picturesque costume of the country dweller reinforced the impression of well-being and idyllic pastoral existence that the tourist wished to see. Not merely in their dress but in their very presence the people were welcome decoration. Loudon gave instructions; "there would always be children playing and villagers passing to and fro, to contribute to the rural effect of the scene". Again, much later, in one of the Batsford publications on "olde worlde" village life,[5] the book ends with the words, "and now I come to the greatest charm of all, far greater than storied minster, palatial manor or picturesque cottage, and that is the villagers themselves. They are the real charm of our picture." Just as in many pictorial representations of village life, a self-conscious verbal whimsy clouds the view and the stage is set with fittingly costumed, acquiescent "folk".[6]

The status of the people in pattern-book terms was comparable to that of the cows and sheep which were also encouraged to drift across the landscape, if they were not a nuisance. Just as at Nuneham Courtenay the cows had been provided with a special underground passage in order that they could pass from one field to another without spoiling the view, so by the nineteenth century W.S. Gilpin was able to introduce the possibility of a path through the grounds from which "the occasional group of villagers supplying an additional embellishment to the landscape" could be seen. The presence or disappearance of entire communities hung on the whim of a fashionable landscape gardener or on the patron's reading of the Picturesque theoreticians' opinions on the subject — although Price did let a whisper of social concern creep in among the lengthy chapters dealing with thatch, creepers or chimney stacks. He wrote:

> "...I could wish to turn the minds of improvers from too much attachment to solitary parade, towards objects more connected with general habitation and embellishment... it may be truly said, that there is no way in which wealth can produce such natural unaffected variety, and such interest as by adorning a real village and promoting the enjoyments of its inhabitants."

However, Rights of Way were still determined by the "cheerfulness" the walkers might impart to the view and their cottages, if not destroyed, were so overladen with Picturesque additions that they were closer to theatre than reality. Lord Essex at Cassiobury embellished and built ten cottages on his estate (including one in the form of a Swiss cottage which was used for summer picnics) which were "distinguished for their exterior Picturesque features and for the Domestic comfort they offer to their humble occupants".[7] They were designed "with the twofold object of being both useful and ornamental. They are occupied exempt from rent and taxes by men and women who are employed by the noble landlord in various offices about the park, the gardens and the house...". It was becoming necessary to offer social justification for such building, but the accommodation was only a porch, sitting-room, and, at most, two bedrooms and a wash house, and far more care was taken over the embellishment of the Cassiobury cottage with pieces of split stick set in patterns over the entire wall surface. The language expressing some social concern was becoming obligatory but was little more than a gesture.

The early nineteenth-century landlord who bothered with the aesthetic prestige to be gained by affecting connoisseurship in architecture was advised by such a plethora of printed matter and had to watch the swings of fashion moving at such speed that he risked being caught in the ensuing reaction. Thus the man

Cottage at Old Warden, a direct example of the influence of pattern books. P.F. Robinson worked at Southill and may have been concerned with the building of Old Warden

advised by Brown and his contemporaries to raze his village to the ground might occasion the strictures of Repton, who longed to find a simple cottage in the parkland which he could cover with creepers and bargeboards, weigh down with convoluted chimney stacks smoking with evocative wisps and where, under the rustic porch, a villager could be placed. As has been noticed, the Picturesque was concerned with architectural styles but also increasingly with people, living reminders that even beneath their heavy disguises the cottages were still essentially functional; places in which villagers lived.

However, in addition to pattern books which made no attempt to provide any conscientious remedies to housing problems, whose pages were full of ramified dog kennels, hermitages and ornate garden seats, there were those which proposed cottages constructed in the most practical and economical way possible and which sometimes went so far as to suggest a plan for an entire village. Before dealing with these, it is important to emphasise the distinction between the cottage proper and the *cottage orné*. The former was regarded as of minimal interest until Nash and Repton began to reinstate the architectural values of smallscale buildings, while the vogue for the gentleman's retreat, the *cottage orné*, was gathering momentum. The interaction of the two categories is completed with Blaise Hamlet (and all the hamlets and villages which came in its wake), where Nash combined essentially *recherché* elements with a practical motive, the housing of Harford's estate workers.

The *cottage orné*, popularised by the royal lodge in Windsor Great Park (1814) and the Duke of Devonshire's at Endsleigh (1810), was, in terms of size, closer to a villa, but it mocked small-scale traditional buildings with its thatch and fancy detailing. Newspapers in the Regency period are filled with advertisements for cottages for sale in Roehampton, Richmond — all the fashionable areas around London were peppered with these modish little houses. Meanwhile, the cottages lying around a great estate were given a new ornate skin and became just another part of the garden furniture, along with the hermitages, temples and grottoes. This is exemplified by the *Essay on the Villa* (1807) by John Wood Jr., in which he labours to distinguish between cottage and villa — "my cottage is a species of villa and my object to point out what ornaments and accompaniments may be introduced to mark it as the residence of a gentleman without destroying its

53

character as a cottage". These distinctions were all-important in the hierarchies, both social and architectural, that ruled life, and he goes on to point out that the position chosen could be critical. "The cottage of a labourer may occupy many situations but that of a gentleman must be secluded." It is clear that a number of Picturesque cottages were regarded as an indication of status, as earlier the number of garden ornaments and buildings had been seen to illustrate the degree of grandeur the patron aspired to; obviously the presence of an entire village at the gates was the ultimate sign of position.

When William Howitt wrote his lengthy work *The Rural Life of England*[8] he presented country existence in an unusually objective light for the period. "Ah! Cottage life! There is much more hidden under that name than ever inspired the wish to build *cottages ornés*, or to inhabit them." He continued "by sobering down... our poetical fancies of cottage life, and bringing them within the range of human trouble and suffering, still these rustic abodes must inspire us with ideas of a peace and purity of life, in most soothing contrast with the hurry and immorality of cities". But, he adds, "it is the *ideal* of these picturesque and peace-breathing English cottages that has given origins to some of the sweetest paradises in the world — the cottages of the wealthy and tasteful".

It is this *mélange* of reality and fantasy that found the rich confined to gingerbread cottages; though by the 1860s they were unsaleable and often in a state of collapse, when forty years before they had been a desirable acquisition.

In Europe the landed gentry had weathered more storms to retain or regain their position, and the English aspect of an idealised country life was very attractive, allied to romantic imagery of the country. The association of pastoral life with an apolitical state of limbo must have been additionally attractive in the post-revolutionary period in France, when men risen to new eminence in the Napoleonic regime were busily feathering their nests. This time they did not attempt to assume fatuous roles, as Marie Antoinette had done in her hamlet at Versailles, but expressed a more mature understanding, that expressed by Laborde, when he wrote in 1808,[9] "*il semble que la vie de la campagne acquiert un nouveau charme après les grandes révolutions, lorsque les hommes, fatigués des évènements, aiment à se réposer quelque temps dans le calme de la retraite... un autre bienfait de cette existence nouvelle est la conservation de notre propre dignité.*" It

Early Picturesque pattern-book cottage at Redleaf, built in 1826 and illustrated in Loudon's Gardener's Magazine *in 1839; perhaps by E.B. Lamb*

was still the attitude of the sophisticate retreating and had little relation to actual conditions, the hardships of life for country people; aesthetics and romanticism had blunted the perceptions of the French just as much as the English. The village at Ermenonville, with its lodge "similar to those found in many English parks", and the hamlet at Raincy, described as an elegantly built village forming a part of the dependencies of the castle, are both merely decorative appendages, just like many of their English counterparts.

The pattern books, from the first dating from 1775,[10] dealt with the cottage as a single building, comparable to the dairy or dog kennel, rather than as a part of the whole. However there were two exceptions to the rule, and these demonstrate clearly the different approaches to planning that have already been noted in the early rebuilt estate villages.

John Plaw in his *Ferme Ornée or Rural Improvements* of 1795 provided a plan that was by no means Picturesque, but a rational and common sense solution to the problem of rehousing a group of labourers on an estate. The village took the form of an oblong central area with four convergent roads and a village green, surrounded by basic single and two-storey cottages — which might equally be those proposed by Nathaniel Kent or John Wood (*Plans for Cottages*, 1781) a few years earlier; practical, cheap and well-built housing. Certainly Plaw, in 1795, was not proposing anything drastically original, but his ideas were obviously well thought out and practical, the logical approach to building as contrasted against the aesthetic.

The village, on a main road, was "intended to unite symmetry and utility" with the houses designed to be enlarged according to the status of the resident. Plaw had in mind equally the client for whom he was constructing the cottages and the tenant, not often the case at this period. Each cottage was to be built as one of a pair, with a garden area surrounding each. The oval green would have a centrepiece; "a church or chapel would be both convenient and picturesque", and he suggested a four-sided temple with cupola as a suitable design. Pumps would be provided on the angles of the green and "a good idea for building a village of one continuous street is, to place the houses singly or in couples, facing the opening or space allowed for garden ground for those opposite. The views would thereby be preserved and the air circulate more freely." This was to become a standard idea in planning, and even a century later Parker and Unwin at Hampstead drew up a plan showing how each house was sited with an uninterrupted view, exactly the same theory as Plaw's.

Plaw had an intelligent grasp of certain essentials in even the most straightforward building exercises. It is not recorded which of his schemes were built, but it is certain that his book was widely read so that his ideas, if not carried out to the letter, were influential.

He must have agreed with Nathaniel Kent, who earlier had written: "I am far from wishing to see the cottage improved or augmented so as to make it fine or expensive: no matter how plain it is, provided it be light and convenient" and Kent had backed these words up with plans of double cottages (very like those at Nuneham Courtenay, as has been noted), together with estimates of building costs and a suggestion that each house stand in two acres of ground. This approach, the cottage costed and designed with minimal frills and maximum space and facilities, was equally that of John Wood.

The second plan referred to was that drawn out by Joseph Gandy in 1805.[11] Gandy had worked in the office of John Soane and was a much more visionary designer than Plaw, his work being Sublime rather than Picturesque. It is an extension of his design for a House of the Winds. "The idea of the last design is here extended to a village: so that eight of the groups formed into a circle compose sixty-four cottages for labourers and their families whose common centre must be a chapel or parish church." Each housing component consists of three small rooms, and a kitchen with a courtyard attached with "Hovel, for the shelter of a Cow". On precisely the same system, Ebenezer Howard distributed his six satellite cities around a central point.

The cottages Gandy designed were not the rich men's playthings, nor the plain common sense answers proposed by Kent or Wood; quite unique among the pattern-book writers, he was using symbolism to emphasise the social grouping of the community, just as Ledoux used the most overt symbolism at Chaux.[12] It was distinctly designed to remain on paper, in the realm of ideas and theory, not to be constructed but to provoke thought. However, in the United States, a spiritualist community, Spiritual Springs, New York, built c. 1852–57 ten oval houses which are as visionary in reality as anything Gandy had dreamt up.[13]

Although ostensibly even less practical, the Picturesque pattern books put out a flood of designs combining observance of current fashion with an obligatory nod in the direction of practical housing necessities. Newly conceived Picturesque theory treated the village as a related part of the landscape, no longer holding to eighteenth-century ideology, which felt that the landscape was an extension of the architecture.

There was an endless search for variety which eventually led the authors of these innumerable volumes into the realms of the ridiculous as the inappropriateness of the cottage designs, and the sheer impossibility of even trying to construct them, finally reached such a peak that further excesses seemed out of the question. All this was in answer to Price's request: "the characteristic beauties of a village are intricacy, variety and play of outline; whatever is done should be with a view to promote these objects". He cannot have anticipated the seriousness with which his words would be heeded. On a wider front, the licence that such

Plan for a village by John Plaw in Ferme Ornée, *published in 1795*

publications gave set off an interest in historical styles and their re-use, not always too appropriately, that continued up to the building of Port Sunlight — the culmination of historicism in small-scale domestic architecture.

In P.F. Robinson's *Village Architecture* his average village High Street included a range of almshouses built around the three sides of a court, with the doors hidden from sight "in order to avoid the appearance of any uncleanly habits". The half-timbered workhouse "...is composed from old buildings in Gloucester and as these are daily removed to be modernised it is

Plan for a village by Joseph Gandy in Designs for Cottages, *published in 1808*

59

well to preserve some features of our ancient street architecture". This interest in traditional domestic housing, rather than in the churches and mansions, was an active force in the eclectic choice of styles long before the Domestic Revival sanctioned the return to local vernacular styles or their equivalents. The more restrained Picturesque pattern-book authors were resuscitating every conceivable regional variation and the less restrained were gleaning details from Egyptian buildings — so that it was not surprising that a practical interest in renovation came about. As early as 1826 an architect submitted a design at the Royal Academy for a cottage restoration at Penshurst "in the ancient English style", and Picturesque village building often now consisted of the restoration of buildings rather than the laying of new foundations. Most pattern books were derivative but even the feeblest and silliest reached a considerable public; many ran into numerous editions, and they must be credited with encouraging a genuine interest in tradition in architecture.

The early Picturesque cottage consists of a symmetrical and minimal core with an overlay of decoration and detail. As the pattern books continued to proliferate so the buildings illustrated became more florid, the cottages rambling across the page in ever more irregular fashion. Malton was an early writer[14] to introduce entirely asymmetrical buildings, and often as the symmetry retreated so did historical accuracy. English national styles mingled with mongrel compilations of features learned abroad, and added to this was a much greater professional skill at presenting the buildings on paper. This made it possible for country builders to follow such examples. Previously their guides had been nebulous and lacked plans or any practical information as to their construction.

While the pattern books suggested the form of the buildings, the actual form the village should take was, on the whole, not dictated provided it fulfilled Picturesque ideals. Numerous text books and some practical efforts had provided the starting-point, and then the moment came to pull all the theories and the practice together and to begin constructing new villages according to the new ideas.

A very large proportion of the villages built in the first half of the nineteenth century are Picturesque to the letter, and in the following chapter it can be seen how, taking Blaise Hamlet as the prototype, the form, and perhaps more important still, the image of the Picturesque village became established to the extent that in our own century it still holds good.

Notes

1. Uvedale Price, *Essay on the Picturesque*, 1794.
2. Loudon's *Encyclopaedia of Cottage, Farm and Villa Architecture and Furniture*, 1842 edition.
3. *Gardener's Magazine* was published from 1826 onwards.
4. Murray's *Hertfordshire, Bedfordshire and Buckinghamshire*, 1895.
5. P.H. Ditchfield, *The Charm of the English Village*, London, 1908.
6. "Instead of a fence, the children of some poor but worthy cottagers, prettily disguised as shepherds, might be employed to keep the sheep from straying." William Mason, *The English Garden*, 1772.
7. John Britton, *History and Description of Cassiobury*, 1837.
8. William Howitt, *The Rural Life of England*, 1838.
9. A. Laborde, *Description des Nouveaux Jardins*, 1808.
10. Nathaniel Kent, *Hints to Gentlemen of Landed Property*, 1775; see also articles on pattern books in *Vernacular Architecture*, 3, 1972; *Architectural History*, Vol. 11.
11. Joseph Gandy, *Designs for Cottages*, 1805. Dedicated to Thomas Hope.
12. Ledoux's *"Ville Sociale"* around the saltworks at Chaux was the largest of his schemes for housing and was of considerable importance in town planning: for example R. Pemberton's *The Happy Colony* (1854), a major project for New Zealand, with ten districts each of 20,000 acres, led on to Ebenezer Howard's schemes and may have been partially inspired by Ledoux. See Rosenau, *The Ideal City* and *Social Practice in Architecture* for discussion of the links between French and English planning.
13. See Dolores Hayden *The Architecture of Communitarian Socialism* 1790–1975, Cambridge Mass., 1976.
14. James Malton, *Essay on British Cottage Architecture*, 1798.

Dairy at Blaise Castle. This was the first Picturesque building on the estate to introduce the cottage orné style, built c. 1804

Chapter 4

Blaise Hamlet and After

Despite the economies that the Napoleonic Wars necessitated, it was precisely in the middle of wartime that John Scandrett Harford decided to build himself the first fully Picturesque village. Although the manifestoes of Picturesque aesthetics were by then widely known — Price's *Essay on the Picturesque* had been published almost twenty years before — and although scattered *cottages ornés*[1] had been constructed, no one had grouped them into a village format. Existing villages had been prettified with rebuilt chimneys, accentuated thatched eaves and latticed windows,[2] but it needed more nerve wholeheartedly to take up the message of Picturesque rulebooks and redesign the landscape in their image.

Blaise Hamlet, built in 1810, was the village that lay behind the planning and form of almost every subsequent Picturesque village. By bringing together the qualities of cliché, nostalgia and escapism (which were already well in evidence in literature and painting), and expressing them in architectural form, Harford and his architects made their gesture of confidence in the Picturesque. Blaise was in fact Romanticism in a highly appropriate form, and all over the country in succeeding years extensions of the same idea sprang up; it was an architecture based, somewhat flimsily, on the vernacular of the regions. Thus, the large-scale buildings of the later nineteenth century were based on the unpretentious work of the early builders, reintroduced by a new awareness of tradition and association. It was a notable reversal and the Picturesque movement was instrumental in it. By providing housing for the poorest section of society, in Harford's case the elderly, which would be new and soundly built, the patrons could reconcile their extravagance with their social consciences.

Harford was a Quaker banker and his village, outside Bristol, was the final complementary touch to the surroundings of Blaise Castle. His architect was John Nash, who worked in close association with George Repton on the project, and between them they built what is without doubt the prime example of the Picturesque village pure — although it is in reality only a small cottage group around a village green without a church or public buildings to substantiate its claims to a separate entity. The cottage core in each case is a rather cramped little house, while the exteriors play upon an extraordinary series of variations — the Picturesque rampant. Harford had already worked closely with Nash on the Castle from 1802 onwards, and Nash and John Repton had already built a thatched dairy in the grounds which gave a foretaste of the style of Blaise.

Nash outlined the ideas for Blaise and then transmitted them from wherever he was working (usually Ireland) to Repton, who drew them in detail and sent them on to Harford and his builders. On one occasion there was some confusion over the placing of a cottage,[3] for the general plan was distinctly random; the nine cottages, one double, eight single, being ranged round a central green with a sundial, each with a garden and well hidden behind its hedge. Nash had laid down pegs in the field to indicate where they were to be built and Repton made a rough sketch from this; this was as sophisticated as the plan ever became. Much more important was the depth of thatch which was to hang over a window, or the exact dimensions of that window.

Unlike so many newly built villages, Blaise was not a replacement for an earlier, destroyed settlement. No one had been dislodged to make way for the fancies of their landlord and the village could be planned without the restraints imposed by existing roadways, public buildings or any other relics of established communities. In addition there was no time-lag while leases expired or obstinate tenants were persuaded to leave.

The cottages typify everything that Price wished in a Picturesque cottage. They are hung with creepers, and have steep roofs (three of them had heavy overhanging thatch, the rest were tiled), ornate chimneys and curved verandahs; all the signs of irregularity, roughness and variety are there. The cottages have names such as "Jessamine" and "Sweet Briar", and the front doors face in different directions — supposedly to discourage gossip, though more likely in the cause of irregularity.

A lithograph produced in 1826, showing all the cottages at Blaise Hamlet. Built in 1810, Blaise had become a port of call on Picturesque tours of the West Country and publications such as this helped popularise it further

The pursuit of variety was a priority; George Repton wrote to Harford pointing out that although the pantry and cellar in some of the cottages were inside, "if we make them *all* so it will very much injure (if not entirely destroy) the picturesque effect of the different cottages where so much depends on the lean-tos and sheds". At Nuneham Courtenay, that much reviled example of regularity and symmetry, the lean-tos and sheds were carefully hidden behind the cottages. But at Blaise, as in all respects, an opposite course is taken.

Nash was particularly adamant about his design for the chimneys being executed correctly: "he considers the chimneys to be a great feature in the cottages, he recommends you to have moulded bricks made for them, which will very much increase their effect. Should you wish it, I will send you 2 or 3 different designs for them..." Repton reported to his employer that Nash had written that "these kind of chimney stacks are frequently seen in old cottages and generally in old Manor Houses and buildings of the reign of Queen Elizabeth and invariably produce a picturesque effect. Their character requires that they should be *very high*..." Today, hidden behind encroaching building estates, busy roads and fast traffic, it is the towering chimneys that indicate where Blaise Hamlet is to be found behind its hedges. These chimneys became the most imitated of all the features introduced at Blaise; by the mid-century mass-produced moulded chimney stacks of different designs were being advertised in the architectural periodicals and no rebuilt or newly built cottage was complete without them.

In October 1811, Nash had sent a lengthy list of comments on the shortcomings in the buildings which he had noticed on one of his two visits to the site, mostly concerning external details (thatching, arrow slits and window heights), but also dealing at length with the positioning of the privies — those for numbers 4 and 5 to be "back to back and close in the hedge" — and giving instructions on the coppers and ovens. He comments that "the glazing is very badly done" on one cottage, and appears to have subjected the work to the closest scrutiny, despite his absence which made Harford impatient on more than one occasion, orders having to depend on the vagaries of the post. The interest in the practical as well as the more esoteric details contradicts the

Site Plan of the cottages at Blaise, showing the random way in which they were located. The plan of the double-cottage interior shows how limited the interior space was

66

commonly held view that Blaise is little more than a far-fetched attempt to employ aesthetic theories.

Harford spent considerably more on his Picturesque exercise than the architects had originally estimated; their sum had been less than £2,000, he wrote, but "I have expended upwards of £3,000... most of that amount had nothing to do with the building". This was written in 1812, and presumably the extra expense was connected with landscaping or materials.

However, Harford can hardly have considered his village a waste of money. Firstly he had created a perfectly Picturesque environment, secondly he had housed his elderly employees — in both respects he could expect praise. In 1826 a series of lithographs were published[4] bearing the following introduction: "a visit to them [the cottages] has long formed a favourite excursion from the village of Clifton and the city of Bristol". It then goes on to describe at length the different Picturesque features exhibited in the hamlet which can "offer a variety of subjects for the pencil". Blaise Hamlet in fact presents a compilation of Nash's work in small domestic architecture — several of the cottages had in fact already been built elsewhere.

One of the three thatched cottages at Blaise: the others were tiled

It has come to light, at Attingham Park, that Nash built a village on this estate too. Paintings exist showing the lost hamlet as a half-hearted attempt, a scattered incoherent group of cottages lacking entirely the finesse of style of the hamlet at Blaise.[5] In fairness to Harford, whose village is always held to be the exemplar of Picturesque futility, it should be remembered that he was a prominent member of the anti-slavery lobby, and in 1815, his social concern was exhibited in his pamphlet drawing attention to the appalling conditions in Bristol gaol — both sanitary deficiencies and bad administration — which forced convicted men to share the terrible quarters, and it is a document showing great concern and humanity which ill accords with a man who might force his old employees into sub-standard housing.[6] At the same time Blaise Hamlet was an exercise in fashionable taste which was to attract many travellers as they journeyed round the West Country. According to the introduction to the set of lithographs, Harford had "gratified at once, by this final work, his love of the Picturesque and his feelings of benevolence". The two were felt to be compatible.

When asked to give his occupation, Charles Buxton replied, "enjoying my thoughts, chiefly on architecture, that is what I turn to for enjoyment — planning Picturesqueness". This, after the great impact made by Blaise Hamlet, became a favourite nineteenth-century hobby, and a string of villages emulating the fantasy of the architecture at Blaise and its "unplanned" informality followed in its wake. Closest to the spirit of Blaise was Somerleyton, a village near Lowestoft, which was built for estate employees in the early 1850s. Sir Samuel Morton Peto, its builder, was a ubiquitous figure who had collected a great fortune building railways and undertaking major construction works such as Hungerford Market and the Reform Club. One of the guarantors of the Great Exhibition of 1851, he was a Liberal MP for Norwich and cropped up repeatedly in newspapers of the period in a variety of guises including that of sponsor for a parliamentary deputation from the Association for the Suppression of the Dog Show Nuisance in Populous Neighbourhoods.

At the gates of his great mansion, Somerleyton Hall, he built what was described at its sale as "twenty-eight cottage residences, of a most substantial and a highly ornamental character — showing, in the domestic arrangement and in the sleeping apartments, a singular and rare attention to the comfort and morality of peasant families".[7] These are placed around a great open green with a pump, a few carefully planted trees and a school building. The church remained closer to the house so that the effect is again more of a hamlet than a village. However a new church was originally planned in addition to the wooden Independent Chapel. Eventually Peto merely reroofed the extant church and left it *in situ*. An order diverting the road was made in 1848 and the village dates from shortly after. John Thomas, the architect of the house and Barry's assistant on the Houses of Parliament, was thought to be responsible for what is in fact a highly derivative group of pattern-book cottages. The school-house particularly shows all the Picturesque features; it is built in traditional black and white East Anglian timbering, and has a thick thatched roof, ornate clustered chimneys, a trellised porch and much irregularity. The gardener's cottage is built from rustic wood work, presumably to indicate the occupation of the inhabitant — one of Loudon's maxims. Somerleyton is a larger-scale exercise in the same vein as Blaise and today, still unchanged and remote, it probably remains the most successful functioning

Cottage at Somerleyton. The village, like Blaise, is grouped loosely round a large green with each cottage built in an individual style

Picturesque village. Smothered in creepers and sunflowers, Price would have found it very much to his liking.

How practical the cottages were is less immediately obvious but they are considerably larger than those provided by Harford. In 1899 at Penshurst, some old men were overheard discussing the well in their mock rustic village.[8] "Might so well have gi'ed us a pump, mightn't they?" "Lord love ye, that wouldn't have been quaint fashioned enough," replied his companion. The inhabitants of Somerleyton were not necessarily experiencing the latest developments in improved living conditions, but they found themselves guinea-pigs for an architectural pattern book come to life.

By chance, after the 1866 Overend and Gurney Bank crash which ruined Peto, the estate was bought by the Crossley family, industrial village builders from Yorkshire.

The progeny of Blaise are numerous[9] — all Picturesque to the letter, though the conditions the villagers found varied considerably according to the motives of the landlord.

Unsuspecting villagers in different corners of England were being herded into pattern-book hamlets to fulfil the aesthetic or philanthropic dreams of their landlords: one such was Holly Village, Highgate.

Baroness Burdett Coutts had established herself as one of the leading philanthropists of the mid-nineteenth century. She had inherited £2,00,000 at the age of twenty-three, as a result of which she was pursued by a diligent fortune-hunter for fourteen years. The Baroness's concerns were firmly on the side of the practical alleviation of misery in the city, and she carried out housing schemes at Bethnal Green and devoted all her energies and riches to the assistance of the working classes through improved education and housing. While doing so she pursued an active social life, in the cause of her charities (Augustus Sala wrote, in 1884, that he had dined with the Baroness "who gave me a letter of introduction to the King of the Sandwich Islands, whom I had previously met at her villegiatura at Holly Lodge"). She even found time when she was in her sixties to shatter polite society by marrying her American secretary, who was less than half her age. She was on terms of friendship with many of the leading figures of her time and was very far from the stereotyped Victorian lady.

It was, then, all the more surprising that she should choose to house her elderly servants in a Picturesque escapist paradise, at

Creepers and turrets ornamenting one of the Picturesque cottages at Holly Village, Highgate, surrounded by open gardens and a central green

Holly Village. The small group of cottages, like Blaise, is loosely grouped around a central green with ample gardens and well planted with trees — the monkey puzzle predominant. Her architect, as at Bethnal Green, was H.A. Darbishire, but it is suspected that much of the originality and impetus came from the Baroness herself, for Darbishire was a rather dizzy, inconsequential figure, blowing in the winds of fashion. He wrote disarmingly of his efforts, around 1864, to enter a competition for a town hall near Salford. "I did my best to express my admiration for Gothic architecture but was told by well-meaning friends that it would be well to get out an alternative design in the Classic style." In fact he won on the Classical design and readily confessed himself to be insufficiently versed in medieval architecture, as adapted to nineteenth-century requirements.[10]

Certainly Baroness Burdett Coutts was no aesthete, yet she put her old employees into a practical exercise in Picturesque taste that is oddly in conflict with her every other action. It can only be supposed that such provision was genuinely considered reasonable, even an improvement; and that when the surroundings were so carefully planned, then the deficiencies — the dingy rooms, for example — were thought to be minimal.

Entered through an ornate arch, inscribed with the date 1865 and with statues perched in niches, the "village" consists of seven cottages and a gateway (which is also a double cottage) grouped around the grassy inner area. The housing is built from yellow-grey brick with much wooden detailing, including medieval sculptures and an abundance of bargeboarding, fancy chimneys and creepers, all of which add to the atmosphere conveyed — that of an untouched rural community. It is far less urban in every respect than its counterpart of forty years earlier, Nash's Park Villages.

The Picturesque did not come unannounced to Highgate. Long before this, Wyatville had made sketches for various rustic ornaments for the grounds of Holly Lodge — the original house including a pergola, dairy and labourer's hut. This must have given the lead, just like the dairy at Blaise, and was no doubt the reason that the inhabitants of Holly Village found themselves in small, high-ceilinged rooms with strict instructions not to fence their gardens or in any way alter their cottages. However convinced a philanthropist was the Baroness, comfort and convenience were only two of many considerations at Holly Village.[11]

While, as has been described, numerous villages were actually built to emulate Blaise, others took as their starting-point more generalised Picturesque qualities — carefully chosen sites, well planted surroundings or suitable associations all qualified a location. Therefore it was no surprise that when Jesse Watts Russell

72

commissioned George Gilbert Scott to build a village at Ilam, Scott should trim down his Gothic into a more Picturesque vein and play up the advantages of this unique site to the best of his ability. A situation which had been commented on by innumerable travellers to the Peak District, and Dovedale in particular, Ilam (or as Boswell called it, Islam) lay at the foot of a considerable hill with a winding stream and meadows before it. In 1857 Scott built a collection of cottages with steep tiled roofs and dormer windows and a neat black and white school, with a little turret, in a manner more Picturesque than anything an Alpine traveller might find on his path. The cottages had large gardens and facing them was a memorial to Mrs Watts Russell inscribed with the appropriately Romantic lines:

"Free as for all these crystal waters flow,
Her gentle eyes would weep for others' woe,
Dried is that fount but long may this endure,
To be a well of comfort to the poor."

In fact, the village is a far more notable monument to Watts Russell wealth (they were industrialists) than Ilam Hall, which is

The Gatehouse at Holly Village, Highgate, the only symmetrical building among the cottages. Decorated with Gothic statuary and details, its inscription commemorates Baroness Burdett Coutts and the date of the building, 1865

a rather forbidding building standing a way off, by the church. The associations of the place, where both Congreve and Johnson spent considerable time (the latter writing in 1774 that it "was a fair abode for pastoral virtue"), are far better echoed by the smoking chimneys, a profusion of flowers in the gardens and the cosily positioned cottages than by any stately mansion of cold grey stone. Above all, the village echoes Price's emphasis on buildings considered in relation to their surroundings — these cottages placed out amidst flat arable fields would hardly achieve the same impact.

Subtlety of landscaping and particularly delicate architecture are the Picturesque qualities of Old Warden in Bedfordshire, where Lord Ongley improved his village in the mid-century after earlier work had been carried out by the Whitbreads, local landowners at Southill, the adjoining parish. *Murrays' Guide*[12] describes it:

> "the quaint houses with curved bargeboards and red painted doors and windows and some covered with ivy and honeysuckle and all Picturesque, were for the most part devised and arranged by Lord Ongley in whose time Old Warden was one of the sights of Bedfordshire — the inhabitants, by aid of red cloaks and tall hats, being made to harmonise with their dwellings."

Cottages built by G.G. Scott in 1857 at Ilam. The tile-hung gables are polychromatic and cottages are carefully clustered

The words "devised and arranged" have appropriate overtones of theatricality — almost as pronounced here as at Blaise. But the truly Picturesque feature of Old Warden is the care with which the cottages are placed, surrounded by hedges and trees which are the result of a very fully planned exercise in planting. Evergreen trees and bushes in particular are banked up almost under the eaves of the houses, and are used to tie together the scattered groups of the village, which lies in two main sections, along the road.

The cottages, intricately thatched, colour-washed a pale honey colour, with exotic latticed windows, some with half-moon-shaped casements, convoluted bargeboards and white-trellised verandahs and porches, suggest a village where the hand of some leading Picturesque architect might be traced, perhaps P.F. Robinson who had worked with Henry Holland at Southill nearby.

As has been noted, a further category of Picturesque villages were those where a core of older cottages were given an overlay of architectural decoration, while new cottages in the same idiom were slipped in to complete the picture. This was one way in

Cottages at Old Warden in which such Picturesque details as the deep projecting eaves, latticework porches and fancy casement windows are particularly elaborate. This group probably belongs to the 1830s

which a landowner whose village was flourishing and who could find no justification, or possibly could not afford to start anew, could prove himself to be conversant with the currents of fashion. One such village was Harlaxton, the Lincolnshire village described at length by Loudon.[13] The house, one of the most extravagant creations of its period, was built by Salvin in the years 1831–38 for George de Ligne Gregory, and the village seems to have been remodelled during the same period. The type of ornament to be found in the garden of the great house, stone terraces and pergolas in a curious primitive style, is echoed in the decoration which was loaded on to the cottages, which, according to Loudon, had been built in plain style by Gregory's predecessor. Much attention was paid to detail "the great value of Mr Gregory's improvements... is that all the leading features have some kind of relation to use, and are, in fact, to be considered more as parts added to the very plainest cottages, in order to render them complete, than as ornaments put on to render them beautiful". The gardens were ornamented by architectural features, wells "rendered architectural", walls and gateways, all different; even the paving stones were chosen with care and Loudon considers the cottager "now becoming a reading and thinking being" should be able to put sculptural ornaments in the garden, should he wish.

Harlaxton also impresses Loudon for the variety of its architectural styles; in his opinion, to use the same manner too frequently would "lead a stranger to suppose that it has been done through ignorance". This variety also extends to the adaptation of the cottage to suit the occupation of its inhabitant — provision for livestock, workshops or the special modifications necessary for a house for the schoolmaster or the clergyman. The carpenter's shop and the smithy "when properly introduced, can never be mistaken", a form of architectural symbolism which became increasingly common. Harlaxton is something of a visual oddity, even for its period, and the heterogenous aspect of its appearance rivals some of the most eclectic products of a later period. Harlaxton, described in all its detail by Loudon, is the Picturesque village *par excellence* in all but one respect, its site, which is unexceptional.

Those responsible for the building of Harlaxton apparently paid lip service to the ideas of a moral architecture — the attainment of a level of taste which could not fail to uplift the most

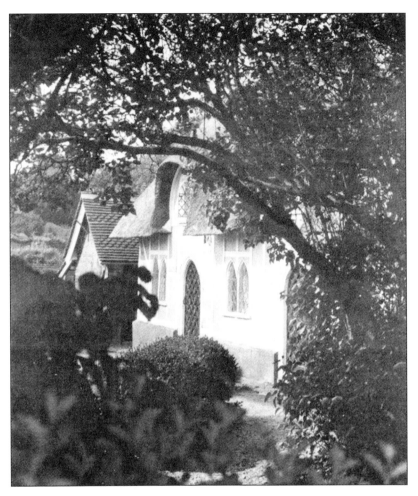

Evergreen planting at Old Warden complements the Picturesque qualities of the architecture and produced vistas such as this, details framed by foliage

doltish soul, encouraging him to litter his garden with sculptural oddments and not to question the novel decorations with which his cottage became suddenly laden, leaving him a better man as a result. This questionable thesis was the popular justification of all manner of dubious extravagance and should not be taken too

Bargeboards, fine chimneys and crescent-shaped windows at Old Warden

Porch and stonework on a cottage at Harlaxton built during the 1830s. The odd flattened forms are also found among the garden ornaments at Harlaxton Manor

seriously — the villagers of Harlaxton were quite comfortable where de Ligne Gregory found them and the renovation of their cottages was probably rather immaterial to their daily lives.

Inconsequential is perhaps the fairest description of many of the further excesses of the Picturesque Movement — but the ideas it introduced in the wider sphere of planning were crucial to future developments and never more so than in the area of suburban villa building, starting with Nash and Pennethorne's Park Villages in London.

Notes

1.   For example the several *cottages ornés* by Thomas Wright on the Badminton estate.
2.   Erlestoke was one example which Cobbett particularly noted.
3.   "The second cottage from the top north side looking south-east": all quotations are from the Harford Papers, at Bristol Public Library.
4.   Published by George Davey.

79

5. See Nigel Temple "In Search of the Picturesque", *Architectural Review*, August 1976.
6. J.S. Harford, *Pernicious Influence of Bristol Gaol*, 1815.
7. Used as endpapers in Mark Girouard, *The Victorian Country House*, Oxford, 1971.
8. *Country Life*, 23 December 1899 (quoted in Girouard, *op. cit.*).
9. Two interesting examples are at Selworthy Green, Somerset, and Little Bredy, Dorset.
10. H.A. Darbishire, *An Architect's Experiences*, 1897.
11. G.W. Thornbury and E. Walford, *Old and New London*, 1873–78, 6 vols. Also *Country Life*, 5 December 1968.
12. Murray's *Hertfordshire, Bedfordshire and Buckinghamshire*, 1895.
13. Supplement to *Encyclopaedia of Cottage, Farm and Villa Architecture and Furniture*, 1842 edition.

Chapter 5

Villadom

Although the first examples were constructed in the 1820s, the exclusive residential suburb began to proliferate in the 1830s and 1840s. A number of factors had combined to produce a pattern of development, detached housing set in sizeable gardens on an informal ground plan, which corresponded to the need of the time. That is, the need within the expanding middle classes for exclusivity without the responsibility and cost of a great estate.

Nash and Pennethorne's Park Villages, the suburban fringe of the great scheme for Regent's Park, date from 1824 and can be pinpointed as the first attempts to place the villa, a type of housing that Nash had excelled in designing, within a setting both rural and urban and, in essence, Picturesque. On the same model, but a village in the true sense, was Edensor, the Chatsworth model village built with advice from Joseph Paxton for the 6th Duke of Devonshire from 1838.

P.F. Robinson's *Village Architecture*, produced in 1830, was in his words "illustrative of the observations contained in the *Essay on the Picturesque* by Sir Uvedale Price". It was a supplement to his own pattern book on cottages, *Rural Architecture*, and gave instructions for the building of principal landmarks of the village; the inn, the schoolhouse, almshouses, market house, shambles, workhouse, town hall and church. As the final plate to the book he illustrates an entire village street, "a village street of ancient architecture" as he termed it. He assembled a highly unlikely variety of buildings side by side, a sort of dictionary of historicism which might seem unlikely in reality, were it not that the village of Edensor is just this.

Edensor was merely a particularly grandiose estate village built by the Duke in a distinct and spacious style. He expanded other neighbouring villages on the estate, but Edensor is the only

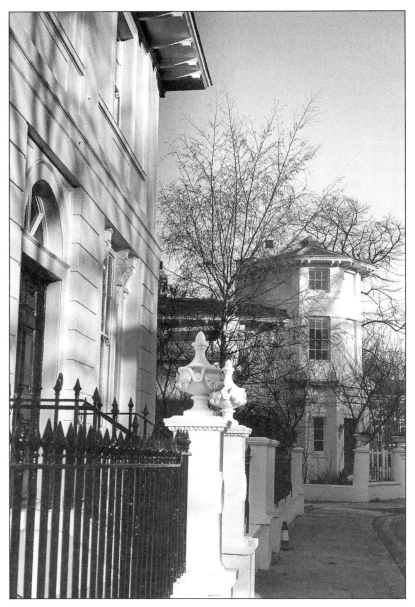

Park Village West, by John Nash, 1824, the model for later estates of suburban villas and an influence on Edensor

complete exercise and was a new creation in every detail. The overall planning of the village was in the hands of Paxton, whose efforts were presumably intensified at this expression of faith in his abilities from his employer. Like the arrangement between Nash and Repton at Blaise, Paxton was in charge of the general, John Robertson his assistant being given charge of the particular, the supervision of the construction. Robertson had previously been J.C. Loudon's draughtsman, so he was imbued with the Picturesque as deeply as any architect of this generation.

It seems likely that Paxton knew P.F. Robinson's books. The second edition of *Rural Architecture* began with a long panegyric on the virtues of traditional cottage architecture as contrasted against "modern tradesmen's villas!" However it was not a sequence of creeper-hung Picturesque little cottages that was built at Edensor, but a number of sizeable stone houses with slate roofs, representing an extraordinary selection of styles — just like the street in *Village Architecture*.

In the previous century Capability Brown had been employed on the Chatsworth landscape, and this had involved the first of the two demolitions the village was to suffer.[1] When Bray visited Edensor in the 1770s the inn had recently been moved closer to the village but he found the then Duke of Devonshire far from an empty minded aesthete.[2]

> "However little the noble owner may be inclined to lay out his money in disposing his grounds according to the modern, simple and beautiful style, he is not backward when he is there, in distributing it to the distressed. The poor, the widow and the fatherless bless the providence which has bestowed such wealth on one so ready to relieve their wants."

However, it was not that the Duke was unconcerned in architectural matters, but he was at Buxton laying out a spa to rival Bath, and it was left to the 6th Duke to enter into the reconstruction of their local estate village.

The first efforts at emparking had left a single cottage — which was then given a Picturesque treatment — and a portion of the village had been left hidden behind a hill. It was this section which was demolished in 1835, leaving just the church which was rebuilt by Scott for the 7th Duke.

Plate from P.F. Robinson's Village Architecture *showing a village street. The variety of historical styles is comparable with those at Edensor*

In the entry in his diary on 8 December 1835, the Duke of Devonshire wrote that he and Paxton had been to Blaise Hamlet, "The most perfect cottages... I ever saw... Paxton was struck with the chimneys." The fact that a visit to Nuneham Courtenay two days later aroused no comment proves which way their sympathies lay; they were attracted by the irregular Picturesque hamlet and not the symmetrical vernacular lines of the cottages at Nuneham. There is no doubt that the Duke took a very decisive part with Paxton in deciding on the form of his village and by September 1839, on his return from a year's trip to Europe, he could note in his diary, "Fine day. Happy village. New cottages."[3]

When the works were finished, a correspondent from the *Gardener's Chronicle* of 1842 described the cottages as follows:

"...the buildings embrace houses of almost every calibre, from the spacious farmhouse to the humble cottage and they are distributed with admirable skill; some on the level ground at the mouth of the dell and others on gentle declivities, while not a few overhang the brow of a precipice or occupy a snug position that has

84

Edensor. The village dates from 1838, the church from the 1860s

been excavated out of the solid rock. The buildings are entirely of stone, except where enriched wooden gables or other ornamental carvings have been introduced; and they present a perfect compendium of all the prettiest styles of cottage architecture from the sturdy Norman to the sprightly Italian."

Included in this range of styles are Swiss, Tudor and castellated Gothic — each house is entirely distinct, set in a sizeable garden, and the whole ensemble in its artificially steep valley is hidden from the view of Chatsworth House and park by its surrounding hills.

Edensor was the village which best exemplified the potential of the Picturesque in larger-scale building. In a category quite apart from that of the *cottages ornés* and their progeny, it was a blueprint for the perfect shell for the middle classes. They adopted it, not merely in Britain but in Europe and the United States as well, taking the elements of earlier developments and adding to them the distinct, rather rigid, eclecticism that Nash had already made respectable.

In France various aspects of the Picturesque had long been in evidence, as the French pursued an independent path towards the same ends. Ledoux's complex of detached housing at Meaupertuis was a speculative scheme consisting of retreats for the almost-wealthy, surrounded by their own gardens, and designed in a brutal neo-classical style. The concept was novel for its date, 1780,[4] and although never built and not included among his published works, it demonstrates the direction in which so innovatory an architect was moving. Housing for the bourgeoisie was to become the mainstay of the architectural profession in the nineteenth century.

As has already been mentioned, French architectural publications made great play with the village idea, and perhaps the most perfectly Picturesque of all villages was that built at Clisson by the brothers Caccault in 1817. This was based on memories of the

Chimney profiles at Edensor. Each house at Edensor is detached and sizeable, in marked contrast to earlier Picturesque villages

Roman Campagna, in every detail a facsimile of a painting by Claude or Poussin — the artists whose vision gave rise to the entire Picturesque aesthetic. The combination of this imagery and the new pattern of housing led to suburban "villages", the best known of which is Le Vésinet, outside Paris, planned in the mid-nineteenth century. The Avenue Frochot in the 9th arrondissement of Paris is a French Picturesque version of Park Village West, though considerably later in date, with its half-timbered entrance lodge, Gothic and Italianate villas set along the winding roadway.

American links were forged through the friendship[5] of Andrew Jackson Downing and J.C. Loudon, and when Jackson Downing brought out his *Cottage Residences* (1842) in America it exerted an enormous influence on the course of domestic architecture from then on. This publication was strongly influenced by Loudon's own works, and through him, the work of earlier theorists of the Picturesque. Certainly the European Picturesque ideology landed on fertile soil when it reached America. Llewellyn Park, New Jersey, was an early villa park consisting of housing in a miscellany of styles and designed as "a retreat for man to exercise his own rights and privileges". Not merely the physical form of the early Victorian villa estate crossed the Atlantic, but also its premises — exclusivity and privacy. Llewellyn Park dated from 1853–69 and another important early imitation of the prosperous purlieus of the rich industrial towns of Northern England was Riverside, Chicago. Here Olmsted and Vaux, from 1868 onwards, paid respects to Paxton's Birkenhead Park (which Olmsted was strongly influenced by) and laid out a complex system of winding roads and well planted surroundings in which to place Vaux's mixture of villa designs. Although not designed to be self-sufficient communities in the way that utopian settlements had been, these American estates soon took on the proportions of towns even if they were essentially merely extensions of existing cities.

The potential in America for this type of building which paid little regard to the European pressure for space was endless, and as the later changes in planning fashion wavered between the Beaux Arts, the Picturesque or the rectilinear, the suburban villa might be built in a cul-de-sac, by the side of a winding road or among a series of gridiron blocks. Wherever it was situated, the form of the housing was decided: it was to be relatively small-scale and Picturesque.

The English had taken to the villa avidly. Alexander Pope and his friends were one of the earliest groups to do so and by the beginning of the nineteenth century no less a personage than Humphry Repton himself was living in a small villa at Harestreet[6] — the garden of which, once the village green, he landscaped with all the care that he might have lavished on his most grandiose stately house commission. He was making enormous efforts to emphasise the country aspect, framing the vista of the village street, its inn and village green; in his own words "the cheerful village, the high road, and that constant moving scene, which I would not exchange for any of the lonely parks that I have improved for others".[7] Small wonder then that the convenience and fashionableness of the villa should take the nineteenth century by storm — leaving only the very richest to continue to construct immense ostentatious heaps.

The residential estates already mentioned as successors to Edensor or Park Villages East and West fall between villages proper and mere speculative housing development. Certainly the architects were aiming at emotional association with the village. Decimus Burton's Calverley Park at Tunbridge Wells provided certain community facilities, such as shops, and he had sited the housing near an existing church. These estates, residential enclaves guarded by romantic castellated lodges, surrounded by high walls and pierced by winding roads, proliferated around the edges of the newly expanding northern industrial towns and at the fashionable resorts, both inland and coastal. They show the full vocabulary of eclecticism and echoed the contemporary passion for the romantic medieval era as expressed elsewhere in the lightweight costume dramas of historical painting, the tales of Walter Scott and the reinacting of a tournament at Eglinton in 1839,[8] an event which had enormous influence and caught the public imagination forcibly.

One significance of these residential parks lies above all in the emphasis they gave to the nurturing of natural surroundings, heavily planted with shrubs and mature trees, the houses almost vanishing back into their wooded settings.

Therefore when the speculators moved into this field they tried to seize on a newly sophisticated manipulation of planning which would immediately raise the level of their schemes. Speculation, neatly characterised in these lines, was big business from the early nineteenth century onwards.

Tudor detailing on a cottage and a Swiss "chalet" side by side at Edensor, built by Paxton and John Robertson

"The richest crop for any field
Is a crop of bricks for it to yield.
The richest crop that it can grow,
Is a crop of houses in a row."[9]

Speculative schemes, at their worst, were confined solely to the provision of cheap, fashionable housing and relied on neighbouring town centres to provide any further facilities. The tradesmen's villas, so deprecated by P.F. Robinson, but so influenced by his works, were the quickest growing housing type in all industrialised countries.

At their worst, the villa estates, with no effort made to induce any sense of community, were oases of detached villas left isolated behind their sturdy hedges without the social hierarchy or the traditional elements of village life to provide any points of contact. It was this settled exclusivity that the nineteenth-century residential developments, whether in Britain, Europe or America, bequeathed to later suburbia — the loneliness of affluence.

Notes

1. Stephen Heath makes the point, in his thesis *Picturesque Villages* (typescript, Architectural Association, 1974), that the original village as depicted in the painting by L. Knyff of 1701 — was in fact extremely picturesque.
2. W. Bray, *Tour Through Some of the Midland Counties into Derbyshire and Yorkshire*, 1777.
3. Quotations taken from the 6th Duke of Devonshire's diary and accounts, in the Library, Chatsworth House.
4. Illustrated M. Raval, *Ledoux*, Paris, 1945, Fig. 101. Other schemes of detached housing carried out by Ledoux were those for the Maisons Saiseval, the Hosten estate (both speculative) and the Eaubonne park scheme. His published works undoubtedly were of great influence in the formal sense, just as Marie Antoinette's Hameau (perhaps by Hubert Robert) at Versailles was a foretaste of *cottages ornés* and the furthest reaches of the Picturesque.
5. Loudon, reviewing Downing's book, wrote that it "cannot fail to be of great service in adding to the comforts and improving the taste of the citizens of the United States".
6. Before and after versions of the improvement were illustrated in *Fragments on the Theory and Practice of Landscape Gardening*, 1810.
7. Quoted in *ibid*.
8. For a good account of the influence of the Eglinton Tournament see John Steegman, *Victorian Taste*, 1950.
9. From Tarbruck, *Handbook of House Property*, 1875.

Chapter 6

Reformers
and their Villages

As the nineteenth century progressed there was a mounting pressure for housing reform in practical terms, and the inadequacy of the average cottage, poorly constructed with meagre accommodation and dingy interiors, however charmingly situated around the village green, became apparent. Efforts to appeal to the conscience and to activate a sense of social responsibility began to place an onus on the landowner which it became increasingly difficult to ignore, and these voluntary appeals were backed up by official investigations and the first stages of legislation which aimed at a generally higher standard of living. This was the beginning of state intervention in a field formerly exclusively the domain of individuals who might or might not feel responsibilities incumbent on them to improve the lot of their tenantry. A rare example of tenants' own reaction to their housing is provided on the Duke of Bedford's Thorney estate where their opinions were recorded — for example against the name of Albert Darves are the remarks "the organist at Thorney; two cottages have been formed into one house for him; it is a very good one and he is perfectly satisfied and thankful." The other side of the coin is represented by Joseph Simpson. "This man, his wife and two grown-up sons (with one daughter occasionally at home) were all living in a house with one bedroom and all sleeping in it: the husband and sons were quite intent to go into the new house — but the wife who is a notorious shrew, disliked the change, and did all in her power to disparage the cottage and dissatisfy her neighbours." Thus it is not until the mid-nineteenth century that the voice of the villager is heard and only then in exceptional circumstances.[1] In many respects the country labourer was living in conditions more intolerable than those of the industrial worker but as a more longstanding problem it was more easily overlooked than the acute and dramatic situation which rapid industrialisation had brought about.

The eighteenth century had seen the expansion and, equally, the disappearance of villages due to enclosure and emparking, the nineteenth century had to deal with the legacy of ancient communities which were crumbling, literally and metaphorically.

A good example of the depth of concern felt when the conditions were brought into the open is illustrated in the correspondence between Sir Henry Acland and his fellow Trustees administering the Ewelme Charity in the village of Marsh Gibbon in Buckinghamshire. Acland, in his official capacity as Regius Professor of Medicine at Oxford, was Master of the Trustees and instigated a programme of cottage improvements, on which he based his writings on village health and sanitary reform. One local landowner, Sir Harry Verney, wrote to him in 1869 that the state of the village was worse than anything he had seen in England and that he was ashamed to be unaware of the situation, only five miles from his home. This is a typical reaction — showing that more often than not it was not callousness, but short-sightedness, that prolonged the agonies of these rural slums. Verney outlines in his letter a common sense and practical rationale. "Owners of landed property or they who manage landed property for others, are not justified in receiving the produce or profits of the land without providing that those whose labour brings the profits are properly and decently cared for." But in this period no such standards obtained and paternalism was far from the guiding sentiment of the majority of landowners.[2]

Verney mentions that the land around Marsh Gibbon is good and that there is stone in the neighbourhood for house building. He continues,

"if land is properly drained and improved, its increased produce will pay the interest of the money spent on improving it and I believe, not it only, but also that of the dwellings of the labourers who work on it. Increased produce will give more work — more work will bring better pay, so that the cottagers will be able to pay rent sufficient to pay interest on the money spent on their cottages. If they could not still it is a duty incumbent on the Ewelme Trustees to provide better dwellings."

In other words, simple economics would justify any work carried out and it would prove to have more than paid for itself.

However, it took Acland's crusading energies and Ruskinian application to encourage the other dozing trustees, and it was similarly left in the hands of a tiny number of conscientious men and women throughout Britain to effect the necessarily enormous reforms.

Even as late as the 1890 Housing Act, progress was sporadic. Effective local authority responsibility for housing was still well in the future, and the burden remained with the landowner, who needed either the purest philanthropic motives or a strong belief in the expediency value of improved housing as an incentive to labour and a stable workforce.

In 1884, Sir Henry Acland's *Health in the Village* threw light on the realities behind the creeper-hung porches of the delightful cottages so beloved of English water-colourists. He listed the essential requirements for a healthy environment in the following order — firstly, the dwellings, then water supply, removal of refuse and drainage, education, occupation and recreation, and finally medical treatment. He suggested that the standard house size for a family of seven (two adults, five children) should be three bedrooms — in this he was using the standard accommodation in prize-winning cottage designs, the size advocated by Henry Roberts, James Hole and John Birch, three of the most prolific figures in the field. Acland describes the sight that would meet any foreign traveller in the countryside — he "would also see the ornate and carefully arranged habitations that are near the parks and features of this island..." This is the same hypocrisy that Alexander Somerville noted in the late 1840s when he observed the enormous disparities between a village and its outlying dilapidated hamlets.

Genuine philanthropy was a rare motive in village rebuilding or foundation until the mid-century. Earlier, at the turn of the century, Samuel Whitbread and John Howard the prison reformer had vied with one another in considerable pioneer housing improvement schemes. Howard, known as "The Torch of Philanthropy", constructed a number of cottages around the green at Cardington, near Bedford, which were eminently sensible solutions to the problem of decent rural housing.

Philanthropy was a bandwagon which attracted a miscellaneous selection of adherents.[3] Apart from overt frauds, such as the nicely named Laudable Institution, it also became a fashionable pursuit, so that the well-advertised distribution of a little largesse around an estate became virtually obligatory. However, philanthropy, in its best sense, attracted men and women of great wealth with the highest principles who were prepared to spend fortunes fighting the apathy and entrenched attitudes to poverty that were paralysing official circles. In some cases the philanthropic village-builders formed tight-knit circles — for example the Quakers or the mid-Victorian heiresses — so that the news and experience of one enterprise could be passed to receptive ears and applied again elsewhere. Just as fashions in architecture spread into every furthest corner of the country, and beyond, for example the village built according to Picturesque vision, so too the pressure of example activated landowners into consulting the pattern books, hiring a builder and setting in motion work on a new group of cottages, or, often enough, an entirely new village. The philanthropic concern could usually be measured by the financial arrangements; there were some who ploughed back all the money they received in rent into further improvements, while others took a very nominal return. In fact it soon became obvious that it was virtually impossible to profit from such ventures.

In his book Acland nominated a familiar group of landowners, the men who were consistently praised for their efforts to ameliorate the generally appalling conditions; they were the Duke of Bedford, the Duke of Northumberland and Earl Spencer. Above all, he praises West Newton, the Sandringham estate village. Sandringham had lately acquired its royal status and celebrated its new eminence with a village consisting of numerous new cottages, all with three bedrooms, and which instead of a pub could boast a village club, restored church and cottage hospital all built by the Prince of Wales. Certainly, for the reformer in search of exemplary material, it was a well ordered picture, but it must have been a cheerless one for the inhabitants of this remote Norfolk community who, no doubt, walked to the next village in search of the missing ingredient.

Acland saw the answers to the problem as lying in the rebuilding of existing areas and infusing new life into moribund communities, but saw that England could not offer the possibilities for full-scale replanning, such as obviously existed in the United States. Yet five years after this, Ebenezer Howard published his key work, *Tomorrow, a Peaceful Path to Real Reform*,

Henry Roberts's plan for an agricultural cottage. It has three bedrooms, by the 1860s recognised as a minimum requisite. The rustic porches indicate the continuing pervasiveness of the Picturesque

which saw no such objections even if there were no "virgin prairies" on which to build.

However, from a mixture of motives, landowners — particularly new landowners — were making individual efforts to remedy the gloomy situation. Sindlesham Green, in Berkshire, was built in its entirety at the gates of Bearwood for John Walter and his son, another John Walter, chief proprietors of *The Times*. Workshops were set up specifically to manufacture materials for the village and its mansion, which Robert Kerr had been building, amidst disagreements and squabbles, from 1865 onwards. The housing in the village is well designed and is built of the red and black bricks produced on the estate. It is grouped around a green, while opposite one of the lodges to the house stands the church and the Walter Arms. Without making any effort to rival the strident and amazingly intricate structure of the house, the village sets the building within its context — the great mansion with the village at its gates — just as the eighteenth-century equivalents suggested their feudal origins merely by disposition. The source of employment and the *raison d'être* of the community is announced by housing which plays the same tune, but in muted tones.

School at Sindlesham Green, typical of the better class of estate building during the 1860s

Similar examples of this — an extension of the activities of the great Victorian country house builders — can be found throughout the country, and while they offer much improved housing, they consolidate the position of the landowner in much the same way that the industrialist who surrounded his factory with a model village was hedging himself around with a cast-iron security.

The building of model housing was the favourite activity of Dorothea, George Eliot's heroine in *Middlemarch*. She saw one of the advantages of marrying that unenviable catch, the pedantic Dr Casaubon, as the possibility of carrying on her cottage building: "everything seems like going on a mission to a people whose language I don't know unless it were building good cottages — there can be no doubt about that. Oh, I hope I should be able to get the people well housed in Lowick!" Although the novel was supposedly set in the early 1830s, the situation reflects that of the time in which George Eliot was writing, 1870.

No pamphleteer or reformer could have stated the position better than George Eliot through the mouthpiece of Dorothea:

Cottages at Combrook

"I think we deserve to be beaten out of our beautiful houses with a scourge of small cords — all of us who let tenants live in such sties as we see around us. Life in cottages might be happier than ours, if they were real houses fit for human beings from whom we expect duties and affections."

She had even consulted Loudon's publication for the designs.

One person who might almost be the model for Dorothea, so energetic and idealistic was she, was Louisa, Marchioness of Waterford.[4] A very remarkable woman, humane, intelligent and practical, she is best known for her considerable achievements as a painter. She was the daughter of an architectural amateur, Lord Stuart de Rothesay, and, immediately after marrying Lord Waterford (whom she had met at the Eglinton Tournament), she threw herself into the fray. She wrote:

"I am collecting in a book an immense mass of evidence about our labourers [at Curraghmore, the Irish estate] and hope, before I die, to see them thoroughly comfortable and if I can I shall do the same for every creature on Waterford's property. W. is at this moment at some race. I am reading every book Ruskin ever wrote. I delight in them!"

Waterford himself seems to have been tolerant of her activities, but considerably more at home on the hunting field. However, at the time of the Famine he ceased to hunt until 10pm as previously. Meanwhile, his wife was planting trees along the streets, painting the village inn sign of a turkey and consulting with a neighbour, Dr Coghlan, over housing, schools and a woollen manufactory they had set up nearby at Kilmacthomas. In Curraghmore she had set up a woollen industry also and supplied the thirty poor women employed with a uniform. By 1848 the situation was becoming intolerable, mobs from Portlaw attacking the house. Lady Waterford spent much of the year in England but insisted on returning. In 1849 she wrote in her diary: "called on Mrs P. in a hovel scarcely 12 feet square for 15 persons. Children almost naked and not an article of furniture of any kind — some heath for a bed. Stopped at various other cabins, in almost all cases 15 or 18 in one small room."

Already in the early years of her marriage, she had visited Ford, the family estate in Northumberland. Here she noted: "the cottages — I never saw people so clean and comfortable; it is

Lady Waterford, in a contemporary photograph

quite a treat to see them so", and her sister, Viscountess Canning, mentioned the strong contrast between the two properties; Ford being "such a prosperous place — so surrounded by good cultivation and good cottages".

In 1859 Lord Waterford was killed in a hunting accident and his widow decided to move to Ford Castle. Her diary is full of accounts of cottage visiting and she seems to have immersed herself even deeper in her interests of architecture and painting. Soon Augustus Hare, in a letter to his mother, could write,

> "the ugly village has moved away from its old site to a hillside half a mile off and picturesque cottages now line a broad avenue in the centre of which is a fountain with a tall pillar, surmounted by an angel, a memorial built by George Gilbert Scott to Lord Waterford. Schools for boys and girls have sprung up, a school for washing, adult schools, a grand bridge of three full arches over the dene; it is quite magical."

Lady Waterford had a lively interest in contemporary architecture and had visited Salvin's great house at Harlaxton. She felt that Augustus Hare, author of the Murray's *Guide to Durham and Northumberland*, which he was then engaged in compiling, "cares for everything that belongs to other times... but this, I think, is a taste that wants mixing up with a more onward march".

Lady Waterford was a notable painter and frescoed her school at Ford with considerable panache, but when Ruskin passed by one morning, "he condemned (very justly) my frescoes", as she self-effacingly phrased it. She allowed herself to comment that she admired his mind more than his personality.

Ford village consists of grey cottages placed off a wide roadway which leads to the smithy with its horseshoe doorway.

Apart from her unremitting interest in Ford, where she combined her pursuits of philanthropy and architecture within her model village, Lady Waterford also kept herself fully occupied at Highcliffe, the Hampshire estate left to her on her mother's death. Here she set up a milk shop to further her temperance beliefs, and painted another sign, this time a cow. Living here she came into contact with Miss Talbot of Bournemouth, another model village builder and energetic philanthropist.

Georgina Charlotte Talbot, and her sister Mary Anne Talbot, were two immensely wealthy women who set about spending

Stone horseshoe marking the forge at Ford: many village smithies were distinguished by this motif. Identical ones exist at Dunmore in Scotland and Enniskerry, Ireland

Almshouses at Talbot Village

their fortune in rehabilitating the considerable number of poor families who had been dispossessed of land on the hills outside Bournemouth by the enclosures of 1802 and 1805. The scheme for a few cottages grew considerably during execution in the 1860s and the outcome was Talbot Village, consisting of nineteen cottages, six farms, a church, school and almshouses with provision for seven couples or single inmates.[5] Georgina Talbot claimed that her scheme came directly from the inspiration and ideas in a German book, *The Goldmakers' Village*, and also those presented in the writings of Robert Owen. The village is basically Picturesque, with carefully sited cottages hidden behind pine trees and blackberry bushes; it is gnomish in scale and has the full complement of porches, verandahs and tall smoking chimneys.

The Misses Talbot, however, were more concerned with the idealistic theories of influence of environment on morals than with the petty details of depth of eaves or the arrangement of the lattice work. Above all, the provision of an acre of ground for each house was their practical solution to the problems of the families whom they were attempting to rescue from destitution and the deepest poverty.

Georgina Talbot was the prime mover of the two, although Mary Anne continued, up to the age of ninety-nine, to administer the estate after her sister's death. Georgina Talbot was a formidable matriarch, with a tendency to make awe-inspiring swoops upon her village, but she was also refreshingly aware of the evils of over-rigid religion and put her faith in the beneficient properties of an acre of ground and the absence of alcohol. "The outset of this village was anything but encouraging or cheerful. The first inhabitants were unused to any restraints; the women many of them, lax in their behaviour; the surrounding gentlemen and clergy having no sympathy with improvements or amelioration for the lower classes," wrote Miss Talbot, who persisted to overcome most of these obstacles. Of the numerous buildings in the village the church was in fact the last to be constructed, the school doubling as chapel for some time.

Lady Waterford called her "La Talbotina" and on her death referred to her as an old and very dear friend. In Mary Anne Talbot's will, one of the principal legatees was Lady Waterford. It is a nice thought that a considerable part of the time these lady philanthropists spent together must have been spent, not in conversations dealing with gossip and the weather, but in the finer details of cottage construction and model village building.

Cottage among the pine trees at Talbot village, built during the 1860s and one of the outstanding examples of practical philanthropy of the period

Canford Magna, an early postcard referring to "the model village"

Many of the great estates encouraged a higher standard of building, reinforced by the institution of national competitions for improved housing and the production of pattern books aiming specifically at practical rather than aesthetic advances.

The Bedford estate had one "industrial" village which was entirely devoted to servicing the building works in the area, and Viscountess Canning, writing to her mother in 1854, talks of a stay at Woburn where the conversation was of "pictures, cottages, planting". She describes the buildings in impressed, if rather breathless, terms:

> "...the cottages are very good very plain indeed, but not ugly. Each holds only one family and is not the least too large for it to avoid the temptation of lodgers, but by their leases the cottagers are also absolutely debarred from taking them. The walls inside are whitened brick, not plastered and the whole is very plain but substantial and well finished. The inhabitants seemed enchanted with them and very dirty people became neat and clean in them."

In 1885 the Duke of Bedford wrote to Henry Acland, "you may do good, if you will teach me to house the poor as an example to others and not as a rich man's fancy".[6]

There were numerous estates where landowners seem to have heeded Loudon's strictures against the "many formal and disagreeable villages designed purposely to be ornamental". In Gloucestershire, R.S. Holford, a notable Victorian connoisseur of the Italian Renaissance period, had rebuilt the villages of Westonbirt and Beverston using as his consultant architect Vulliamy, who had also built his mansion at Westonbirt, and his London palace Dorchester House. The housing is an excellent example of the best combination of good design with improved standards; the terraced cottages, lodges and model farms are carried out in a warm golden sandstone and are sparingly decorated with bargeboards, finials and Gothic porches, though never obtrusively so. Holford, who had inherited a massive fortune in his twenties, lies under an intricate Gothic stone canopy in Westonbirt church, far the most flamboyant Gothic detail in his village. The village there was a late product of emparking, and the church remains close to the house.

In general the picture of mid to late nineteenth-century cottage building is one of the monotonous repetition of an extremely limited architectural vocabulary. G.G. Scott, architect of Ilam and concerned in the planning of Akroydon, wrote strongly in *Domestic Architecture*[7] of the standards of vernacular domestic architecture when it was neither informed by philanthropic intentions or artistic precept — what he termed "the spontaneous productions of our builders where no external influence is brought to bear upon them". He continues, "Can anything be more execrable? Can anything be more utterly at variance with what one would think should be the character of a country village or more deadening to all the natural feeling of the labourer of his house?", but it was precisely the scarcity of influential architects' interest in the field that caused this low general standard. Architects such as Teulon, Vulliamy, Waterhouse and Butterfield made contributions to cottage building, but in general patrons were not commissioning small-scale domestic buildings — churches and the great exuberant productions of the country house architects absorbed their energies, and builders were left to construct pattern-book designs.

One of the less happy attempts to break away from tediously repetitive architecture was made by the Hon. Henry Hanbury-Tracy, who decided to construct his estate cottages around Gregynog, Montgomeryshire (Powys), in the new material, con-

*Cottage detail at Beverston: one of the numerous near-identical terraces
there and at Westonbirt, designed by Vulliamy*

crete.[8] This experiment led to the sale of the estate by the family in 1894, "for over-extending themselves in various industrial and commercial experiments, e.g. the early use of concrete". Unfortunately the concrete sweated, making the cottages uncomfortably damp, a trouble which still persists, but contemporary reaction to the use of the revolutionary material was favourable, "the building, if well done, is almost imperishable", and Tracy was praised as an exemplary landlord with the interests of his tenants at heart. In the 1880s John Birch, the prolific author of cottage designs many of which were constructed by leading landlords, published *Concrete Buildings*. Norman Shaw used the material too.

Landowners were set an example in housing their tenantry by Prince Albert,[9] who had designed, in collaboration with Henry Roberts, a pair of slightly bizarre cottages for the Great Exhibition (now reconstructed at Kennington). On the Windsor estates good cottages were built, some by one of the best known architects to turn his hand to cottage building, S.S. Teulon. With the various prizes offered for good designs and a great deal of agitation in the architectural press — most notably in *The Builder* — the situation was bound to improve, not just where new villages were built but wherever a farmer needed to house a family of employees. The result was that the new improved standards brought about a uniformity of design. Brick or stone built housing with steep pitched tiled roofs and a little superficial Gothic or Tudor ornamentation became the order of the day and the eccentricities of earlier efforts in the century became rarer. One refreshingly flamboyant exception were the flint and brick buildings scattered by the Earl Lovelace over the villages of Ockham and East Horsley, in Surrey; it had certainly not occurred to him to ask his builder to run up a cottage in the Henry Roberts or John Birch mould, with the result that the area is marked by some of the most atypical small buildings anywhere in the South of England.

Notes

1. Quotations from unpublished thesis by Paul Birch (Architectural Association, 1976) *Aspects Affecting the Labourer and His Cottage 1770–1860, with particular reference to the Duke of Bedford's*

Bedfordshire and Buckinghamshire estates which gives a detailed technical analysis of the construction of agricultural cottages in the period.

2. Quotations from Acland MSS, Bodleian Library, Oxford.
3. A good history of philanthropy is D. Owen, *English Philanthropy*, 1965.
4. Augustus Hare, *Two Noble Lives*, 1893, 3 vols., giving the biographies of Lady Waterford and her sister Viscountess Canning.
5. A description of Talbot Village published together with "Views of the Founder", 1873.
6. Acland MSS.
7. G.G. Scott, *Domestic Architecture*, 1857.
8. *Concrete Quarterly*, 95, October–December 1972.
9. Prince Albert's interest in housing was emulated by Louis Napoleon who subsidised workers' housing in 1849 and, in the following year, arranged for the translation of Roberts's book as *Des Habitations des Classes Ouvrières*. At the 1867 Exposition Universelle there were four model houses on show.

Chapter 7

Orphanages and Aesthetic Retreats

While commendable efforts were being made to improve rural living standards — though the agricultural depression during the 1880s slowed this down — the village was being taken up in other quarters for its social advantages and its visual qualities.

One area in which the village was considered an ideal format was that of charitable institutions — proliferating in the late nineteenth century as practical philanthropy prospered — such as orphanages, almshouses and centres for the physically and mentally handicapped. A village form was the obvious choice for the almshouse. Since medieval times the northern European almshouse had been a courtyard of cottages, but orphanages were a new type of institution. Following the Ragged Schools and other efforts to take destitute children off the streets, the first cottage orphanage was opened at Farningham, Kent, in 1864. This was the Home for Little Boys,[1] which housed, educated (in both religious and secular matters), trained and employed the children. The use of a cottage-village form rather than cramming the hundreds of children into a great all-purpose barracks was a humane wish to introduce something of the family atmosphere into such a place. By breaking down the numbers into smaller family groups the overbearing institutional character was minimised — the organisers were after all only following the plan of the public schools, institutions with which they were doubtless familiar.

In fact the principle of cottage-villages was originally tried out in France and Germany, and it was the example of these, and the Farningham experiment, that Barnardo had in mind when he set up his Village Home for Girls at Ilford, opened in 1876. This was a considerable complex, with cottages dotted around the circumference of a great open space, and was planned with the needs of small girls particularly in mind: a place where "family life and family love might be reproduced".[2] They had an orchard in which to play, and every effort was made to minimise the impersonal aspects of the home.

Certainly the philanthropists who founded these villages were working along the same lines as the landowners who held that good housing might help to reinforce the moral fibre of the ordinary tenantry — giving them the first taste of self-confidence and pride in their surroundings. They felt that the less fortunate, finding themselves in a close-knit society, particularly ready-made villages such as these, would resolve themselves to better their character defects, moderate their antisocial behaviour and immerse themselves in this substitute family. Perhaps the hopes were over-optimistic, but such foundations proliferated. A colony for alcoholic women founded by Lady Henry Somerset at Duxhurst, near Reigate, claimed that "the first aim of our work is to restore the lost feeling of self-respect, and we can do this better in cottage life than in any institution".[3]

Perhaps the most ambitious of plans for a private charitable exercise in village building was that outlined by Alexander Beresford Hope but never realised.[4] In 1851 he wrote of founding a model village for his labourers, to include a hospice which was to function as a retreat for clergymen, "a Christian watering-place so to speak", a memorial chapel, almshouses and a reform school whose pupils would be put to work on a farm and on the reclamation of bog land, "an ideal training for future emigrants". All this was to be a memorial to his mother, and presumably by grouping such diverse elements as delinquents, clergymen and country labourers together in rural Kent (at Bedgebury) he hoped for the best for everyone concerned.

The use of such cottage homes — practical rather than utopian — has continued with such groups as the Pestalozzi Villages or the Dutch village, Het Dorp, where an entire village for the physically handicapped has been built.

The other attraction of the village, apart from its social advantages, is its physical form. While uniformity was becoming the hallmark of the otherwise worthy building schemes around the country, some architects were seeking a source for their small-scale buildings in the vernacular of the different regions. From the mid-nineteenth century onwards the movement for a revival

Peaceful Dutch-style terrace at Bedford Park

Cottage homes for reformed alcoholic ladies set up by Lady Henry Somerset at Duxhurst, near Reigate. The inhabitants are indulging in a Victorian panacea, gardening

Rustic cottage illustrated in P.F. Robinson's Rural Architecture of the usage of traditional materials and styles began to gather impetus. From the moment that the battle for minimum cottage standards had been fought and virtually won, then the emphasis could fall back on to the inessentials, the choice of tiling rather than polychromatic brick, casement windows rather than intricate lattice work and plain chimneys rather than intricate moulded ones.

One key figure was Eden Nesfield, an architect in whom several influences met; his father was a water-colourist and landscape gardener and he himself had been the pupil of the topographical illustrator J.D. Harding, illustrator of P.F. Robinson's works. With Norman Shaw, whose partner he was for a time, he had travelled in France, Germany and Italy, sketching predictably Picturesque subjects, and it was scarcely surprising that when he carried out work on the Crewe estates, and later at Radwinter in Essex, his work should be steeped in regional details copied with antiquarian precision and remarkable historical accuracy.

It was not surprising that the recreation of village life should appeal to artists, in particular those artists whose work dealt with this type of subject matter. Myles Birket Foster was a relatively minor yet immensely popular water-colourist and illustrator who painted countless scenes of cottage life and rural incidents. He first took a cottage at Witley in Surrey, to which he could commute from London and where he found numerous other kindred spirits[5] sharing his addiction for this sort of pastoral life — one foot in town, where the work could be found, one in the country, where the quiet and relaxed atmosphere were conducive to carrying out the work. Eventually he built himself a great half-timbered mansion, a monument to his success, and gave up the journeys to London.

Areas such as Kent and Surrey became full of enclaves such as this; William Wells at Penshurst gathered a circle of artists around himself, and others lived nearby at Cranbrook.[6] Such people had clear ideas about the countryside they wished to live in, and correspondingly about the type of cottage or villa they wanted — usually new, but in the traditional style. It was George Devey who carried out the best work in this vein, though in his footsteps other competent, if less original architects spread the style so that the villages of Penshurst, Leigh, Benenden and Cranbrook are laden with tile-hung mellowed cottages built only a century ago.

Earl Lovelace built his estate buildings in idiosyncratic style, using materials from his own brickworks

The sort of vision that the Victorian artists, especially landscapists and illustrators, shared with the architects was a rather whimsical vision of the past where rotund country folk are seen in front of overwhelmingly pretty, if decrepit, cottages. Devey took this Picturesque viewpoint and gave it a systematic practical outcome. His cottages for Lord de L'Isle at Penshurst, some newly built, others restorations, have little of the *cottage orné* about them. Practical considerations determined their construction, so that the half-timbering was often faked to prevent danger of fire while tile-hanging was considered as good insulation. But the materials were the best, the wood the hardest oak, the brickwork and tiling done to the highest standard. But however firmly Devey stood against the imitation of authenticity in materials and sham short cuts, he made a conscious effort to recreate the village proper. The saddler's shop, butcher's shop, forge and rustic well all enforce the references to the past and emulate the ancient form of a village, even if the artistic inhabitants were now coming out to the country by train to blow away the ennui of town life. The construction of these cottages, which was phenomenally expensive, paralleled the minuteness of vision of the topographic draughtsmen or, indeed, the sort of observation that gives Victorian narrative painting an almost three-dimensional effect.

Butterfield's village for the Dawnay family at Baldersby St James in Yorkshire was another example of this new attempt at veracity. Here the origins are less in local style than in observations of foreign buildings, the brick of medieval Germany for example. The village, consisting of a church with a great spire, a school, parsonage and several cottages arranged freely in a roadside group, sets a precedent for low-key informal domestic architecture which before very long was to become of great importance.[7]

In the north-west, the work of Douglas on the Grosvenor estate, and his later work for Lever, made the same sort of clean break. His use of grouped housing, as in the three-sided group at Eccleston, anticipates the closes and culs-de-sac that Parker and Unwin were to use to break the thrall of dreary terracing. This type of planning also relies on traditional forms, in the case of the quadrangle, the precedent being the almshouse, or medieval college or monastery, which again helps to relate the buildings to their past.

"Cottage at Wheeler Street, Witley" by Birket Foster. A popular Victorian watercolourist, he used his surroundings to produce a pastoral, nostalgic imagery which became increasingly potent

The rise of the Arts and Crafts Movement and the adoption of the Domestic Revival in respectable and influential circles took many by surprise. Foreign entrants to the Royal Academy in the 1890s continued to show florid designs based on totally catholic taste, and the revolutionary activities of the English small-house builder prompted the Prussian government to send Hermann Muthesius to investigate the situation from 1896 to 1903 and to produce his influential three-volume work *Das Englische Haus*. He illustrated houses at Bedford Park Suburb, Bournville and Leigh as well as numerous examples of traditional cottage building and larger houses. Ironically, it was now the smallest and humblest houses which began to dictate styles in architecture.

It was not surprising that when Jonathan Carr chose to plan an estate in London, originally as a speculative venture, he should attempt to present it in the light of an elite artistic community on the lines of those at Penshurst or Holland Park.

A close of cottages at Leigh, designed by Ernest George and Peto

He was prompted to found Bedford Park because of its easy access by public transport to central London (it was half-an-hour from the City on the Blackfriars-Richmond line) and although he started with the idea of merely building an estate, the introduction of a church, inn and shopping area, as well as clear efforts to appeal to a particular type of resident, meant that the outcome was an urban village and a pioneering attempt in the planning of detached medium-sized housing.[8]

This artificially created community, self-consciously retreating into "village" life, was naughtily characterised in The Ballad of Bedford Park in the *St James Gazette* of 1881:

> "Thus was a village builded
> For all who are aesthete
> Whose precious souls it fill did
> With utter joy complete."

One resident wrote that he felt himself to be part of a water-colour, and indeed the architecture emphasised this quality; the tasteful housing rested in large gardens well shaded by the trees that had been left to complement the scheme. The "Flannelled faddists all prying into each other's gardens" that Voysey saw as

Lych-gate and school at Baldersby St James, by Butterfield

1850's cottages by Butterfield at Baldersby St James, in a style which points towards the Arts and Crafts

the product of the garden suburb cultivated an arty exclusivity, and there was no pretence at the sort of genuine social integration that Dame Henrietta Barnett was to envisage for Hampstead Garden Suburb.

Bedford Park represents the type of estate with which we are now fully familiar, roomy detached housing standing in generous gardens in an area of quiet tree-lined streets. At the time, however, it struck an entirely fresh note. As the *Building News* commented in its notes on one of the terraces of "middle-class houses" as they were determinedly called, "it could be wished that such a treatment was more general in all our suburbs". The Park was well known in architectural circles, for one of the original residents and propagandists was Maurice Adams, who also was a leading contributor to the *Building News* and who drew immaculate elevations and plans of many of Shaw's and Godwin's designs.

Plan of Bedford Park with inscriptions and a list of early residents. Arty self-consciousness was characteristic of early days in the Suburb

When some Architectural Association visitors were taken round in 1879 only eighteen houses had been built but Carr was already talking of an eventual 600. The hand behind the actual plan is not known: the principal roads converge at a point near the railway station, the Tabard Inn, the stores and the church while three straight avenues form the central area with a freer curving section to the west and a stricter grid plan to the east.

Godwin's plans were the first commissioned. He was a suitable architect as his ideas were best developed in the field of relatively smallscale domestic architecture — he, in fact, was responsible for the most important houses in another venture for an artistic community, in Tite Street. During his affair with Ellen Terry he was moving in artistic and bohemian circles and thus was the architect most favoured in this group. His designs, without basements, were, however, more criticised than acted upon, and it was Norman Shaw whose stamp was to lie indelibly upon the entire scheme. The calm, gentle proportions of the inaccurately named Queen Anne style used were a far cry from the massive, heavily detailed houses of the earlier estates aiming at a similar class of resident.

Voysey cottages in traditional manner at Elmesthorpe

There is no doubt of the intense clannishness that living in Bedford Park promoted, as witnessed by its short-lived magazine.[9] It was also still physically isolated, and a social club and group activities catering for every conceivable interest were set up to remedy this. The residents' protection was ensured by a much derided fire brigade and an early forerunner of the amenity group, a Vigilance Committee. The economics of the housing — rent for the terraced Dutch-style housing was around £40 per annum — and the sizeable accommodation provided, with sometimes as many as seven bedrooms, dictated that the residents would be middle-class.

Bedford Park combines two aspects of nineteenth-century building; the efforts to create community, although not in this case socially integrated, together with a more sophisticated attitude to physical planning. It combines nostalgia, in the form of its architecture and the recreation of village life, with the beginnings of self-determination in housing on a wide scale — the spirit of the early Garden City enthusiasts and the co-partnership supporters.

Notes

1. *The Story of the Little Boys*, printed at the Homes, n.d., *c.* 1870.
2. See the catalogue, *The Camera and Dr Barnardo*; exhibition at the National Portrait Gallery, London, Summer 1974.
3. Jennie Chappell, *Noble Work by Noble Women*, n.d. (1890s?). Contains a section on Lady Henry Somerset and material on Baroness Burdett Coutts.
4. Note in John Newman, *West Kent and the Weald* (Buildings of England series), 1969.
5. H.M. Cundall, *Birket Foster*, 1906.
6. Described in two-part articles in *Country Life* by Mark Girouard: "Devey in Kent", 1, 8 April 1972; "Early Norman Shaw Commissions", 30 August, 6 September 1973.
7. Paul Thompson, *William Butterfield*, London, 1971.
8. *The Daily News*, 5 May 1880, reported: "nothing could differ more widely from a brand-new rectangular American township than the charming London suburb at Bedford Park". T. Affleck Greeves "London's First Garden Suburb", in *Country Life*, 7, 14 December 1967. See also A. Saint, *Richard Norman Shaw*, 1976.
9. *The Bedford Park Gazette* was published July 1883–July 1884; thirteen issues in all. It gives by far the best sense of the spirit in which the suburb was conceived, and is entertaining reading.

Chapter 8

The Early
Industrial Village

The advent of the Industrial Revolution meant that the living conditions of an entirely new section of the population had to be considered. The men instrumental to the functioning of the new industries needed housing, and needed it far more urgently than the estate workers for whom the rural villages were being built.

The conditions in which workers were living in the expanding areas, particularly in the textile producing districts of the north-west of England, varied from appalling overcrowding in existing, quite unfit, cottages to newly built quarters which were often worse, offering single room accommodation and a total absence of facilities. The "necessary room", to give it its euphemistic name, if it existed at all, emptied into open drains which ran down between the rows of back-to-back houses carrying disease and polluting the atmosphere with a foul stench. *The Builder* described, in 1863, the state of affairs — the outcome of fifty years of building without planning and without even rudimentary standards:

> "[Places] where the factory smoke pollutes the air, and the dye-houses poison the streams; where streets cannot well be described than as canals in wet weather: where it is difficult to get air at all, and impossible to get it untainted by the chimneys and sewers; where the refuse of a thickly populated district lies rotting in the open streets, and the gutters do duty for more than surface drainage..."

The actual form that industrial housing took did not, in the early stages, present any revolution — in the way that the architecture and planning of many of the estate villages did — but it repre-sented a more important step forward, the first flickering evidence of humanitarian concern. It is hard to disentangle the

Housing at Akroydon with elaborate Gothic window details

motives of the early industrialist who provided better housing
and facilities for his workers. If he was merely concerned with
expediency why was he so rare?

Certainly, unlike the landowner who built himself an estate village, little prestige in aesthetically-aware circles came to the man
who built his employees lines of drab cottages, even if he did provide gardens, schools and marginally better working conditions
than the owner of the next mill down the valley. Many of the
early employers who might be called paternalistic were particularly religious men, often Quakers, and as a result they did feel a
genuinely heightened concern for their workers, even if by present standards they were exploiting them and their families
mercilessly, with the intolerable hours and child labour that were
the norm at the time.

It took very little to better the average state of affairs, and
people regarded as particularly enlightened employers, the
Strutts and the Gregs for example, were building cottages in the
late eighteenth century that were only reaching a minimum standard. At Styal, Samuel Greg used the cottages he built as an
incentive to obtain labour — with housing close to the mill he
could depend on a good amount of overtime per worker but he
provided a shop for fresh produce (long before he built them a

chapel, surprisingly), and doctor's records go back as far as 1804 although medical attention was probably available before that.[1] Certainly the warring forces of expediency and conscientiousness fought a hard battle, but on evidence it is clear that good materials were used for building, the cottages were built to last, and they used certain recent inventions — the Strutts used special fireproof, cast-iron window frames — but their contribution to reform was their attention to education and recreation. They were not content to employ mere sweated labour in their factories and mills.

The general public, those whom the Industrial Revolution did not touch, viewed the whole spectacle in its romantic aspect — the drama of the roaring furnaces, the Sublime of the soaring mills and the Picturesque of the labouring man. One tour which had already visited the great houses of Derbyshire continued to Cromford, while another, heading for the noted scenery of North Wales, stopped for a while at Coalbrookdale where, noticing the great iron bridge built by Telford, "a stupendous specimen of the powers of mechanism", the author wrote of his "indescribable sensation of wonder" as he looked at the furnaces by night, which reminded him of the "workshop of Vulcan".[2] This dramatic impact, the scenes that appealed to painters such as Wright of Derby and de Loutherbourg, masked for the majority the growing and insidious problem of housing conditions in industrial areas.

Different industries gave rise to different patterns of housing; for example in Derbyshire, mining was carried out by staking claims, which meant that temporary ramshackle hovels would be erected, or existing sheds converted into living quarters. Around the mills tighter communities grew up, sometimes based on the nucleus of an earlier village and sometimes newly founded. At Cromford, Bray[3] noted that "Mr Arkwright carries on the business (of spinning cotton) with great advantage to himself and the neighbourhood. It employs about 200 persons, chiefly children... (who work by turns day and night). Another mill, as large as the first, is building here, new houses are rising round it and everything wears the face of industry and cheerfulness..." and, he adds, "Mr Arkwright was born a barber but true genius is superior to all difficulties."

Already in the eighteenth century there was a foretaste of later problems of polluted air and smog-laden atmosphere. Skrine described the sulphurous atmosphere near Swansea, caused by the effluent from the coal-mines and copperworks, and only paused to mention Morristown as an example of a company town built on new principles — a "curious place" with regular streets, wharfs and a church — before hurrying on to cleaner parts.

Some landowners found themselves industrialists during this period; many large estates were discovered to have mineral deposits, and where their land extended to the coast, ports were established to ease the transport of materials to and fro. Other landowners set their sights further afield, envisaging grandiose schemes; some remained on paper, others exist in fragmentary form, the victims of misfortune or miscalculation.

One such is Bucklers Hard on the Beaulieu estate. The neat red brick line of houses is all that remains of a plan for Montagu Town, a great port to rival Southampton and

A plan of 1727 for a sugar port at Bucklers Hard to be named after the Duke of Montagu, its founder: sophisticated planning at an early date

*Tremadoc view of central square of William Madocks' planned town,
built c. 1805. The arcaded building was the market hall cum theatre,
and next to it the inn*

Lymington.[4] The Duke of Montagu drew up plans and a
prospectus in 1724, including housing, a chapel, an inn and a
bath-house, with the proviso that the house fronts be
constructed from local brick in order to give uniformity.
Incentives to build were the nominal rent, 6s. 8d. per annum,
and the gift of three loads of oak from the estate woods.
However, the economic basis for the town went aground; it had
been planned as a sugar port when the Duke had seen the
potential for trade while he had been Governor of St Vincent
and Lucia. He sent an expedition to promote the scheme and
set up the necessary export arrangements, but the French
forced them home and the plantation failed, losing some
£40,000. By this time, however, a quay had been built and
roads and the first of the housing were under construction, so
the port was turned into a ship-building centre and timber-
loading port. It continued as such into the nineteenth century
and even after, with spasmodic moments of activity, including
ship building in the Second World War. The little that remains
stands as a monument to a great failed enterprise.

Seaton Sluice in Northumberland was the port built by the Delavals to export the coal which had been found in massive quantities on their, and other, estates in the area. In 1720 the beginnings of a village, planned around a square, were constructed and a great berth for shipping was built. For a century it flourished and then Blyth took over its function, leaving the port to crumble away, leaving fewer clues to its former importance than Bucklers Hard does of Montagu Town. Such failed schemes are numerous, and nowhere more so than in Highland Scotland and Ireland where the obstacles to such foundations were inevitably more insuperable.

Of the great unrealised schemes, that of William Madocks at Tremadoc was the most visionary.[5] Madocks began with a great land reclamation scheme, taking an embankment across marshland to form a port principally aimed at shipping out the locally quarried slate. Twice the bank was breached and as a result Madocks became bankrupt. However, this hardly deterred him and, like Lord Leverhulme a century later, he scrawled plans on the backs of envelopes and plotted the town of Tremadoc on the spot. In Peacock's novel *Headlong Hall* the three philosophers inspect the almost completed embankment, visit the factories at Tremadoc, and then discuss their impressions of industrialisation — as it seemed to them in 1816. Presumably Peacock chose Tremadoc because of his friend Shelley's connection with fund-raising for Madocks's reclamation schemes but the tenor of the discussion would seem to be more fitting to Coalbrookdale than to the early stages of Tremadoc, which was hardly in the league of major industrial centres. However, during the talk we are presented with the opposing views of Mr Foster, who sees the potential of great industrial wealth, despite the iniquities which he admits. The riches and scientific advances to be gained, the "employment and existence thus given to innumerable families, and the multiplied comforts and conveniences diffused over the whole community", are more than adequate recompense for the shortcomings. Mr Escot, on the other hand, might well be the voice of William Morris before his time. He sees, firstly, the human degradation, the avarice of newly found "needs" and the inevitable decline of "the industrious cottager". The machine and the "little human machines that keep play with the revolutions of the iron work, robbed at that hour of their natural rest as of air and exercise by day: observe their pale and ghastly features, more ghastly in that light... they are mere automata, component parts of the enormous machines which administer to the pampered attitudes of the few...".

Tremadoc itself was full of imaginative concepts. Set beneath and against the sheer rock face, it was planned around an open square, which belies the scale of the village which peters out just beyond. The town hall provided a meeting room above and the school doubled as an open-air theatre complete with an arcaded auditorium. As a whole the village was hardly that most fitted to the wants and climate of the North Wales coastline, but the inception was remarkably ambitious.

However, on the more mundane level of the housing necessitated by vast influxes of labourers for the ever-expanding mills in the North of England, much of the building was sub-standard and built entirely out of expediency to induce the workforce to remain at hand. The Strutts at Belper and Milford advanced the standards and by 1812 had set up a farm nearby specifically to provide good quality fresh vegetables and dairy produce.[6]

However, even they, representing the enlightened Nonconformist element in employers, were liable to have managers who drilled holes in the shutters to observe which workers stayed up late — a step far beyond benevolent paternalism.

The cottages Carr built on the Wentworth Woodhouse estate for miners have already been mentioned as a very early example of a notable architect being involved in such "routine" work as industrial housing.[7] In general, a far lower standard of accommodation was provided even in the most advanced industrial centres than in the country estate villages. Possibly this is because at this period pattern books were aimed exclusively at the landed gentry, and it was not until the efforts of hygiene reformers or such publications as James Hole's book on *Homes for the Working Classes* of 1860 that industrial housing entered into the consciousness of the vast majority of those exploiting the ready labour at hand.

The Royal Commission of 1844, the first such report on housing conditions, contrasted the housing provided by the Ashworth brothers near Bolton with the back-to-back cottages at Preston which were used to illustrate the worst in minimum standard housing. The Preston cottages stood on a waste ground of mud, without gardens or vegetation, and backed on to an open drain common to all the houses. The misery of the situation was com-

Terraces of good quality housing built at Barrow Bridge during the 1830s

pleted by the view, the smoking chimneys of the factory the housing was built to serve. There was nothing exceptional about this — it was the norm, and activities of men such as the Ashworths were all the more remarkable for that. The Ashworths were cotton spinners, a Nonconformist family whose motives were overtly practical.[8] They realised the expediency of well-housed, content operatives in the mills and built hundreds of houses at Turton, New Eagley, Bank Top and Egerton between the early 1820s and the 1840s, when their fortunes fell.

As the workers were provided with the best available living standards, so their employers expected the best from them. The mills were hung with rule boards on which were written the golden words "thrift, order, promptitude and perseverance". Fines were handed out for any signs of remiss behaviour, but holidays and free days were relatively frequent, schools and shops were provided from very early days and by 1844 Egerton had a library and news-room, and by 1855 several chapels. The mills were provided with lavish gardens and the ground around the cottages was planted with evergreens.

Cottages were of variable size, and the Ashworths worked on the principle that pride in the cottages would be induced gradually, and that the workers would aspire to bigger houses once they had seen the advantages of their present homes. By 1835 piped water was provided and each house was presented with twenty feet of shelving, with the result that the cottagers filled them with lines of books and considerable trouble was taken over the furnishings. Conditions were checked by the Ashworths themselves and provision was made for the cottages to be whitewashed annually, painted every two years and papered at the expense of the company.

Another similarly advanced scheme was the housing provided at Barrow Bridge, where particular attention was paid to the attractive layout of the terraces which stood above a stream and wooded valley, and where the housing itself was well-designed, with crisply detailed window surrounds and door frames. The mills here were operational from 1837, but the housing dates from 1830 onwards, although the plan had been mooted long before in the 1770s. The cotton textile workers were housed in five terraces, each of six houses, placed on a slope and surrounded by ample gardens. There was a cooperative shop, and the two mills were nearby; the industrial function of the community was masked by the beauty of the countryside, which is still unblemished.

In far less auspicious surroundings is Bromborough Pool, which, because of its proximity to Port Sunlight, affords an interesting contrast with later developments.[9] The creation of the Wilson brothers, enlightened proprietors of Price's candle factory, the village was laid out by a London architect, Julian Hill. The cottages, very plain and unimaginative, were provided in a variety of sizes — two large bedrooms or one large and two small were the standard provision — but some had four. Sanitation was advanced, internal lavatories being provided rather than backyard privies, and very sizeable gardens were attached to each house. An article in the *Illustrated London News* said that "the cottages will attach the people much more closely to the place", and certainly this had become noticeable in the Ashworth villages, where there was a remarkably low labour turnover. But closer to the later paternalistic industrial schemes was the Wilson's real innovation, a branch of the Belmont Mutual Improvement Society "for instruction and intellectual recreation and to promote generally their intellectual, moral and social advancement". This became the focus of life at Bromborough Pool from 1854 onwards, providing lectures and a library and catering for and encouraging a considerable variety of interests. There is no doubt that this was one of the most genuine efforts to broaden the horizons of a working community, and cannot be attributed to motives of expediency or self-interest.

In the mid nineteenth century there was still a very deep gulf stretching between the wordy utopias of the idealists and the conscientious employer who made some attempt at building a satisfactory community for his workmen. The new worlds prophesied by the variously plumaged reformers had little bearing on the sinking standards in intensively industrial areas.

One exception was Sir Titus Salt, who doggedly pursued his ideal of an industrial community away from the heavy atmosphere of Bradford. His mills would be Italian Renaissance palaces, the housing would offer the best in hygienic living standards, and every opportunity for education and advancement would be at hand. Salt had made his fortune by spotting the potential of alpaca wool for the manufacture of worsted, and the

Designed by Lockwood and Mawson, Titus Salt's magnificent Italianate mill at Saltaire proclaimed the fortunes to be made in the mid-nineteenth century

Saltaire, almshouses: "they attract the notice of every visitor, and have the appearance of Italian villas, with walks and flower gardens in front, and creeping plants by the windows . . . the qualification for admission are good moral character, and incapacity for labour by reason of age, disease or infirmity"

same foresight marked his village, Saltaire.[10] Two reputable local architects, Lockwood and Mawson, built the village, which looked across to open country and to a great park by the riverside which emphasised the rural setting. Salt's village combined the practical lessons of earlier and sporadic philanthropic efforts with his own precise vision of the community he wished to create. It is said that he was influenced by reading Benjamin Disraeli's novel *Sybil* (published in 1847), with its description of the model village around the mill which is contrasted against the neighbouring squatters' village. Disraeli, who also describes another such village in *Coningsby* (which is possibly based on Ashworth's initiative), used the image of the ideal village to illustrate the path ahead.

By the mid-1860s, when James Hole was writing, Saltaire which had been founded in 1850 was already largely built. Five hundred and sixty houses were grouped around the magnificent soaring mill, and a church and temporary buildings for dining rooms, school room and a lecture hall were in use. Later buildings for an Institute and almshouses were ornate and expensively detailed but at this stage the terraces were given light Italianate detail and varied by the use of three storeys in the centre and on the ends of the blocks. Yet the housing at Saltaire was, strictly

Copley: Akroyd's earlier housing experiment from 1847 onwards

speaking, still back-to-back. A steam laundry was provided to obviate the necessity for lines of washing, an unsightly feature of back-to-back housing, and the identity of the community — now surrounded by outer suburbs of Bradford — is still preserved in its replacement, "The Village Launderette".

With the example set so notably by Sir Titus Salt, other employers began to follow suit. In Somerset, Clarks the leather manufacturers, a Quaker family, consistently provided good conditions for their workers, from the foundation of their company in 1825 onwards. The railway companies, too, constructed unimaginative but solid villages around 1840–50; as Palmerston put it, "the rage for railways is in our favour because railways create station-houses and station-houses beget villages and little towns are springing up everywhere upon the lines of railways".

In Halifax there was an element of competition in the establishment of model villages; Colonel Edward Akroyd, a local MP and textile manufacturer and a figure of great importance in the working-class housing movement, built two; the Crossleys, carpet manufacturers and local chieftains, built one. Titus Salt had had his eye on Paxton's Crystal Palace for the central feature of Saltaire, after the closure of the Great Exhibition, and certainly neither Akroyd nor the Crossleys thought quite as grandly as Salt. However, more modestly, these three villages all made their distinctive mark on housing history. Copley was Akroyd's first

The entrance to Copley Mill, an imposing classical arch with the date inscribed

venture, begun in 1847 (the same year as Bessbrook in Ireland), and although the housing was back-to-back it was situated in open country and on this count *The Builder* let the deficiency pass, noting that at least the windows could be opened for fresh air. Shops were provided, later a church, and the mill stood a little way off, while the housing was built in terraces of sturdy Gothic-detailed cottages. Akroydon, closer to Halifax, was the second of his villages and a much more advanced scheme. G.G. Scott was in charge of the overall plan, based on a large square with a central market cross, and Akroyd and the acting architect, W.H. Crossland, carried it out although Scott built the fine church. The cottages were to be built in blocks in the Gothic style, "to awaken the innate taste of the people for the beautiful in outline". Hygiene and advanced facilities were priority — running water and gas were provided and drainage was by "sanitary tubes". Local warm golden stone was used, and each cottage was identified by a stone monogram of its occupant's name over the door. Dormer windows were planned, but the future residents objected on the grounds that they smacked of the almshouse.

Even more interesting than the architectural details were Akroyd's ideas on social integration. He had pronounced views on this subject; as *The Builder* reported,[11] he wanted to mix the grades of housing so that "the better paid and better educated might act usefully on the desires and tastes of others in an inferior social position" the recurring hope of every idealistic village builder up to Henrietta Barnett at Hampstead.

The Builder also made some interesting comments on the interior arrangements of the housing, pointing out that a single large livingroom with a scullery was better suited to the needs of a family than two rooms, both needing fires. This would stretch the budget and mean that one room would remain virtually unused, as is still the case. A chilly parlour for Sundays and holidays stayed empty while the other room would be used for all pur-

Aerial view of Akroydon, an enlightened industrial housing project built by Colonel Akroyd from 1859 onwards. Note the ramshackle housing deliberately shown in the background for contrast

poses. Akroyd's cottages were the two usual sizes, two- or three-bedroomed versions, with similar exteriors. The building activities at Halifax were closely allied to the early days of the Halifax Building Society, an organisation which for the first time made the purchase of a house over a period of years a viable proposition for the working man. In Halifax itself, it was the influence of the Crossleys that was most felt. John Crossley had built himself a Gothic mansion, Francis Crossley a French château, and the family had laid out a fine park, given almshouses, churches and the town hall and built a sizeable estate on the fringes of the town at West Hill Park.[12] It is appropriate that when Sir Francis Crossley looked for a stately home in the latter part of his life, he should choose the mansion and perfect model village built by Sir Morton Peto at Somerleyton. The interests of benevolent landowner and philanthropic industrialist came neatly together.[13]

Notes

1. John Cornforth, "A Mill and its Master", *Country Life*, 28 December 1972.
2. W. Mavor, *The British Tourists*, 1798.
3. W. Bray, *Tour Through some of the Midland Counties into Derbyshire and Yorkshire*, 1777.
4. Conservation report, Brandt Potter Hare.
5. E. Beazley, *Madocks and the Wonder of Wales*, London, 1967.
6. *Industrial Archaeology*, August 1973.
7. Sydney Smirke was another architect who at an early date (1834) put forward ideas for improved industrial housing. In his *Suggestions for the Improvement of the Western Parts of the Metropolis* he wrote, "Portions of unoccupied ground should be taken in the skirts of the town... and let a village, expressly dedicated to the working classes, be there erected." He proposed an open layout with avenues, recreation areas and houses "totally differing in every respect from the small, close, inconvenient tenements usually let out into lodgings".
8. R. Boyson, *The Ashworth Cotton Enterprise*, Oxford, 1970.
9. A. Watson, *Price's Village*, Bromborough, 1966.
10. James Stevens Curl, "A Victorian Model Town", *Country Life*, 9 March 1972. Holroyd, *Saltaire and its Founder*, 1871.
11. *The Builder*, 14 February 1863.
12. Mark Girouard, "A Town Built on Carpets", *Country Life*, 24

September 1970.

13. Later, in 1883, utopianism and industrial housing schemes came together in the Society for Promoting Industrial Villages; chairman was Henry Solly who wrote on the subject, finance came in part from Samuel Morley (of Leigh). Contrasted against the practical work of a man such as Edward Akroyd, the whole scheme, though idealistic, smacks of hot air and produced no positive results.

Chapter 9

Bournville and Port Sunlight: Two Approaches to a Problem

In 1861, as Saltaire was rising in its valley outside Bradford, George Cadbury took over the family tea and coffee firm. He had spent much of his spare time working in Sunday Schools and had a Quaker conscience for the welfare of others and an unusually clear sight of what needed to be done to improve life for his employees.

However, it was not until later, when the firm moved out into the countryside to a new large factory, that the situation offered itself for a real advance, not merely in the smaller details but for a change in environment. The essential difference between Cadbury's plans at Bournville and others, before and after, was that they were designed not merely as improved *industrial* housing, but as improved housing equally suitable for office workers as for packers in the cocoa factory. The planning was revolutionary; low density suburban villa development was the starting-point with large detached housing replaced by various cottage forms, both terraced and semi-detached.

The first stage of the enterprise was the sixteen houses that Cadbury built for the foremen; they were surrounded by ample gardens planted with fruit trees and there were a swimming pool and sports ground nearby. Physical fitness was one of Cadbury's prerequisites for a contented employee — in the official photographs taken in 1912 of the workers in the grounds around the factory, enormous emphasis is laid on groups of men doing press-ups and women doing gentle gymnastics. Equally, gardening and the learning of efficient horticulture were encouraged, with teaching plots provided and instruction on their use.

Cadbury thought that employees could achieve a measure of independence and self-sufficiency, as well as health, by cultivating

Girl employees passing an idyllic lunch hour at Bournville

their own vegetables, and he rightly felt that gardening was the perfect antidote for repetitious work. He had a much more perceptive attitude to the problem of stifling industrial paternalism than others such as Lever, and to this end he kept the housing for his employees to only 50% of the total at Bournville.

The scheme really got under way in 1895 when W. Alexander Harvey and Cadbury began to plan a complete community; a great central green with shopping facilities and institutional buildings formed the hub of the village and from this wound informal roads with houses set in gardens around them. Profits on the scheme were ploughed back, and the administration was carried out by a Trust.[1]

The factory was surrounded by gardens, where the white-gowned workers could idle by the rose bushes in their lunch breaks, another palliative for the tedium of assembly-line work. One of the problems that the Bournville architects came up against was that of restrictive by-laws which governed road widths and meant an enormous wastage of valuable land; laws

Aerial view of Bournville, showing the clear distinction between the housing in the village, with its large garden areas and winding roads, and the areas beyond

framed for typical urban planning were laughable applied to a fresh approach such as Bournville represented.

The village exerted an influence world wide; from Germany the architect of the Krupp village of Margaretenhöhe was sent over to visit Bournville, and it was of great interest to those planning similar ventures in Britain, Lever, Rowntree and Henrietta Barnett.

Surveys were conducted on the Bournville residents — one proved that the children were two to three inches taller there than in slum areas of Birmingham, and after the leader of the Labour party in the Reichstag had paid a visit in 1912 he wrote to Cadbury "... I have repeatedly exhibited the pictures you gave me and was asked by those who saw them to what the gymnasium, swimming baths, park etc. belonged. They all thought they were looking at pictures of a watering place and it did not occur to anyone that these places were for the use of factory hands". Another observer said "the Bournville community differs from

Morris's dream only in being healthier and truer". There could be no doubt of Cadbury's utopian sincerity; he lived by a set of standards befitting a staunch Quaker, leading the sort of unostentatious existence that did not conflict with his attempts to improve the living standards of others. Cadbury's personal campaign, together with those of his friends and colleagues in the same field, was of immense importance in applying pressure to Parliament and in passing the onus of housing reform into the hands of government.

The cottages were built with emphasis on economy; building costs were falling in this period as the processes of mechanisation and mass production, together with simpler construction, made themselves felt. In the late nineteenth century £300 was considered the minimum sum for a good cottage, while by the 1920s the figure was little over £100. At Bournville plain brick was used, the houses had large windows and were grouped either singly or in groups of up to four as courts. The effect was lightened by ingenious chimney designs and sometimes by porches and verandahs, while inside were such innovations as the "patent adjustable cabinet bath" and the inglenook. Both the practical and the decorative were attended to.

William Hesketh Lever, like George Cadbury, started his empire from expansion of a family grocery business. His acumen was such that in 1887, after just three years in operation, Sunlight soap was the best selling brand on the market. From a strong Nonconformist background — his father had been Church of England converted to Congregationalist — Lever decided, when moving his factory and expanding his business, to go one further and to build a self-contained and model community.[2]

From the earliest moments when he scribbled his ideas on the backs of envelopes, until, after years of constant absorption in the project, he actually came to live at Port Sunlight, one can trace the ever-present figure of Lever. On 3 March 1888, as Mrs Lever cut the first sod with a silver spade, Lever addressed the crowd:

"It is my and my brother's hope some day to build houses in which our workpeople will be able to live and be comfortable — semi-detached houses with gardens back and front in which they will be able to know more about the science of life than they can in a back-to-back slum, and in which they will learn that there is more enjoyment in life than the mere going to and returning from work and looking forward to Saturday night to draw their wages."

141

Kitchen of a cottage at Bournville. The sunken bath, economising on space but not hygiene, was a great innovation

Like a possessive parent, Lever could not, as Cadbury was able to, leave the village which he had founded any measure of independence. With the brooding presence of the factory, the sole employer of every man in the village, the constant respect required for its founder and the extraordinarily hermetic effect of the village plan, it is hardly surprising that one union official commented that "no man of an independent turn of mind could breathe for long in the atmosphere of Port Sunlight".

"The individual or community which has no ideal is to be pitied" were the opening words of an early book written on Port Sunlight.[3] Certainly, it was not the profit motive that prompted men such as Cadbury and Lever, who had amassed fortunes within a short period, to pour their money into altruistic schemes for their employees. Religious conviction bringing with it a highly developed sense of responsibility was the motivating force.

Life at Port Sunlight still bears the marks of an oppressively paternalistic regime, though the 1st Lord Leverhulme died many years ago and the overlord is now an amorphous company. That a man's house, workplace, sport and

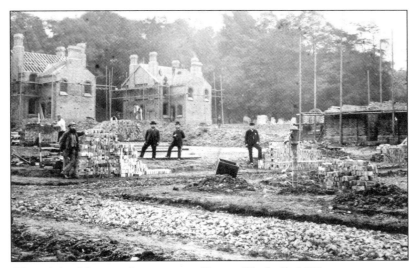

The original foremen's cottages at Bournville, built 1879

entertainment are all provided by courtesy of one agent is suffocating and induces a depressing feeling of being bespoken for; this is shown in one recent account of the village.[4] One woman who came to Port Sunlight on her marriage is glad to live close to the edge of the village to retain a sense of connection with the "outside world". The soapy pall which obscures the sky is a constant reminder that the factory is just around the corner.*

However, the inception of the scheme was to provide low-cost housing, secure employment, pleasant surroundings and a full range of facilities at hand. The housing is uncommonly attractive and of advanced design for its date.

From the first the unions were strongly against Lever's plan. His attempt to exonerate capitalism — industrial housing being one of the open sores of the system — was not welcomed and his

*Recently Polly Toynbee returned. In *Hard Work: Life in Low-pay Britain*, (London, 2003) she records the changes at the Unilever factory with its "slimmed-down, self-supervising, multiskilled workforce". The village of Port Sunlight is now almost entirely owner-occupied and houses much sought after.

143

abortive co-partnership scheme was resented as high-handed despotism, though Lever called it "enlightened self interest".

The aims of the village were "a conveniently planned and healthy settlement laid out with all possible artistic thought on sound business lines". Economics and sanitation were to be wrapped with taste. In architectural terms Port Sunlight was more important than Bournville, though both shared the garden suburb planning which had come down from the Victorian residential parks of the larger northern towns. Port Sunlight represented a many-faceted retreat into a stylistic retrospective view of English cottage building, rivalling the eclecticism of Edensor, and one writer referred to its "chaste antique design". Anne Hathaway's cottage is faithfully reproduced, Kenyon Hall reappears as a cottage group, and every material is used — half-timbering, patterned brick with ornate turrets, plain white plasterwork and much else. Many architects were involved, but in the range of styles it is Douglas (the Eaton estate architect) whose hand is most noticeable. The housing is placed above the roads and much of the frontage consists of open grass, giving a smooth landscaped unity at the expense of individual gardens, which were ordered behind the houses. Economics were a relatively minor consideration. No cost was spared on the decoration and high quality craftsmanship that went into the cottages.

Owen, the company architect and personal friend of Lever, drew up the first plan for twenty-eight cottages and an entrance gate in December 1888, and over twenty years later, in 1910, he won the Grand Prix at Brussels for his cottages. The natural landscape, a wooded dell being the prominent feature, was incorporated and the fully developed plan was for a great *beaux-arts* scheme centring on the church and later, the art gallery. This was not completed, and Port Sunlight has some of the unsatisfactory marks of a grand conception that has fallen short of its aim.

Port Sunlight exhibited many aspects which were to be of great influence; the cloaking of working-class housing in a middle-class disguise was one, and as at Thornton Hough, Lever's country estate village nearby, it was becoming obvious how influential the architecture of the small house was becoming.

The village was continually in the public eye: Gladstone opened the Recreational Hall in 1891, King Albert of Belgium visited

Port Sunlight incognito in 1903 and was so impressed he encouraged Lever to build settlements in the Congo (one was called Leverville), and in 1914 the King and Queen visited the works and paid a "surprise" visit to one of the houses.

Port Sunlight was obligatory on Town and Country Planning Association itineraries and a musical produced in 1912 took Port Sunlight for its setting. *The Sunshine Girl.*

Lever was a Liberal MP and in 1919, as Lord Leverhulme spoke in the House of Lords of "a deep-rooted suspicion between employers and employed which ought not to exist. I think it arises entirely from misunderstanding." He had campaigned unceasingly for old-age pensions, arranged for a shorter working day, believed in the workers' right to strike and was deeply committed to bettering housing conditions in his capacity as a Trustee of Hampstead Garden Suburb and a member of the Garden Cities Association. He had also sponsored the Department of Town Planning and Civic Design set up in 1909 in Liverpool University. It is perhaps churlish to emphasise the aspects of Port Sunlight that, with hindsight, appear suffocating and misdirected. The plethora of organisations, social clubs, educational and recreational facilities were all non-profit-making concerns, intended to widen the outlook of the families living there, though Lever may not have foreseen that they would soon be educated to reject just this sort of environment, for one where self-determination was more important. He showed an inkling of the problem in one speech when he noted that "the workman is not to be kept turning as a machine by satisfying his wants. Every fresh aspiration of the workman that we grant today will lift him higher and give him new aspirations tomorrow and so we shall always have what we call labour unrest if we are to be a healthy community."

Port Sunlight, together with Bournville, represented the breaking down of distinctions between housing for workers, and housing for others. Excellent housing of the highest available standards had been the privilege of the few — Lever's efforts were instrumental in extending this privilege to the many.

From the late eighteenth century, Britain, as the first extensively industrialised country, had been watched from elsewhere with considerable interest. The same problems were looming all over Europe and in America, and attention was focused wherever attempts were being made to solve them. New Lanark attracted innumerable foreign visitors and so too did Bournville and Port Sunlight in their turn.

However, by the late nineteenth century many other pioneering attempts had been made and the currents flowed both ways. For example Lever made a number of visits to the Van Marken village, Agneta, outside Delft. Here the Dutch yeast and vegetable oil concern had founded in 1883 a ten-acre park of cottages for their workers, grouped around a circular road with a central lake. Eighty families were housed here, and together with traditional-style cottages went numerous small thoughtful details such as wooden rubbish boxes and special clothes horses for outside airing of clothes. The motto at the works was "the factory for all; all for the factory", and the general scheme was far more cooperative than anything Lever set up. The housing was owned by the Common Property Society and the aim was to keep an air of self-determination throughout.

Early aerial view of Port Sunlight. The surroundings, railways and smoking factories are in marked contrast with the village itself

In Germany, around Essen, the Krupp's villages moved gradually towards a garden village image, though those built in the 1890s were designed as mock-medieval settlements. In France there was a tradition in industrial housing almost as well founded as that in Britain by the time the Menier chocolate company built Noisiel in the 1870s. Here neat housing, generous gardens and a full range of facilities made it a genuinely enlightened effort at building a pleasant community around the place of work. Examples from Europe are innumerable,[6] but in America the picture was less happy.

Despite the example of early religious communities and frontier settlements, the American industrialists achieved less visionary results with their foundations. Basically they were faced with the problem of creating new centres — few existing sites of towns were suitable for this type of expansion. Many centres were run on restrictively Puritan lines but tended to ignore the compensations offered by their European counterparts — good education, facilities for recreation and a fair standard of housing.

Apathy in the direction of social concern was common, and where paternalism was practised, as at Pullman, it made Lever's oppressive regime seem freedom by comparison. Pullman, the most ambitious of American foundations[7] built in the late 1880s, was gripped by a desperate strike in 1894, and behind the façade of a model settlement were found hidden the skeletons of a truly appalling situation where the workers were exploited more than many who lived in unambitious tenement communities elsewhere.

Leclaire, Illinois, was a rare example of a profit-sharing organisation with a pleasant company town to back up the benefits of cooperation between workers and their management. Yet the fact remained that the influence Bournville and Port Sunlight exerted in America was not in the area of industrial housing, but in that of suburban development. The social message had little meaning in a country where the rich very rarely considered crossing the divide to assist those who had failed to match their own achievements.

Notes

1. *Report of Bournville Village Trust 1900-1955,* Bournville, 1956. Also A.G. Gardiner, *Life of George Cadbury*, 1923. See also Alexander Harvey, *Model Village: Bournville*, London, 1906.
2. Described in innumerable articles: also C. Wilson, *History of Unilever*, Vol. 1, London, 1954.
3. Raffles Davison, *Port Sunlight*, 1916; also W.L. George, *Labour and Housing at Port Sunlight*, 1911.
4. Polly Toynbee, *A Working Life*, London, 1971.
5. For Lever himself see *Viscount Leverhulme* by his son, the 2nd Viscount, London, 1927. A more balanced biography is given by Nigel Nicolson, *Lord of the Isles*, London, 1960, an account of Leverhulme's unhappy attempts to practise paternalism on the crofters of Lewis and Harris from 1917 onwards. He planned to redevelop Stornoway (Raffles Davison produced an extraordinary sketch), and then, failing that, to found Leverburgh (formerly Obbe) as a fishing harbour. This scheme produced only a few cottages and some warehouses; for the first time, one of Leverhulme's plans was a disastrous failure.
6. Budgett Meakin, *Model Factories and Villages*, 1905. The most important early pioneering attempts in Europe were those at Le Grand-Hornu by De Gorge-Legrand (architect Renard) from 1819–32 and the work at Mulhouse by textile manufacturers culminating in the Société Mulhousienne des Cités Ouvrières, founded in 1853. See *Industrial Archaeology*, Vol. 6, 1969.
7. S. Buder, *Pullman*, New York, 1967. Another account of an early American industrial enterprise is John Coolidge, *Mill and Mansion*, New York, 1942, which deals with Lowell, Massachusetts.

Chapter 10

Utopias

Community building on paper has always proved an easier task than community building in reality. The experience of utopian thinkers of the past, it is equally the experience of planners now. Fortunately, against the weight of evidence, optimists have always added the positive note which ensures the continuance of a search for an environment which will match aspirations.

One such optimist was John Bellers[1] who, in 1696, presented his plans for a community to the Houses of Lords and Commons with these words: "I humbly pray you would please to consider it, and as may be agreeable to your wisdom (like the summer sun to a fruitful tree) ripen these proposals to the nation's advantage." The proposals he put forward were to produce "an epitomy of the world, by a collection of all the useful trades in it; so it may afford all the conveniences and comforts a man can want, and a christian use... regular people (of all visible creatures) being the life and perfection of Treasure, the strength of nations, and glory of princes."

He saw his "regular people" settled in a self-supporting "college", and proposed that work would be shared, so that the "mechanicks" would help on the land at harvest time, while education was to be emphasised above all else. His idea, a great advance on the workhouse on which it was based, fell on stony ground at the time, but in 1819 Robert Owen reprinted the pamphlet, which contained the seeds of many of his theories.

The firmest basis, however, for idealistic experiment was religion. The monastery provided the nearest equivalent to successful community living and from this came the early religious settlements, which expanded monasticism into larger-scale village units. The first such villages in Britain were founded by

Chapel at Fulneck Moravian village, surrounded by school buildings. The crisp classical style is typical of Moravian settlements

the Moravians, a German Protestant sect who used a set formula, both of planning and social organisation, wherever they founded a settlement. Between 1744 and the 1780s seven villages were built in England and Ireland, all based on the German prototype, Herrnhut.[2]

The first village was Fulneck near Pudsey, which was also the most lavish. Wesley kept a close eye on the Moravians and commented that "the Germans suppose it will cost by the time it is finished about £3,000. It is well if it be not nearer £10,000. But it is no concern of the English brethren. They are told (and patently believe) that "all the money will come from beyond the sea".[3] In fact, building the nine houses and essential communal facilities cost £15,000, chiefly because of problems posed by an awkward site, a ledge on a steep hillside. Fulneck was built as a long terrace, with another row of housing running parallel which included the chapel and brethren's housing.

Front view of the principal buildings in Fulneck, which form a single block facing over the valley

The members of the village carried on several trades including textile work, and received a salary while the profits reverted to the community. Wesley commented sourly, "I do not see that the mighty power of God can hinder them from acquiring millions," adding, "but can they lay up treasure on earth and at the same time lay up treasure in heaven?"

Whatever Wesley's views, the fact remains that, unlike so many subsequent cooperative schemes, at least three of the Moravian communities were successful in economic terms.

The later villages were based on a square plan and were built in a traditional eighteenth-century urban style. Each one had a chapel, marked by its superior classical architecture, schools, houses for the single brothers and sisters, and other housing as well as shops and workshops. Life was not particularly circumscribed, great emphasis was placed on pleasantly planted gardens and surroundings, and the schools became noted for their exceptional education. Richard Oastler, a notable campaigner against child labour in factories, had been a pupil at Fulneck and commented that the emphasis was on character formation and knowledge treated as something stimulating to inquiring minds, rather than on stern discipline and grim tasks.

Housing at Fairfield

James Silk Buckingham, a later utopian theorist, described the Irish Moravian village of Gracehill in one of his magazine.[4] The textiles produced by the sisters were sold in their own shop on the spot, and as far afield as Dublin, and the general picture drawn is far from the misery of factory workers of the period, or indeed, from the desperate poverty of agricultural workers, particularly in Ireland. Gracehill became an object of wonder, as an oasis of calm and order throughout all the political upheavals, and even in the Rebellion of 1798 it had escaped pillage. The village was approached through an avenue of ash trees and the housing was situated round a central green, where was a gravel walk for "relaxation and recreation" while the evening service consisted of short prayers and much hymn singing. The burial ground had an "air of peculiar quiet and repose" and this was a feature of all the Moravian villages, especial care being lavished on the planting and landscaping of the graveyards. Death was to be anticipated as an arcadian pleasure ahead, not as hell-fires and brimstone.

Fairfield, close to Manchester, was the last of the English communities to be built.[5] To arrive there now, approaching through the arid red brick miles of Droylesden and drab outer Manchester, is a curious experience. A neatly paved eighteenth-century enclave, with tree-lined streets and well detailed brick housing, Fairfield seems to have been swallowed whole by the nineteenth century (there is remarkably little evidence of the twentieth). Originally the village had its own inn, shops, baker, laundry and farm together with a fireman, night watchman, inspector of weights and measures, overseer of roads and doctor; all for some two hundred people.

Early print of Fairfield, the Moravian village near Manchester. The chapel is in the centre, with houses for male and female single brethren segregated to either side

The village dates from 1785 and is planned as a square within a square, with a fine chapel and large school.

The building of these Moravian villages was in the hands of a board, but it is interesting that the birthplace of the great American architect, Benjamin Latrobe, was Fulneck, where his father was schoolmaster. The man who designed the Virginia State Capitol in Romantic Classical style and who helped spread this style across America was brought up amid the neat classical lines of this remote Yorkshire religious community.[6]*

Charles Kingsley felt that the Moravians had succeeded where other socialist experiments had failed because they were "undertaken in fear of God, and with humility and caution... and acted up to their own creed, that they were brothers and sisters, members of one body..." These principles, instilled through the excellent schools, "the steam engine of the moral work", allied to an emphasis on personal happiness, meant the continuance of these tightly knit settlements into the mid-nineteenth century, while the schools are still flourishing. The emphasis laid on cooperation, discipline, "brotherly love and harmony", advanced education and a non-doctrinaire attitude to religion all tend to make later efforts to achieve the same ends seem heavy-handed and dictatorial.

Fairfield particularly, situated close to the epicentre of industrial expansion, attracted a great deal of interest; one observer wrote in the 1790s that the village was visited by considerable numbers from Manchester. Against the background of exploitation and virtual slavery by industry presented by this period, such an oasis of civilised existence in its calm and pleasant surroundings, where religious tolerance and humane principles were all important, was an extraordinary rebuke to employers. The obvious contentment of those who lived there proved that the level at which employees elsewhere were expected to live was inhumane and bestial. In addition, it exemplified the success of a system of cooperation and self-sufficiency, provided that the administration was efficient and that the principles upon which the settlement was based were adhered to.

The Moravians were mentioned wherever plans were being laid for new communities; William Allen consulted Latrobe before

*In fact it turns out that the 19 year old Latrobe designed the buildings for Fairfield. See Gillian Darley, "The Moravians: Building for a Higher Purpose", Architectural Review, April 1985.

founding Lindfield, John Minter Morgan took his schemes to Moravian leaders for consultation, and J.S. Buckingham, as has been seen, devoted space to lengthy descriptions of Moravian settlements.

That the man who effected the greatest revolution in industrial conditions should have spent his youth in Manchester is hardly coincidental. Robert Owen lived there from 1788 until 1799, and he can hardly have been unaware of the newly built community at Fairfield, with its notable educational and economic successes. Even the physical form influenced him, for he used the principle of interlocking squares for his Villages of Cooperation, the same plan as the Moravian village.

In June 1819, with New Lanark behind him and far more ambitious plans ahead, Robert Owen addressed a meeting to consider his plans for "village settlements according to new principles". A distinguished company heard these plans and observed models for his establishments for one thousand people. One of the principal objects was to "have children educated in habits of industry and morality", to which end all children aged three or over would be

Shaker housing in the Berkshires, USA, the only utopian sect to develop its own architectural style

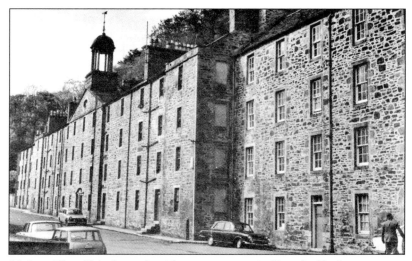

Main mill at New Lanark with tenements extending the block

placed in dormitories, attended by the community as a whole and visited by their parents. Owen visualised each settlement with a minimum of 300 and a maximum of 2,000 inhabitants, each village being placed within range of similar communities so that they "will be found capable of combining within themselves all the advantages that city and country residence now afford, without any of the numerous inconveniences and evils which necessarily attach to both those modes of society". This arrangement, on a reduced scale, pre-figures the satellite cities proposed by Ebenezer Howard, and even New Town planning of the present. Confidence in the village as a suitable unit has not wavered.

Concluding his meeting, Owen declared "that he had no ambition to qualify in introducing this measure: he never would accept of any fee or reward from any party for any service he might render to the country. In the act of performing these things he secured all he wished or ever for one moment contemplated." Owen was undoubtedly sincere in this statement. As the son of a post-master in Newtown in mid Wales, Owen, whose first job was as a draper's assistant, was self-educated and closely in touch with working-class realities. His utopian schemes were infinitely more applicable than, for instance, those of his French counterpart, Charles Fourier, whose theories were presented cocooned in verbosity and near-unintelligible phraseology. Fourier was always jealous of Owen, whose charm of manner had won him influential and rich support.

The most successful attempt to follow Fourier's theory for a great multi-unit single building, to be called the Phalanx, was Jean-Baptiste Godin's Familistère at Guise, built after his death. Another attempt was made at the North American Phalanx, New Jersey, which was established in 1849, and the Fourierists were highly influential in the community building movement in the United States through the many adherents who joined other settlements in following years.[7] Owen, on the other hand, was generous towards Fourier's ideas which, apart from the emphasis on a single block rather than Owen's square, and admitting the importance of individual independence within such a community, were not dissimilar to his own. He recognised this fact in later years when recommending his American followers to pay attention to Fourierist experiments there and to be friendly towards the participants.

Undoubtedly, Owen's personality went far towards smoothing his path; he did not rant or threaten but was always "fair, open, practical and kind". In an article in the *Calcutta Journal* it is remarked that the "same spirit of kindness which produces so much visible good in Mr Owen's establishment at New Lanark enables him to make way in a remarkable manner among all classes of people".

He did, however, succeed in upsetting three boards of directors at New Lanark with his tolerant Deism, and William Allen was only one of the many offended parties. Despite constantly questioning Owen, he was unable to receive a satisfactory reply to his well-intentioned but pestering letters: "It is now the general opinion [he wrote in 1815] that my friend is the determined enemy of all revealed religion".

New Lanark, where Owen first had the opportunity to practise and develop his theories, was only the first of many schemes but is of particular interest as a link between the early years of the industrial age, a period when improved conditions were considered rather for their expediency in labour relations than for any profound motives, and the epoch of genuinely enlightened industrial philanthropy, usually recognised as beginning with Sir Titus Salt. New Lanark was a highly profitable concern where Owen could afford to make experiments in education and social reform,[8] from which experiences and observations he could build utopian schemes based on practical knowledge. Although the later plans for socialist communities far outran anything attempted at New Lanark, once his success there was widely acknowledged he could afford to introduce his more visionary ideas. In 1800 Owen had been faced with 1,800 unruly and rough Scots, and by applying regulations, temperance, discipline, cleanliness and economy, he had turned this rude material into a law-abiding contented community. It was an enormous achievement, but one he never repeated owing to a fatal lack of judgement and impatience with detail.

Having married David Dale's daughter and become his partner, he was managing the mills by 1800. Highly successful in this capacity, he was soon able to devote more attention to the wellbeing and education of his employees, child and adult alike. Dale had already initiated some schemes which, despite the use of child labour and appalling hours, were relatively enlightened for the time, and Owen built upon these foundations. In 1816 he opened the Institution for the Formation of Character, the crowning achievement of his years at New Lanark.

As these initial aims became realised, so Owen set his sights higher and proceeded to mould his workforce into a community into which individual desires would be absorbed, on which he based *A New View of Society* published in 1813, and from which he evolved his plans for New Harmony and other American Owenite experiments, and Harmony Hall in Hampshire.

A view of New Lanark is presented by John Griscom, an American who visited the village in 1819.[9] On meeting Owen he commented, "I know no man of equal celebrity, whose manners are less imposing, and who has more of the candour and openness of a child." He remarks on the cleanliness of the place, the cheerfulness and courtesy of the people "whose appearance bespoke health and satisfaction". The factories closing at half past six, the rest of the evening was given over to schooling, music and dance. The dancing master was the village painter and glazier who "took up the fiddle in the evening, and instructed his motley group in the profound mysteries of the Highland Reel". Owen placed great emphasis on dancing as a fit amusement, a happy and relaxing alternative to the hours of labour, and an excellent method of keeping people out of trouble. Griscom was foolish enough to indulge in religious argument with Owen and seemed slightly taken aback at the breadth of his views; though holding to no particular creed himself, "he is willing others should enjoy theirs, provided they fulfil its duties without molesting their neighbours".

On his second day at New Lanark, Griscom was shown the schools, where children remained until they were about ten years old. This was one of Owen's most important innovations since children of six and seven were employed for a full day as a matter of course at this period. Other novel features were the infant school, enabling mothers to continue working, and the warming of the main buildings by steam. As far as the community went, Griscom was bowled over by admiration for the system: "There is not, I apprehend, to be found in any part of the world, a manufacturing village, or a community of equal extent, composed of persons indiscriminately brought together, without any peculiar bond of fraternity, in which so much order, good government, tranquillity and rational happiness prevail." Of Owen's own ideas, he had less flattering words to offer. He saw no future in his shining schemes, mostly because of their lack of Christian principles. The Shakers and Harmonists succeeded in their communities, he felt, because of the unity of their aims through their faith.

The lack of reasoning and logic were, in his view, the weak point of Owen's plans as, in fact, they proved to be and Griscom, after an infuriating evening of inconclusive discussion with his host, remarked, "You may encircle him with the cords of reason and argument, but instead of labouring to untie the knots, he snaps the string and takes his stand in another position."

Though William Cobbett greeted Owen's schemes as "a species of monkery", there were many others who found inspiration and motivation for their own plans.

The publication of Owen's schemes and his work at New Lanark were recognised from the beginning as being of considerable significance, stretching far beyond the confines of conventional industrial relations, and his example sparked off other attempts to revolutionise patterns of living around factories and in rural areas. A new recognition of social responsibilities meant that more landowners and industrialists were being forced to admit to certain basic human rights, which had to be granted if there was to be stability in the future. All over Britain schemes were being put into action, some merely fly-by-night ventures that vanished as fast as the cash contributed to their foundation, but others the product of deep conviction and earnest effort.

One of the least known of Owen's followers was John Moggridge, a Monmouth magistrate and industrialist, who published the account of his villages in the *Oriental Herald*,[10] another of the ubiquitous J.S. Buckingham's many publications. Moggridge's schemes were an antidote to emigration — at this period a favourite cure-all — and he quoted Milton to uphold his view: "There cannot be a more ill-biding sign to a nation, than when the people, to avoid hardships at home are forced by heaps to foresake their native country."

Having discussed his schemes with Owen, he went home to Wales and set about providing conditions conducive to self-help and which would help combat defeatism. These were firstly the provision of land on which colliery workers and farm labourers could build their own homes, and secondly considerable loans to enable them to do so. Financial rewards were not his aim and he seems to have been a genuine idealist.

The villagers were to pay ground rent, build their own houses and cultivate their gardens, repaying the loans over a set period. There was a ready-made landscape of mature trees and a central green, and nine years after its foundation in 1820, Blackwood, the first of the villages, consisted of more than 250 houses. Medical services, shops, workshops for craftsmen and small tradesmen, school and market house — which doubled as chapel for some time — were provided, and despite industrial problems at the collieries in 1827 which caused a temporary halt to activities, the village was reported to be still expanding. Two other settlements, Yuisdd and Trelyn, were formed on the same principles, and the total population of these three villages was over 2,000 by 1829.

Owen influenced at least sixteen American communities and seven in Britain. Many other cooperative experiments owed their conception to the rapid spread and enormously widely publicised interest in his ideas and the great enthusiasm of his close followers. The common denominator of these attempts at resettlement, such as those at Manea Fen[11]* or Ralahine in Ireland, was either

---

Dreamed up by Octavia Hill's passionately Owenite father, James Hill.

the lack of strong and efficient guiding personalities in their formative stages, or, at the opposite extreme, an overpowerful leader who alienated his settlers or single-handedly wrecked the scheme. An example of the latter was the Irish landowner, John Scott Vandeleur, who set up Ralahine in an excess of enthusiasm to solve the problems of the Irish tenantry. He built a great hall and six cottages, and then, with the aid of E.T. Craig who was a leading Manchester follower of Owen, set up an advanced and successful agricultural settlement with school and social security system. From its conception in 1830 until 1833 the community flourished, remarkably in view of it being situated on an Irish estate, but Vandeleur gambled away his land and the scheme crashed to the ground.

This sort of rapid failure was common. The extraordinary problems of complex organisation and of putting into practice a novel social structure overwhelmed the idealists, and only with a determined leader such as Owen himself could the settlements be pressured into existence, let alone continuance. Added to this, instead of the careful selection of men advocated, they were motley crowds of misfits — the type of people the Chartist land colonies also attracted — and the original ideals of the community were often followed only by those in charge.

In 1824 Owen divested himself of responsibility for New Lanark and irrevocably turned his back on life as a manufacturer. He put a very large proportion of his personal fortune into his American scheme, New Harmony, which he had taken over from the German religious sect, the Rappites. His chief collaborator in this scheme was William Maclure, a radical, whose great interest was in the educational possibilities of applying Pestalozzian principles (which held the village unit to be the ideal community), and who brought to New Harmony distinguished teachers and scientists on his boat "The Philanthropist" — the Boatload of Knowledge. Even this core of intellectuals was not enough to make an ideal community and Owen returned to Britain in 1827 (although New Harmony itself continued under Maclure in the thirties), having lost a considerable fortune. At this stage, already world famous and lauded as the inspiration and driving force behind the successes at New Lanark, Owen did not plan and organise as necessary. In addition, he and Maclure had had conflicting ideas in various respects and so Owen's return was under clouds of collapsed plans and financial disaster.

Owen had set out bearing plans by his architect, Stedman Whitwell, for a giant square with the principal buildings differentiated by a stark, rather visionary, style — oddly comparable to municipal architecture of the 1930s or even Mussolini's E.U.R. outside Rome. The square was the unit Owen based his Villages of Cooperation upon, each square being equidistant from other identical squares. Whitwell's drawing shows marked similarities to a scheme for almshouses published by P.F. Robinson in *Rural Architecture* (1823),which in turn is based on a college quadrangle or monastic cloister. Owen's architect was a little known pupil of Sir John Soane who was possibly particularly keen to remove himself to America in view of the fact that his work on the Brunswick Theatre was rewarded by its collapse after two performances, but New Harmony was never to rise to vindicate his reputation. Owenite communities never adopted an architectural style as did the Shaker or Moravian villages.

New Lanark attracted visitors from all over the world, including Tsar Nicholas of Russia. It had convinced Owen of his near infallibility but from the moment he rescinded responsibility for that, his sure touch began to falter, in practical terms. The success of New Lanark as a business enterprise had ensured a firm basis for experimentation, but the later efforts to found communities had no such foundation and extravagant innovation without financial stability is a recipe for spectacular failure.

One such enterprise that seemed set for success was Orbiston in Lanarkshire. A local landowner and a tanner, Alexander Hamilton and Abraham Combe, were the men behind the scheme.[12] It was the third attempt to found a settlement in the area, and originally it had been planned to fall directly under Owen's aegis.

Early progress at Orbiston was encouraging. The physical form of the community was a single great building, with a central block and two massive projecting wings. It was in fact much closer to the Phalanx proposed by Fourier than Owen's own Villages of Cooperation. Only one of the wings was built, but this could house 300, and a factory, inn and other facilities were constructed. Plans for a theatre were carried out and the scheme would be supported by its dual activities of agriculture and industry. One of the donors to the fund for the foundation of Orbiston was Minter Morgan, already supporting the cause he was going to contribute his own ideas to.

The potential members of the community built Orbiston themselves, but while the first concrete results were rising the

Orbiston Register was already looking far into the future with plans for holiday houses run for the benefit of members of the community in the Scottish Highlands, Glasgow and Edinburgh. The editor, Combe, was constantly looking ahead and published admonitory notices if he felt behaviour in the village fell below standards. In reality, the least satisfactory aspect was the schooling — it proved very hard to find a suitable Pestalozzian teacher — and the most satisfactory aspect the iron foundry.

The reason for the collapse of Orbiston, however, was the one event that could not have been foreseen or averted, the death of Alexander Hamilton, on whose land it stood and with much of whose money it had been founded. He died in 1827, and with him the prospects of Orbiston.

New Harmony and Orbiston were dealing with two very different problems. New Harmony was a novel attempt to set up a community without a specifically religious bias or commitment; a large number of sectarian settlements were being formed in America at this period, mostly initiated by German Protestant sects. Many of these were long-lasting and successful. Orbiston, on the other hand, was populated with people already suffering the pressures and deprivations of the Industrial Revolution, and

Harmony Hall, Queenwood, a later Owenite settlement built in too extravagant a fashion to survive

163

was an attempt to offer an alternative system based on communal self-sufficiency.

Queenwood, near East Tytherley in Hampshire, was the chosen location for Owen's last experiment on his return from New Harmony. The land was leased at a standard rent from Sir Isaac Lyon Goldschmidt, who was a long-standing supporter of Owenite schemes.

Alexander Somerville visited Harmony Hall in 1842 in his capacity as an observer of agricultural improvements, and vividly described what he found.[13] The main building was built of red brick and "its outward form was tasteful and all its proportions substantial". Nearby was the house which the first arrivals had lived in before the hall had been completed, and all was surrounded by work in hand. Heaps of bricks, logs and newly dug ground marked the beginnings of the cultivation of a garden. In search of a guide, Somerville went into the hall and met a man who took him to the kitchen, from where he could hear the community members singing in the dining room; he also showed him the machinery which carried dishes and food from the oven to the table, a very modern device and seemingly rather futile. This was the first sign of the disregard for economy and of miscalculation, blame for which must be laid at the feet of the architect. Somerville continues, on noting the grandeur of the main house, "A village of cottages, each with a garden, would have surely been more appropriate for a working community, and much cheaper. The sum expended on this building, not yet half finished, is said to exceed £30,000. Such extravagance previous to cultivating the land would stagger most people." Bearing in mind the contemporary value of such a vast sum, the overspending was certainly phenomenal and approximated much more the flamboyant gesture of a newly rich industrialist than the basis for a community of equal opportunity. However the search for invention and technical innovation was another facet of the pursuit of perfection that so many communitarians were engaged in. The Oneida Perfectionists, a mid-nineteenth-century American group, lived satisfactorily off the patents of some of their inventions such as the traveller's lunch bag and the "final shoe".[4]

In contrast, work in the grounds at Queenwood was highly organised and appeared efficient, and the gardener was busy directing operations on the twenty-seven acres of his territory. Elsewhere:

All illustration to Hampden in the Nineteenth Century, *a utopian treatise published by John Minter Morgan in 1834. He used, without any acknowledgement, Whitwell's ten-year-old plan for New Harmony, set in an arcadian paradise*

> "brick-makers were making bricks; builders were building; lime-burners were burning lime; road-makers were making roads; the shepherds were with the sheep; nine ploughs were at work; a hundred acres of wheat were already sown, and more wheat land was being prepared; a reservoir was being constructed to save all the liquid manure; and in short, everything was being done to improve the land which industry and capital could accomplish and skill direct."

Sixty men were on the place and another thirty were about to arrive, and Somerville was highly impressed by the effectiveness of the organisation and the advanced techniques that were employed. By the time the book was published, he was forced to add a note on the collapse of the scheme and he could not feel surprised, in view of the overspending he had noticed, that this had been the outcome. His feelings that many of the members were unfit for manual labour were also accurate. As in many other attempts at community settlements at this period, it was the basic unsuitability of the human material that brought about its downfall.

The plans were for a home for 224 adults and 448 children (a neat equation) housed in a building more like a Fourierist colony than an Owenite one, 330 feet long and four storeys high, with excellent accommodation and advanced facilities, surrounded by one thousand acres of land. In the event, Joseph Hansom, patenter of the Hansom Cab and founder and first editor of the influential architectural magazine *The Builder*, constructed the large mansion-like building which Somerville found. As architect of Birmingham Town Hall, he practised a sort of grandiose municipal architecture hardly compatible with the needs of a pioneering agricultural community. The mahogany on the walls and immaculately detailed finishing throughout ensured that the economics of the place stood no chance. The phenomenal extravagance of the scheme, and the inverted order of priorities which caused effective cultivation of the land to begin after building had already started, meant that Harmony Hall, started in 1839, was defunct by 1845. George Holyoake, historian of the cooperative movement, writing of its demise said, "A community was regarded in social mechanics then as a sort of flying machine and it fulfilled the expectation of the day by falling down like one."

Holyoake, commemorating in 1877 the failure of the Cooperative Movement in general, and of Owen's contribution in particular, said, "The Indiana Community [New Harmony] is as silent as the waters of the Wabash by its side — Orbiston is buried in the grave of Abram Combe — Ralahine has been gambled away — the Concordia is a strawberry garden — Manea Fen has sunk out of sight — the President of Queenwood is encamping in the lanes —": but if these practical experiments were admitted failures, tenacious theorists continued to pursue solutions, though few were original.

In spite of the seriousness with which they were treated, the British utopian theorists had little original to propose. They preached suggestions for changing society with considerable self-confidence but on closer observation most are ideas plagiarised from Owen and his followers. John Minter Morgan was one such man who took up ideas already stated and gave them a religious twist. In 1834 he published *Hampden in the Nineteenth Century*, an odd amalgam of moral teaching, conventional romance and digressions into social commentary. He even uses Whitwell's drawing for New Harmony for his community, without mentioning his source. By 1850 his ideas had gelled into a more cohesive pattern "The Christian Commonwealth". He even took his plans to Pope Pius IX, but the agricultural adviser at the Papal Court made it understood that such schemes were inapplicable in Italy.

The Christian Commonwealth was planned as an agricultural self-supporting community for 300 families housed in a great square again based on New Harmony. Handicrafts and mechanical trades were to be carried on, as well as farming, and there was to be no competition or rivalry. The purpose was "moral and religious improvement", as might be expected from a man whose pseudonym was "Philanthropos". Dedicated to Lord Ashley, the noted reformer, the coloured plate in the book shows another pastoral paradise, with contented folk and cows sharing the scene, surrounded by a text which reads: "Seek ye first the Kingdom of God and his righteousness and all these things shall be added unto you."

Morgan did not only inhabit a dream world however. He gave specific details of cottage accommodation — four rooms per family contrasted against the "damp cellars and dreary garrets mill workers were forced to inhabit". An infirmary and surgeon's house were included in the "private official residences", and the average cottage was estimated at £75.

Minter Morgan, until 1840, was a faithful follower of Owen. His other famed publication — an allegory called, quaintly, *The Revolt of the Bees* — was serialised in the *Cooperative Magazine* and ran through five editions. His own organisation, set up after his break with Owen, was called the Church of England Self-Supporting Village Society, which was, in effect, pleading Owen's cause with the addition of organised religion. One of the supporters was James Silk Buckingham. Morgan himself stated that his plans came very close, particularly in their economic organisation, to the Moravian settlements of a hundred years before. He had visited several in Germany and Holland and secured the approval of their bishops for his "model institution" — a more likely audience than the Pope. In spite of drawing attention to his sources, and the similarities between his ideas and these executed schemes, Morgan then added a self-indulgent chapter on the visionary quality of his project, comparing himself with the luckless men who had been laughed down on the introduction of gas some forty years before.

The list of moral advantages to be gained by this form of settlement then follows; a weighty selection including "the force of habit, discipline equal to that of the army, greater inducements to good, less incentives to vice, increasing attractions of the

167

institution and freedom from depressing anxiety", as well as the more obvious benefits of education and good community relations. Morgan also cites Bellers's College of Industry as one of his many sources of inspiration, known to him from Owen's reprint. Finally, Morgan shows himself as something of a social reactionary — despite its high claims to social justice and communal good, the Model Institution

> "neither interferes with the distinctions of class or of wealth... the families of the aristocracy and of the shareholders, would have an opportunity of visiting and advancing the schools, composed of children assembled in better order and more susceptible of improvement; of promoting horticultural and Botanical gardens and of aiding the rural fêtes etc. etc."

Minter Morgan, for all his "vision", remained close to the prevailing wind, paternalism.

Another prominent theorist was the idiosyncratic figure of James Silk Buckingham. Interested in everything and everyone, he was described in the *Dictionary of National Biography* as having "too many schemes in hand at the same time". He started life at sea and spent a considerable time in India, where he published the *Calcutta Journal* which caused him to be expelled for the anti-government views expressed in its pages. For some years he was a Member of Parliament for Sheffield, and he was an unstinting campaigner for reform in many fields, especially via his many magazines. His scheme "Victoria", named in honour of the Queen and published in *National Evils and Practical Remedies* (1849), was aimed at removing "ignorance, intemperance, national prejudice, commercial monopolies, war and competition", fairly all-embracing aims. It would also alleviate "the helpless and hopeless condition of the unfortunate". Of considerable interest to the Garden City theorists, his city was to hold ten thousand inhabitants in concentric squares, organised according to social standing and the financial status of each class, the whole to be surrounded by a green belt. Again the Villages of Cooperation are the obvious inspiration, but Buckingham goes into considerably more detail as to the provisions of his city and, above all, its physical form.

The housing was to be flat-roofed and built of iron; baths and kitchens were communal. No blind alley or quiet culs-de-sac would be allowed — "no secret and obscure haunts for the retirement of the filthy and the immoral from public eye", as he put it. Each area would be served by a colonnaded walkway where the architectural orders denoted the status of the residents, thus at the upper end of the scale the composite order would advertise the presence of "opulent capitalists". All residents would hold shares as in Morgan's community, and they would be governed by a rigid moral code.

Buckingham surprised himself, he claimed, by finding remarkable similarities between his conception of an ideal community and Wren's master plan for rebuilding London. He also passes comment on other settlements and theorists such as John Stuart Mill, whom he quotes, and he considered Fourier's schemes preferable to those of St Simon, Louis Blanc, Cabet or Owen. "The failure of all former attempts has arisen from their having been commenced without sufficient capital to cover the expense of the first outlay and without a bond of religious faith and a moral control to unite and direct the associated." The remarks on the lack of religion were obviously directed at Owen's communities — at this period religion and philanthropy usually met in the same man.

Buckingham visited two American utopian communities — Zoar, established in 1817, a German reformist settlement founded by the Shakers, and Economy, founded by George Rapp, builder of the early New Harmony.

A standard Chartist cottage at Charterville (Minster Lovell), with considerable grounds and fruit trees. Cottages built by the Chartists at Snigs End and elsewhere are virtually identical

Snigs End Chartist land settlement: the former schoolhouse. The house for the schoolmaster and mistress was in the centre, and schoolrooms for girls and boys to either side

The latter contained about 500 people, living virtually self-sufficiently, and had a symmetric town plan with tree-lined streets, detached brick and wood houses with individual gardens and public buildings including, oddly enough, a Museum of Natural History. "The only thing that seems wanting to make the community perfect, is a higher relish for education, literature and the fine arts..." In such a small community hope for such intellectual refinement seems rather out of place. Buckingham nominates Lowell as a good example of an American industrial community run on satisfactory lines, having a well organised and contented workforce.

The opposing forces of town and country were increasingly marked in the mid-nineteenth century, and in comprehending these contradictions the utopians were able to offer certain viable suggestions. The town was becoming beleaguered by working-class discontent, and with the spectre of revolution over the Channel in 1848 and Chartist and agricultural disruption at home, the poor were seen as a seething threat to the status quo. The rich passed through cities briefly, or made their own exclusive ghettoes, but strange convolutions were taking place in the

170

moneyed section of society too — traditional landowners were, in many cases, becoming richer through new industrial wealth while the newly rich from the manufacturing areas were becoming country patriarchs. The vision of a paternalistic society offered by the village, with its confirmed and complex "natural" order, was attractive and with the rise to prosperity of a large middle-class, suburbia, the imitation of rural life at one remove could take hold. Mr Pooter was in residence. Compromise had been reached and political stability was the result.

Before this state of affairs could be reached, various solutions were being offered, centred on agricultural self-sufficiency. One of Owen's critics on religious grounds had been William Allen.[15] In 1813 he wrote that Owen's plans

> "had been in operation about thirteen years and during that period none of the workmen have applied for relief from public charity, as they had raised a fund amongst themselves which is able to support them under sickness, and provide for them in old age, neither has any one of them been called before a magistrate for any offence."

Two years later disillusion had crept in. He wrote: "... we came into the concern, not to form a manufactory of infidels, but to support a benevolent character in plans of a very different nature, in which the happiness of millions, and the cause of morality and virtue are deeply concerned". By 1821, Allen was contemplating plans of his own.

It was quite in character for Allen to strike out independently for his beliefs. As a chemist with strong Quaker principles, he had refused to supply the Russian army with drugs because of his pacifist principles, and had not eaten sugar for over forty years because of his work with Wilberforce against slavery. His periodical *The Philanthropist*, begun in 1811, became finally *The Lindfield Reporter* and the official publication dealing with his land colony experiment.

He travelled widely, visiting colonies abroad, including Quaker villages and Swiss educational experiments. With the support of John Smith MP (another of Owen's fervent supporters), and the Earl of Chichester, Allen bought a tract of land in Sussex to set up a smallholding community which would be self-supporting and where education would be advanced and considered of great importance, on the lines of the Moravians. Like Moggridge's early settlers, the people would be encouraged to help themselves. In 1823 Allen circulated a fund-raising letter setting out the principles, and by 1831 the colony was in existence with twenty-five cottages, a school and workshops. To emphasise the strength of his commitment Allen took one of the cottages himself. The school charged minimum fees and for large families or exceptionally constant attendance there was exemption from payment. Houses of two standards were offered, those with slate roofs costing 2s. 6d. per week, those with thatch 2s. 0d. Each cottage had one and a quarter acres, and later larger holdings of five to six acres were added. The soil was poor but the experiment was a success and had considerable influence on the other similar attempts in Britain and abroad, particularly through Allen's publication, *Colonies at Home*.

The string of Chartist land colonies[16] set up by Feargus O'Connor from 1846–50 were directly influenced by Allen's ideas. However, the haphazard finances and muddled conception of the Chartist schemes doomed them from the start. O'Connor chose areas with bad soil, no accessible markets for his goods, and was faced with groups of patently unsuitable town people while he himself lacked the necessary mental stability for his task.

Parcelling out land by lottery, and later, when this was declared illegal, by auction, O'Connor started with 103 acres in Hertfordshire, at Heronsgate. With the first steps of this scheme the image of the Chartists changed from that of potential revolutionaries and irresponsible firebrands to one of peaceful labouring men, and the ideals of these plans carried great power. They built well-proportioned roomy cottages with big windows, oak floors and cast-iron gates. The cottages were equipped with bookshelves as an incentive to improvement, and the school was, as in subsequent villages, a fine building including accommodation for the teachers. Some practical details were less well attended to — there was but one well for the entire community, and the problem of selling their produce was acute. No chapel was built and it was not until after O'Connor's downfall — he ended his life insane — that one was built.

Twenty applications were received for the post of schoolmaster and the project continued on a wave of optimism. However, the problem of finding money with which to pay back loans and rent

of the land became crucial and did not bode well for the furtherance of Chartist land colonies.

But O'Connor pressed on regardless; Lowbands in Gloucestershire was bought in October 1846 (six months after the first site
had been obtained) in spite of considerable local opposition. Snigs
End and Minster Lovell — also known as Charterville — were
bought in June the following year, and Great Dodford in January
1848. The latter site, being near to Birmingham, was more suitable
and promised a sounder economic basis but, as always, the recurring problem was that of adapting townspeople, formerly factory
workers, to the hard task of learning agricultural methods simulta-
neously with building up the settlements. The necessary time-lag
between the initial cultivation of land and production was too great
and meanwhile money was being lost at an appalling rate. One settler was said to have thrashed his pig because it squealed, not being
aware that it was asking for food.

O'Connor — "I would rather be the founder of the Land Plan
than monarch of Europe" — was championed in some quarters
(for instance the *Illustrated London News* published various
reports of his activities) and pilloried in many others. As finances
became even more rocky, rural cottage industries were introduced, such as glove-making, and these helped keep a narrow
margin of solvency.

In July 1848 a Select Committee of the House of Commons
reported that the Land Company was in fact illegal and an Act to
dissolve it was passed in July 1851, despite the fact that a
member of the committee had paid a visit to one of the colonies
and reported favourably on what he found there.

The tenants of the land colonies were in some cases intensely
loyal — *The Times* in 1850 reported that fifty colonists were "prepared to manure the land with blood before it was taken from
them".

The villages became increasingly well built as their settlers
learned from previous mistakes. Minster Lovell consisted of fifty-
seven houses built in ten months, while Snigs End was laid out in
a crescent form with sturdy stone-walled cottages. At Great
Dodford each cottage was supplied with a well and, owing to the
poor soil, larger divisions of land per tenant were made, four
acres or more.

In spite of O'Connor's eventual failure and the disillusionment
of the Chartists with his methods before that, the land colonies

continued to function and in some cases, by increasing their revenue with cottage industries and market gardening, carried out more efficiently, they began to flourish. Ironically, when smallholdings were advocated in the period after the First World War, the Chartist land colonies were continuing to carry out their function.

In spite of their pronounced views on a better way of life and improved environment, neither William Morris nor John Ruskin actually achieved any notable results in the realities of community building.

Ruskin had expounded some woolly suggestions for cities ringed by gardens, harking back to his ever-present medieval ideals. More practically, however, Ruskin set up a farm community, the St George's Guild near Sheffield,[17] which he hoped would prove self-sufficient, be a good exemplar of communistic principles and be run without the use of any machinery, even so much as a sewing machine — wind and water power would suffice. However, as usual, the human element proved the weak point in the plan and the head of the project, William Riley, proved its downfall by becoming a despot. Even the eventual object of the farm, to become a notable botanical garden, failed, and it was finally leased and then bought by a single farmer.

Morris spent considerably more energy forcefully putting the case against the city, and used as his answer the utopian dream described in *News from Nowhere*.[18] Morris was fascinated by Bellamy's *Looking Backwards* (1888),[19] and it was this that prompted his efforts at writing a novel transposed into a future century, though his city was London, not Boston. Fascinated by the book, he still found much to criticise; chiefly the setting of utopia within a city. "In one passage, indeed, he mentions villages, but with unconscious simplicity shows that they do not come into his scheme of economical equality, but are mere servants of the great centres of civilisation." Morris considered the village the ideal microcosm and so had to disagree with the main thesis of Bellamy's novel.

The scene painted in *News from Nowhere* is that of a country shorn of all industrial excrescences which has reverted to a pattern of little settlements — England "is now a garden, where nothing is wasted and nothing is spoilt, with the necessary dwellings, sheds and workshops scattered up and down the country, all trim and neat and pretty". The country life that had been lost as a result of rural depopulation, and the cities that absorbed this overflow, were rebalanced in Morris's utopia by the removal of industry. People either lived communally in large houses, "more like the old colleges than ordinary houses as they used to be", or in renewed villages which show "no tokens of poverty about them; no tumbledown picturesque; which, to tell you the truth, the artist usually availed himself of to veil his incapacity for drawing architecture".

> "Like the medievals we like everything trim and clean, and orderly and bright; as people always do when they have any sense of architectural power; because then they know that they can have what they want, and they won't stand any nonsense from nature in their dealings with her."

Faced with realities rather than fictional idealism, Morris supported the idea of tenements for towns as space-saving, and agreed with the solutions provided by various housing trusts in their model dwellings.

In fact, Morris goes further with a short promotion for high-rise housing, provided the accommodation per family was sufficient.

> "It might be advisable, granting the existence of huge towns for the present, that the houses for workers should be built in tall blocks, in what might be called vertical streets, but that need not prevent ample room in each lodging, so as to include such comforts of space, air, and privacy as every moderately living middle-class family considers itself entitled to."[20]

This would mean ample space for communal gardens which would provide an amenity to all the inhabitants. Factories too would be aesthetically landscaped. Morris did not foresee the realities of devastated public space as clearly as he visualised his utopian England.

Morris had taken much of what Ruskin had hinted at or thrown out, amidst ideas on other topics, and made a much more cogent rationale from it. Arcadian simple-mindedness was converted into practical form as the Cotswolds became filled with community experiments at the turn of the century, including C.R. Ashbee's community of 150 East Enders in Chipping Campden, planned to be a return to the medieval Guild system

The village hall, built by colonists at Whiteway in true frontier style

and its values.[21] Morris's own home, Kelmscott, was called by
D.G. Rossetti "the doziest dump of old grey beehives".

Long after the Chartist land colonies had faded from public
view, one practical attempt was made to set up a community
based on a similar brand of self-sufficiency supported by home-
based industry. The village, at Whiteway near Miserden,[22] was
founded in 1898 by a group of Tolstoyan anarchists who built
their own houses, wooden shacks much rougher than the neat
cottages of the Chartists. The colony endured while many other
such experiments failed, and exists today, in some respects still
intact. Although fighting battles against planning authorities,
rating assessors and local government bureaucracy in general,
the colonists of Whiteway still hold their land in common and
support some small workshops. However, their housing is subject
to planning restrictions. In the words of one elderly resident who
came to Whiteway in 1920 the colony was "like the Trade Union
movement — damn good thing to start with but then the 'isms'
began".

The account of the foundation of the colony is idealistic; the
title deeds were burnt to emphasise the joint aspect of the venture. Frictions arose between members as to the degree of

176

communism they were prepared to entertain, and the bakery, most successful of the businesses, was run as a private enterprise. The leather-worker suffered from scruples as a vegetarian and searched for material which would not conflict with his morals. Originally the village was to be run without money, which meant the post and other public services were out of reach. In general, the colony attracted a reputation as a nest of eccentrics as well it might when some of them wore Greek dress, struggled to learn Esperanto (and to converse with Continental Esperantists), and lived in direct opposition to the mores of the period. The early reputation of Whiteway as far as the sober citizens of Cheltenham were concerned was that of a place "where they run about with nothing on and swap wives every night".

The population was boosted by several separate influxes, but a committee of residents is still the governing body of the village and a settler wishing to leave has to relinquish his land and hand it over to the new resident who is chosen by the committee. The test for Whiteway colony came in 1955 when a resident went to the High Court to claim her title to her property. She lost the case and proved indisputably that the colonists hold the land in common.

The village centres on an iron-fronted building, the Colony Hall, and each cottage is surrounded by a considerable area of ground. In spite of suburban incursions such as rustic boards with house names inscribed, there still exists an extraordinary air of an enclave and a historic continuity with the original founding members who laid out the network of earth footpaths which still link one house to the next. If some of the theories of the small group who bought the original house with its forty acres were not carried through, aspects of their communitarian principles still flourish and it continues to exist alone amid the wreckage of many other schemes.

Community ideals have rarely proved translatable into reality, but utopias are a continuing currency.[23]

Notes

1. John Bellers, *Proposals for Raising a College of Industry of All Useful Trades and Husbandry*, 1696.
2. A.J. Dobb, *History of Moravian Architecture in England*, 1951.

Thesis in typescript, R.I.B.A. Library, London.

3. John Wesley, *Journals*, 1770s, etc.
4. *Calcutta Journal*, 9 February 1819.
5. R. Speake and F.R. Witty, *History of Droylesden*, Stockport, 1953.
6. Benjamin Latrobe senior was in charge of financial operations for the Moravians in the country from 1760–81 and laid the foundation stone at Fairfield. He was also a prime mover in the reconciliation between Methodists and Moravians.
7. Fourier was in the tradition of French romantic planners (cf. Ledoux). A Phalanx was attempted in 1832 at Rambouillet and later in the United States (see Hayden *op. cit.*). Godin's Familistère (1859 onwards) flourished and in 1880 the factory and Familistère were handed over to the workers. One great difference with Owenite schemes was the emphasis placed on the retention of the family.
8. J.F.C. Harrison, *Robert Owen and the Owenites*, London, 1969.
9. J. Griscom, *A Year in Europe*, 2 vols., 1823.
10. *Oriental Herald*, Vol. 21, 1829.
11. Near Wisbech; it functioned from 1838–40
12. Alex Cullen, *Adventures in Socialism*, Glasgow, 1910.
13. A. Somerville, *The Whistler at the Plough*, 1852.
14. See Hayden *op. cit.*
15. W. Allen, *Life of William Allen*, 3 vols., 1846–47.
16. A.M. Hadfield, *The Chartist Land Company*, London, 1970.
17. Ruskin's doctrine of education through manual work did not extend to himself.
18. *News from Nowhere* first appeared here serialised in the *Commonweal*, but it appeared in book form in Boston, Massachusetts, in 1891, the first edition in Britain appearing a year later.
19. *Looking Backwards* was published in Boston.
20. Mary Morris, *William Morris*, 2 vols., Oxford, 1936.
21. In addition to his community-building activities in the Cotswolds and elsewhere, Ashbee built some industrial housing at Ellesmere Port and planned a vast competition village at Ruislip, in 1909, on a circular plan which remained unexecuted.
22. Nellie Shaw, *History of Whiteway*, 1935; as she put it, "if our feet were down in the potato trenches our heads were up with the stars".
23. Andrew Rigby, *Alternative Realities*, London, 1974.

Chapter 11

"There is a Boom Coming in Garden Cities"

As has been seen in preceding chapters, the village has been regarded as particularly fertile ground for experiment, both for the architectural theorist and experimenter and for the reformer. It provides a feasible social unit, showing an ideal situation where the needs of those within the community are not ignored, a sort of extended family group. An individual contained by, but not overwhelmed by his surroundings can retain self-respect, and respect for human values in general, which is all-important. This has impressed itself on many looking for remedies to problems social or visual.

A clean start, with new buildings, a new situation and, above all, new ideals, no longer seemed entirely utopian as model villages sprang up around the gates of stately homes, around the new industrial centres and far out in the countryside where groups of like-minded people could share religious or political convictions, and, further, convince others of the efficacy of such ideas by example. But all this positive development became confused with the pressing urgency of providing housing for a vastly expanding urban population, keeping the newly stated minimum requirements in mind, yet never stopping far beyond the lowest acceptable standards. Thus James Hole confused his wholly admirable wish to see the workman living at a reasonable level in pleasant surroundings, in what he terms as a model community, self-sufficient in social terms, with the motives that in fact gave rise to suburbia. "It appears," he wrote,

> "that a better plan for relieving the crowded seats of population would be the erection of "model" villages outside our large towns and on the main lines of railway, so that the workmen might be

179

brought to and from their work each day at almost nominal cost. There the artisan might enjoy the blessed gifts of sunlight and pure air, open space for his children to play in, and a cottage garden to find him pleasant and profitable employment for a spare hour."[1]

He was signposting the path to featureless sprawl, which was already bedevilling almost every sizeable town, as opposed to a clearly defined nucleated centre based on its own efficiency. By advocating a separation between the place of work and the home, Hole immediately undermined the closely knit community he put forward. Suburbia, an emotive word, was the subject of a lengthy article in *Chambers' Journal* of 1835.[2] Speculative estates were beginning to ring the larger towns of Britain, and the author expresses horror at what he terms "the little surprised villages" which become incorporated within the towns by the tentacles of suburbia. He describes the process by which these areas come into being:

Housing by Parker and Unwin at New Earswick c. 1902. Neat detailing, good materials and imaginative planning made this the most successful of industrial villages — perhaps of all model villages

"...you see houses whose sides betray that they were intended to have others stuck upon them all yawning, ghastly, unskinned and irregular; you see infant shrubberies struggling in awkward parcels amidst lots of yet to be occupied ground, and clumps of fine places and squares looking down upon clumps of old half-ruined villages, which the spreading town has taken by surprise, and which have not yet had time to get out of the way."

The description has a contemporary ring.

The suburb, an area "lying on the outskirts" of a town as the dictionary definition puts it, is a non-entity, a bastardised version of any other recognised pattern of living. How can an effective community exist where the individual, cocooned in affluence and isolation, has broken away from all means of regular social contact? It can be argued that today our aim, supported by every possible agency, is exactly that privacy and exclusivity, but while the Victorian strait-jackets of the church and family were in operation, suburbia was undoubtedly a destructive environment nurturing the embryonic middle classes in a state of limbo.

The village and the suburb were regarded as opposing forces — the city served a different function, presented different problems and could be excluded from the picture.

Against the fear of ever-encroaching suburbanisation came encouragement for the re-establishment of village life in its basic aspects. The village, whether as ready-made unit or new foundation, could counteract the detrimental effects of industrialisation of the country. These threats were held off by such foundations as the Arts and Crafts village-based workshops, which retreated into the Middle Ages for their example, and where there could be a resurgence of skills lost since the onset of the machine age. Others preached a self-sufficient life-style, echoing the earlier examples of the Moravians and Chartists, but all forms of reaction shared a common thread of horror at the direction in which "progress" was heading; villages were not merely physically crumbling away, but also rural depopulation and emigration were destructive factors which had to be reversed. Old villages needed to be consolidated, new ones founded. One writer put it in these words:

"If we wish for a real and permanent revival of rural life we must not depend on spontaneous growth, we must create the village and we must create it on the lines of perfect independence. The

181

landowner and the profit-making farmer must be eliminated and plans must be laid swiftly and solely for the good of the village itself."[3]

In rural terms he wished for an equivalent of the most notable recent philanthropic efforts, with the philanthropy replaced by self-determination.

As plans were laid for villages built according to many principles, a general sharpening of the senses with regard to environment was taking place. The *Cottagers' Monthly Visitor* for example, a magazine giving handy hints on religion, health, the kitchen and much else, devoted much of its space in the 1830s to advice on the garden and its cultivation. It was not to be merely a decorative adjunct, or even a productive sideline, but was the key to physical health, morality, and led to a sensitivity to beauty in the surroundings. By the 1840s the gardening magazines had a tremendous vogue.

It took only a short step to make the middle classes enter into the activity, even if by proxy when a gardener or two were employed. William Webb, who had a certain undeclared interest being a horticulturist by profession, recognised the potential of the situation, even to the point where the choice of garden was to be as important a criteria in house-buying as the house itself. For thirty years, from 1888 onwards, he promoted a scheme for Garden First, even putting his ideas into print.[4] Woodcote Village in Surrey is the outcome of all this, really an unexceptional early suburban estate but offering some interesting sidelights on the attitudes towards village and villa building at the turn of the century. It is built in the image of high-class suburbia in its most entrenched form. Webb felt that the "house is but the complement to the garden", and designed his estate specifically for city workers. He planned the village starting with the hedges and trees, next planting out gardens, laying out roads and finally building the housing from 1895 on.

Nearby is "the village", which started in 1900 for men working on the estate, consisting of twenty cottages around a green.

"Somehow or other the workmen did not care to occupy the cottages, which were offered them at a rental within their means: and at one time it looked as though the houses would be empty. On the other hand, the place has since become popular with people of good social position, and artists, authors, city men,

182

Members of Parliament and musicians have taken up their residence there. In fact so popular did this village become, that it was found necessary to take steps to prevent it turning into a colony of weekenders."

This *faux naïveté* was echoed by the planting of a fully-grown chestnut tree by the smithy ("it is not every smith who is good both at horse-shoeing and at some approach to art smithing"), and the placing of a set of totally fake stocks and whipping post on the green, where for a while some geese also were living decoratively; "although they are quaint creatures, they had their drawbacks and were not totally regretted" — they were quietly removed. This scene is one that the missionaries of the Picturesque could claim for their own, the ultimate result of an emphasis on stage effects as an alternative to reality.

A fey quality was creeping into assumed country life that became ever more extreme and stemmed from a complete miscalculation of the realities of rural existence. It was this attitude which Lutyens attacked in Dame Henrietta Barnett, founder of Hampstead Garden Suburb though it was hardly fair criticism in her case. She was, he wrote, "a nice woman but... has no ideas

Folk Hall, New Earswick, in which extreme simplicity and a Scandinavian-style steep pitched roof are the chief features

183

much beyond a window box full of geraniums, calceolarias and lobelias, over which you see a goose on a green ". Reaction against suburbia expressed itself in a romanticism which accorded in no way with the realities of village or rural life. It was also expressed in the writings of Ebenezer Howard, the inspiration of the Garden City movement, where the various elements of earlier ideal schemes were gathered together.

Howard's *Tomorrow; a Peaceful Path to Real Reform* (1898), reissued in 1902 under a significant change of title as *Garden Cities of Tomorrow*, was the keystone of the movement. Howard, a London clerk, had gone to Chicago in 1871 and came back a stenographer with a greatly widened viewpoint. Some years later he read Bellamy's *Looking Backwards,* the book which had influenced William Morris so forcibly. Howard based his own book, which was not a novel but a "practical" treatise, on the image of the Town-Country Magnet, from which he evolved a society which incorporated the advantages of both.

With a fixed population and area, including industry and a full range of services, surrounded by a Green Belt, the Garden City was envisaged as a fresh start in urban planning, a solution to the myriad defects of the city and the social remedy *par excellence.* Robert Owen's *Villages of Cooperation* are reborn in Howard's central unit surrounded by satellite settlements, and there are echoes of Gandy's seemingly visionary circular units grouped around each other.

With the foundation of the Garden City Association in the year after the publication of his book, Howard's ideas came out of the realms of utopian speculation and into the realms of possibility. He needed the assistance of men such as George Cadbury and William Lever to add to the practical experience, idealism and professional capabilities of the partnership of Barry Parker and Raymond Unwin, the architects who brought these plans towards fruition. The airy phrases that Howard strung together needed a social and economic climate sufficiently stable to favour and support the enormous investment of effort and money necessary. By the autumn of 1903 land had been bought and First Garden City Limited was a registered company; the building of Letchworth could start. "Town and country must be married, and out of this joyous union will spring a new hope, a new life, a new civilisation." By taking ownership of the land, all gains from rising values were for the benefit of the Garden City itself.

Howard quotes freely from Ruskin, and indeed the introduction to his work is very much in Ruskin's style; he uses quotations from Richardson's description of the city of health, *Hygiea*, and gives his three sources as Wakefield, who proposed that emigration and colonisation be carried out in an organised fashion, the system of land tenure of Thomas Spence and Herbert Spencer, and finally the model city of James Silk Buckingham, which came, as has been seen, directly from Owen and early utopian planners. Howard saw himself as a descendant of these theorists and mentions how slow a successful invention can be to each fruition, encountering obstacles and setbacks throughout. In the event, Howard was proved right. His ideas incorporated into the Garden City movement were the most influential of all those original thinkers because he had presented them at the first moment when they could, in fact, be put into practice.

He felt confident that by taking a representative cross-section of interests, and including a nucleus of original residents, people could be welded satisfactorily together, without the problems faced in some schemes (presumably he was thinking of some of Owen's schemes and those of the Chartists) where the human material was poor, the distances from commercial centres too great and the settlers inexperienced in the mode of life they were preparing to adopt. These are valid points, but the difference lies in the size of communities projected — while Howard's town contains 30,000, with an additional 2,000 in the surrounding area, the colonies set up by the Chartists and the Owenites never exceeded a few hundred inhabitants and were housed in a village unit.

Howard made the point that street layout is important as a basis upon which the architecture is to show "the fullest measure of individual taste and preference". Communal gardens, and even kitchens (another relic of Owen's ideas) would encourage the sense of community.

Within the city boundaries Howard wished to emphasise the natural, to bring the countryside inwards by allowing generous space for gardens, parks and encircling green belt. Added to this was the informal planning, a radical departure from the stark urban landscape of bye-law regulation streets, the landscape of suburbia at that time. While encouraging the spacing of housing, community atmosphere was engendered in practice by the use of short terraces, culs-de-sac and walkways, and cottages grouped like medieval almshouses around a central space neither private nor entirely public.

Before 1901 Unwin was already expressing his views on the threat of suburbia; in a lecture on "Building and Natural Beauty" he uses the allegory of a rook who chooses to build a nest outside the confines of the rookery — after he has completed it, the other birds remove it, stick by stick. As Unwin puts it, they can recognise the beginnings of "suburban villadom". We admire the towns where demarcation between country and town are strictly marked, not those where town disintegrates slowly outwards. Architects were very conscious of the blight of undisciplined expansion and confused as to how best to combat it. By building smallscale detached domestic housing they were tending, inevitably, to add to the proliferation of this blight. Voysey and Baillie Scott both voiced strong protests along Unwin's lines. The latter reiterated the arguments against limitless suburban expansion and despairingly described what he saw to be the two alternative paths, equally unattractive. These are either the indiscriminate building of small unimaginative houses placed on identical plots or the self-conscious colonies of model cottages "where the earnestness and reality of the ancient village is replaced by complacently picturesque semi-detached cottages which seem to constitute a sort of high-class suburbia". In attempting to ape more sizeable houses they become little villas and in their pretensions fail utterly to succeed on any count. "Art is underlined everywhere and each of these miniature bijou residences seems to pose and smirk in the conscious appreciation of its own artistic qualities."[6]

It was precisely this quality that Marinetti, the Italian Futurist, was attacking in 1914 when he stated himself to be "against Garden Cities with their curfews and artificial battlements". Soon the misused terms Garden Suburb, Village or City began to be synonymous with suburbia.

In the 1920s and 1930s the lowest common denominator of the speculative builder was the garden suburb type of villa; the Redway Estate, Twickenham, was advertised with a touch of overkill as a "model township". "Healthfulness and charm" characterise the place, the houses, "no mere straight rows of standardised dwellings", are surrounded by "garden islands; fields of golden daffodils" and, if feasting the eyes on this perennial spring were not enough, the copywriter rambles on to mention "deep gravel sub-soil with all the advantage to well-being thus offered". The latter sentence is an oblique, recognised way of stating that the house was unlikely to subside — many did. Before the protection of the Trades Description Act the prospective buyer had to keep his feet well on the ground, and his wits about him.

Reaction against what C.R. Ashbee termed "the invasion of ugliness" produced a welter of publications, some dealing with vernacular architecture, others manuals instructing the builder of a small house in the rudiments of traditional construction; all looking back to a time when standards attained by the long practice of high-quality craftsmanship and expertise were the norm. The authors, among them such architects as Ernest Gimson and Guy Dawber, evoked the past with line drawings or photographs with an accompaniment of prose which often bordered on the rhapsodic. Hoping to preach awareness and to educate the public to their traditional past, these books were aiming to improve taste to a point where the phoney and imitative would be no longer in demand. The element overlooked here was that essentially the timber-clad, lattice- windowed bijou villa was itself an evocation of all this but wrapped synthetically, misplaced and misapplied. It had come out of the pretty intricacies of the Picturesque estate cottage, which, itself, was derived from the authentic detailing of traditional country architecture.

This was also the era of a first thorough approach to the restoration of old buildings, and the Society for the Protection of Ancient Buildings had been founded in 1877 to support these efforts by William Morris, its original Secretary. In the Cotswolds Ashbee was concerned equally with restoration and additions to extant buildings, as with the construction of new houses in the vernacular of the area. His work in and around Chipping Campden consisted of many such jobs and there was little noticeable difference between the restorations and originals.[7]

Against this background, and amid a social climate which meant that it was becoming indefensible to visit substandard housing on employees or tenants, came the village built by Parker and Unwin for the Rowntrees at New Earswick. The Quaker chocolate manufacturers, however, made sure that their foundation was not merely paying lipservice to the new standards. Although strictly speaking industrial housing, it was the testing ground for many of the features applied in later Garden City planning, including Hampstead Garden Suburb, and had widespread influence in Europe and America where it was avidly reported and illustrated. In many respects a less ambitious scheme than either Bournville or Port Sunlight, it was correspondingly more successful, in its introduction of a practical yet attractive form of small-scale architecture, based on the rationale of the Arts and Crafts movement rather than the Picturesque.

New Earswick finally closed the gap between industrial housing and other types of small-scale housing. No factory brooded over its rooftops and no pall of smoke darkened the sky. Instead, simple whitewashed terraces with bright red tiled roofs lined the footpaths which led between the rows of cottages and lawns; trees and a small stream were all that could be seen from the main road nearby.

Raymond Unwin had formed his ideas in the intellectual climate of Oxford in the 1880s, where Ruskin and William Morris still held sway, and his brother-in-law and partner Barry Parker was similarly versed in the Arts and Crafts movement which emphasised the basics at the expense of the frills.[8] Unwin's statements on village life and the use of traditional materials in building were pure Arts and Crafts theory; in practice both partners agreed on an emphasis on functional interiors, and the well-lit whitewashed rooms were a natural complement to the essentially simple exteriors. In planning, the emphasis lay on the small unit, a meticulously interwoven pattern of relationships which dictated their own form. This is the quality which makes New Earswick an outstandingly successful whole.

The original conception of New Earswick, which consisted of thirty houses built in 1902–03, has been somewhat lost in later development.[9] It came about through Rowntree's social concern, not to solve an outstanding housing problem, but to provide accommodation for his employees and others within a fully-fledged community laid out on the best principles. Joseph Rowntree was the original mover behind the plans, but much of their execution was due to Seebohm Rowntree, his son. This is important because, as a pioneering sociologist (his work on poverty in York was published in 1901) with industrial interests, he placed particular emphasis on the root causes, recognising that change of environment was 100% more worthwhile than charity meted out later; the model village versus the doss house.

188

Later housing and a typical back path at New Earswick

He gave people independence and the best possible means with which to achieve it. After the initial housing scheme, Joseph Rowntree set up a Trust specifically for village development in the hopes that if the first community proved a financial success the profits could be employed for another scheme, and so on.

Houses were built at twelve to the acre as Parker and Unwin wished, angled to face the sun and surrounded by gardens and common ground. Unwin thought that ground should be left unfenced to extend to the doorstep but this was impracticable. Mature trees were retained, a small stream was emphasised to best advantage, and the factory was a short bicycle ride away. Variety was the hallmark, in roof levels, in the angles at which the housing was set, and in the layout. In the 1903 plan, generous provision was made for leisure facilities, sporting and otherwise — New Earswick was planned to become a sizeable centre and very much a self-contained entity in spite of its nearness to York — but by 1905 it was obvious that the demand for medium-cost rented housing in the area was not great. As Joseph Rowntree put it, "it may be the most useful thing to make a number of small model village communities — say a hundred houses rather than anything approaching a garden city". The other possibility the Trust foresaw was the setting up of cooperative housing schemes on the lines of the Ealing Tenants' Association, although the participation of tenants in their own affairs was always high priority. The village council was already being consulted in the autumn of 1903 when six or seven tenants met Seebohm Rowntree, Parker and Unwin to discuss cottage plans. Rowntree had stated that he did not want to give his community the stamp of charity, and this measure of self-government was crucial to the success of the scheme.

The Institute, renamed the Folk Hall, was planned as the central building. It is notable, and reflects further changes in the structure of such communities, that this building should take precedence over a church as the focal institution provided. Instead of the symbolic church spire, the fine steeply pitched roof of the Hall, built in 1908, rises above the housing, in no way grandiose and entirely suited to its function. It is this quality, the importance of a human scale, that pervades New Earswick, without any doubt the most satisfactory of model villages of this period. The use of space is important, play areas for children, paths and gardens all taking precedence over arterial roads for the estate, and great care was taken to avoid the murky back regions of nineteenth century back-to-back housing.

The use of culs-de-sac, a hallmark of Parker and Unwin's planning here, and elsewhere in later years, gave a varied effect in the best sense of the Picturesque, an ideal antidote to endless urban vistas. Since then the principle has been much misused, producing dismal corners littered with abandoned cars and rubbish.

As the building of the village went ahead, Rowntree kept in touch with George Cadbury, who was much flattered to be told that his village at Bournville had been the starting-point for New Earswick. The Nonconformist philanthropists were a tight-knit body, each contributing to the efforts of the others, and at this point Cadbury was also working in collaboration with Lever to help realise Dame Henrietta Barnett's dream, Hampstead Garden Suburb. Her photograph album included several pictures of cottages at the Rowntree village and it was inevitable that she should choose as planners for her utopia the tried and proven partnership of Parker and Unwin.

Dame Henrietta Barnett was married to Canon Barnett, the founder of Toynbee Hall, and had supported him in his years of work in the Whitechapel area in the East End of London. She could take to her scheme idealism, together with a practical knowledge of conditions at their worst and a fervent belief in the efficacy of social contact between classes. In her booklet to the suburb, written many years later,[10] she said that "the good that each class gains from knowledge of and friendship with another class is beyond price and is not yet valued adequately".

Towards the end of the nineteenth century there had been a rediscovery of the neighbourhood unit within the city as a means to obtaining the type of close community that only the village seemed to offer. The university settlements in poor areas used the principle of introducing educated people into areas of extreme deprivation to break down the vicious circle of social stagnation and the formation of immutable ghettoes. Long before the welfare state this was a well-intentioned scheme to help those almost beyond help. Dame Henrietta was a determined combination of genuine social vision and considerable practical knowledge, with a certain naviete which never adequately protected her from the inevitable disappointments and unfulfilled ambitions. She tells of a conversation with her husband, Canon Barnett: "if we could... buy a huge estate and build so that all classes could live in neighbourliness together the friendships would come about quite naturally and the artificial bridges need not be made". A similar starry-eyed idealism was voiced by her chosen architect, Raymond Unwin, who could see in co-partnership housing projects a vision of perfect community for those "who associate to accept and enjoy the sharing of great things in place of the exclusive possession of small things". With this spirit, he continued, a unity and coherence would emerge — a "harmony of outward expression [which] must in turn react on the life that flourishes under its influence". Finally, out of this would emerge "a new form of communal civic life".

Sadly, this integrated utopian community was not to be realised at Hampstead Garden Suburb. In 1928 Dame Henrietta wrote in conclusion to her history of the Suburb, "I wonder if enough of the residents make real attempts to know intimately the classes which do not belong socially to their own". By offering a highly desirable residential area, an oasis amidst so much inferior housing, inevitably the economics tipped the scheme back into the area of middle-class suburbs. Hampstead Garden Suburb today is an odd mixture of two worlds; houses dripping burglar alarms and lectures on "Bird Watching in the Suburb".

In her own photograph album, Dame Henrietta placed photographs of Whitechapel backyards next to cottages at Port

*St Jude's Church, Hampstead Garden Suburb, just after completion:
the spire was added later, for Dame Henrietta's sixtieth birthday in
1911. Open country and the Heath extension can be seen beyond*

Sunlight, Bournville and New Earswick; she noted the efforts
made to cultivate flowers on window sills and in dingy yards,
"gardening under difficulties", as she characterised it, and she
plotted the eventual progress of the suburb over the peaceful
hedges and fields of Hampstead as it was in 1900. Unwin was a
character after her own heart. Reading a pamphlet by him, she
claimed to have instinctively found the man "for my beautiful
green golden schemes". Together they tramped through the
woods, Unwin expounding the location and routes of roads and
housing positions, Dame Henrietta nervously peering about her
for snakes. In her tribute to him (she could find no such phrases
for Edwin Lutyens who came into the scheme in a consultative
capacity a little later), she wrote of his "rapid adjustment of mind
to my and everybody's point of view, of his unsleeping remem-
brance of the best for everyone, his fertility of imagination used
to provide beauty in out of sight places, his patience with fools —
and their name *is* legion! — his faith in the power of growth in
every tiresome insignificant person, his humility".

Lutyens, on the other hand, came into conflict with her in his
plans for a grandiose central square at the highest point, with two
great churches. He wanted to escape from the village image that
she, and Unwin, had in mind — the image that expressed itself in
her wish to build shops and tea-rooms round the central area. In

192

fact, her sensitivity to the potential of the site was probably greater than his; in many ways the suburb has reverted to the cosy village image that the Dame treasured and the grandiloquence of the square looks oddly at variance with the carefully plotted vistas of trees and hedges leading towards the central church spire, which help to reinforce the traditional village image. In fact, the original intention was to introduce many vistas, making use of church spires further away, but such changes as the increased height of the Temple Fortune shops altered this. Lutyens was fond of his client but found her tiresome in the pettiness of her vision, and one can sense the bold provocation of his work at Hampstead against the understatement of so much else.

The idea for the foundation of the Suburb had first come about in 1896. Transport to the London suburbs was improving all the time and Golders Green Station was to be proposed to Parliament in 1902. The first plans for the Suburb were produced in 1905. The site, which had belonged to the Trustees of Eton College, was an awkward wedge-shape, with one end touching the Heath. This projection was made a feature with a heavy wall to introduce the feel of a German medieval town behind its bastions, but the wall also serves to emphasise the similarities between Hampstead Garden Suburb and the numerous exclusive early Victorian estates behind their fortifications. The German overtones were studied: an early drawing by Charles Wade, carried out as a primitive aerial plan, plays up the German vernacular aspect by showing steeply pitched roofs and whimsical verse in medieval script. In addition, the Temple Fortune shops and the now destroyed Club House were built in determinedly heavy German style, but in general the Garden Suburb provides an unschematised anthology of the best of small domestic building of the period. This includes excellent work by its three principal architects, and in 1909 Edgar Wood designed two flanking groups of flat-roofed blocks which, had they been built, would have constituted an adventurous foray into novelty in Britain at this time. Various co-partnership groups were responsible for parts of the Suburb, as well as the Improved Industrial Dwellings Company who built cottages, and Waterlow Court, a hostel for working ladies, a rather rare breed then, which was designed by Baillie Scott.

In 1911 the King and Queen paid a visit to the rapidly expanding settlement, the King commenting particularly on the provision of gardens for "he could not imagine anything better calculated to give relief from the monotony of the ordinary city worker's life". By this date church services were no longer being held in the builders' hut and a spire had been added to St Jude's to commemorate Dame Henrietta's sixtieth birthday that year.

With the building of the two great churches, one Anglican, the other Free Church, amidst their landscaped gardens and square

Germanic brickwork and iron balconies on the Temple Fortune shops

enclosed on one side by Lutyens's towering Institute, the village found itself with a central area unquestionably magnificent, but hardly in accord with the early ideas of the essentially village character of the place. Lutyens had added an excess of ambition to the Suburb which can be seen best by comparison with the singleness of purpose that New Earswick demonstrates so clearly.

Apart from certain visual characteristics a number of other plans had failed to materialise: a home for the blind, low-rent hostels, a bird sanctuary, an Anglo-American "Hill of Friendship", a home for what were termed "decayed ladies", the Carnegie Library which had been promised but was never delivered, and the Everyman Playhouse which, owing to financial stringencies, found itself in a drill hall near Hampstead tube. Beside the achievements of the indomitable Dame Henrietta, who had single-mindedly pressured through the early stages of her plan and then masterminded its fruition, the few failures and unrealised hopes seem insignificant in the extreme.

Unfortunately, an excess of optimism in the possibilities of human adaptability foiled the real intention of the scheme, the creation of a community with its roots firmly based in the traditional organic village and its balanced social structure. Dame Henrietta was far from seeing a classless community — her wish was for a mutually rewarding integration, not the subordination of individual lives to a general purpose, but the introduction of people of different class and income into a common unit, the village. Neither the co-partnership schemes, which were beginning to proliferate from 1907 onwards, nor the planned industrial villages, could hope for this social mixture; the tenants of such settlements were inevitably of roughly similar economic and social standing, though considerable efforts were made to provide the facilities and central institutions which could mould them into communities rather than duplicate housing estates.

Keeping always the example of the industrial model schemes before it, a Department of Town Planning was set up at Liverpool University, and with the training of architect-planners as such, the professional expertise became available to carry out the changes that were suddenly recognised as essential. The impetus for a change of direction in housing responsibility had been given. The great volume of work carried out by private enterprise, often still enlightened by idealism, was then rapidly overtaken by the private speculative builder and, most important, by local councils as the gradual movement towards state responsibility for municipal housing got under way.

By 1914 there were at least fifty housing schemes on Garden City lines being built, or already completed.[11] In housing design a generally high standard was attained, and similarly, and for the reasons stated above, planning procedures were becoming more sophisticated and enlightened. Often the determining factor between a village attractive in visual terms and one less pleasant, was the use made of vegetation. Hampstead Garden Suburb, following its predecessors, had been planned with emphasis on the retention of mature trees, planting hedges and trees along the streets, and the provision of open green spaces. Very few newly founded Garden Villages had the advantage of outstanding natural scenery — the hamlet set up by the Derwentwater Tenants at Keswick being the exception — and so an attractive environment had to be created.

The 1909 Town Planning Act was not the watershed it should have been. It was introduced to transfer the onus of planning from private enterprise to public authority shoulders, but it was far from instantly effective, not being to any degree mandatory. It set up complicated machinery which was virtually impenetrable, and it acted, in the early years, more as a deterrent than an incentive to action.

Much more important were the publications; the *Garden City* was first published in 1904 and the *Town Planning Review* was the official publication of the new department at Liverpool University, sponsored by Lord Leverhulme's £100,000 libel settlement against the *Daily Mail*. In the same way that early theorists, Robert Owen, William Allen or James Silk Buckingham, had submitted their ideas to the public via a constant stream of information, so the early town planners could illustrate their achievements, plan for the future and take note of overseas work in a specialised forum. No less important, architects and planners abroad, often with far greater facilities for large-scale planning, could profit from the example of various pioneer attempts.

Notes

1. James Hole, *Homes of the Working Classes*, 1866.
2. Chambers' *Edinburgh Journal*, 28 November 1835.
3. G.F. Millin, *The Village Problem*, 1903.
4. William Webb, *Garden First in Land Development*, London, 1919. See also the American equivalent by W.E. Smythe, *City Homes on Country Lanes*, New York, 1921.
5. Raymond Unwin and Barry Parker, *The Art of Building a Home*, Buxton, 1901.
6. J.D. Kornwolf, *Baillie Scott*, Baltimore, 1972.
7. C.R. Ashbee, *Book of Cottages and Little Houses*, 1906.
8. Walter Creese, *The Search for Environment*, New Haven and London, 1966.
9. *One Man's Vision* (report of the Trustees), London, 1954.
10. Henrietta Barnett, "The Story of the Growth of Hampstead Garden Suburb", 1907–28, n.d. *Town Planning and Modern Architecture at the H.G.S.* (Baillie Scott and Unwin), 1909. Many articles, including *Journal of the Royal Institute of British Architects*, October, 1957.
11. J.S. Nettlefold, *Practical Town Planning*, 1914; E. Culpin, *The Garden City Movement Up To Date*, 1913.

Chapter 12

Ireland and Scotland

A very different set of factors governed the planning of villages in Scotland and Ireland than of those in England and Wales although Lowland Scotland has greater affinities with English patterns of settlement. Different social, geographic and economic pressures combined to lead to the foundation of innumerable communities from the eighteenth century onwards. Some of these functioned as centres of considerable importance, far more than was warranted by their scale; others were closer to the traditional village, in the English sense, as contributory settlements within the radius of a larger town.

Both Ireland and Scotland offered enormous scope for the sort of plans feasible in America, but because of high-population density and extant systems of settlement, less possible in England. Builders could spread their wings in the great stretches of the coast of Ireland or the Highlands — and economic necessity in both impoverished areas required that they should do so.

The first planned communities in Ireland of a secular nature were the Plantation Towns, set up by the City Livery Companies and the colonisers to trade with, convert and generally set the Irish on the right path. These heavily fortified villages were to be self-contained and were intended to be sufficiently impregnable to repel all comers. They were equivalent, in form, to the Scottish *fermtoun* (or, in the Highlands, *baile*), which was merely the native population's defence against the greed of its neighbours.

The idea of improving the Irish, and the Highland Scots, by contact with civilising influences soon became considered as a worthwhile and attractive proposition, for, once moulded into amenable material, there was a limitless reservoir of exploitable labour. Once they had been assisted to improve their agriculture and cottage industries, infused with the glow of the Protestant

Rustic porch to a Picturesque cottage at Adare

faith, nothing would be impossible or so the early community founders hoped.

Ireland bears the scars and relics of innumerable settlements born out of these aspirations. It saw the rise, and frequently the fall of many grandiose schemes to industrialise the country or to influence the people by good example or religious pressure. The constant disasters seemed to surprise only those immediately involved — onlookers habitually predicted doom for such enterprises and often were justified.

Certainly the most ambitious scheme for colonisation in Ireland in the eighteenth century, the one which involved most of the eminent figures in the positions of power both in Dublin and London and left as little trace as any to record these efforts, was the proposal to found New Geneva.[1]

In 1782 middle-class liberals in Geneva had overthrown the aristocrats on the city council, but power was restored by the intervention of foreign armies (those of France, Savoy and Berne), meaning that the insurgents had to flee the country. Numerous countries offered them sanctuary but Ireland, at that moment gripped by a period of optimism and idealism, was the home they chose. The Protestant watchmakers, jewellers and intellectuals would form the core of a town to be distinguished by a great University, with an Academy, and would support themselves by their own industry. Parliament found nothing to quarrel with in the idea of re-establishing a Swiss city on the soil of Ireland and granted £50,000 towards its foundation, which was regarded as being of prime importance by the administration in Dublin and particularly by the then Governor-General, Lord Temple. Other members of the highest echelons of Irish society were equally enthusiastic; the Duke of Leinster offered them 2,000 acres and accommodation for one hundred Swiss immigrants in his own house, while Lord Ely wrote: "I am extremely rich — I wish to benefit the most enlightened people in the universe, the first Protestant colony on earth."

When the surveyor Major Ferrers set about looking for a site in 1783, he rejected three possible locations on the grounds that they would all involve the removal of a group of about forty labourers and widows, depriving them of their land and "Potatoe Gardens". The Genevans themselves did not share his solicitude; they rejected the sites because they included part of a Roman Catholic burial ground, not a happy augury for religious coexistence in the years ahead. When Ferrers did find a suitable situation, at Passage West, only ten families were displaced — one of whom was repaid for his ground together with "liberty to take off the materials of the cabbins" and another "with ditto liberty — stones excepted".

The Swiss themselves contributed £30,000 towards the project, but their undoubted enthusiasm was countered by prevarication and torpidity in Dublin, particularly when Lord Temple was replaced by the Duke of Rutland. This was the same inefficiency that occasioned a wistful letter from Ferrers inquiring when he and his employees might expect payment for their year's work.

When the advance guard of the Genevans arrived in Ireland they found that work had not yet begun and there were no signs of any preparation for action. In desperation thirteen went home, but an optimistic and staunch few stayed on.

In 1784 the Commissioners in charge of the project asked for an advance of £14,000 to enable building to begin, and in fact the project did just commence. The form the town was to take was as arguable a point as its situation, or indeed the financing of the operation. Sketches for one proposed plan were sent to Lord Temple by Edward Stratford Earl of Aldborough,[2] who also wrote eloquently on the necessity of inspiring the local population by the example of the Swiss, whose neutral politics, propensity for hard work and honesty seemed to offer an ideal stabilising element. Aldborough was offered sites near his own estates for the proposed settlement, and he put enormous energy and enthusiasm into carrying out the scheme.

The Genevans had already put forward a plan for a circular town, with roads as projecting radii, each sector walled off and the entrance gained through six gates. It bore a practical relationship to German medieval town planning and, for that matter, to the Irish fortified Plantation villages. The Swiss wisely wanted to conduct their life behind a strong physical, as well as moral, citadel of Protestantism. No doubt at the outset they found it hard to share the optimism of Lord Temple and the Commissioners in a favourable reception.

The plan which was chosen for the town, however, consisted of a great curved stretch of buildings flanking the coast for half a mile, well supplied with churches and with the notable absence of a courthouse. The eminent Dublin architect James Gandon was the author of this plan,[3] but none of this was to be. Shortly after the foundation stone had been laid in July 1784, the scheme foundered, leaving a few buildings to be re-used as barracks during the 1798 uprisings; as Lewis's *Guide* put it, "in consequence of their requiring certain privileges and immunities which it was not thought proper to concede, the projected settlement was abandoned". The watchmakers themselves had never stirred from Neuchâtel and the scheme was passed on to Thomas Jefferson for consideration while other watchmakers settled at Constance.

This débâcle illustrates perfectly the hazards and imponderable factors which greeted the smallest and largest of schemes alike. Some other attempts at colonisation were more specifically religious, and several notable settlements already existed in the country. Ballitore, in Kildare, was a Quaker settlement, and its chapel was built as early as 1707. To this were added a school, dispensary and savings bank, together with neat cottages. It was an obvious choice as target for religious protest and was set on fire by insurgents in 1798, though by the time Thackeray visited it[4] he could observe "one of the most beautiful flourishing villages in Ireland... white straggling village surrounding green fields... in the little village I remarked scarcely a single beggar and very few bare feet indeed among the crowds".

The most successful settlement of all was the Moravian community at Gracehill. The residents never made any attempt to antagonise the local population and so the village was left as an oasis; it constantly excited admiration for its rare calm, flourishing and prosperous air and for its particularly attractive planning and architecture which it shared with its English counterparts.[5] Busy "rearing camomiles", the brethren did not have time to interrupt the lives of others, and hoped to set an example rather than to proselytise.

Much less happily conceived was the settlement founded by the Rev. Nangle on Achill Island on behalf of what was called the Protestant Association. The community was built up on barren land and, according to Murray's *Guide*, presented a "cheerful looking square of plain white houses". The Mission consisted of fifty-six families, of which but nine were local people, and its function was placed in some doubt when, after nine years of work amid a population of 6,000, they could claim a grand total of ninety-two converts. As conversion was the object of the foundation, the Mission could reasonably be considered a failure. Not deterred however, Nangle set up schools and an orphanage, larger houses were built for ministers and an agent, and a printing business was started where he "carried on an uncompromising battle with the Roman Catholics in the columns of the *Achill Herald*. The colony which was the result of his labours stands in striking contrast to the other primitive villages of

Achill, but it has not been the means of anything like a conversion of the Roman Catholic inhabitants from the beliefs and practice of their own faith."[6] In fact the local Catholic population, while retaining their autonomy, gained from the introduction of industry and the employment it brought to one of the most destitute corners of Ireland. Ironically much of the money was poured in from England, in the cause of religion. It helped set up a grain mill and woollen factory and finance the construction of roads in a previously almost impassable area all of which benefited the local population enormously, without deflecting their religious views.

Mr and Mrs S.C. Hall took a justly gloomy view of the precepts upon which the settlement was based. Writing about the monthly paper produced at the Printing Office, they noted[7] that it was "scarcely necessary to observe that such a publication is read only by those who do not require to have their zeal stimulated; and that, as paving the way to "conversion" it is totally useless, inasmuch as no Roman Catholic is likely to take even a peep into its columns. The work is intolerant..." The stated object of the newssheet was "to expose the doctrinal and practical abominations of Popery", but in quite literally preaching to the converted, it was printed to talk only to itself. Nangle was, it seems, just another member of the long line of loud-mouthed religious fanatics that Ireland has had the misfortune to harbour; a legacy from early Plantation days.

On a much wider front, the great estates throughout Ireland, the main obstacle to progress was the absentee landlord. When Arthur Young travelled through Ireland he found few enough landlords to praise, and by 1830 it was estimated that one and a half thousand lived in London and Paris and a further four and a half thousand remained in Dublin, virtually never visiting their lands. These were administered by an usually infamous breed of agents who, as John O'Driscoll, editor of the *Irish Observer*, pointed out, were often "petty and rapacious despots because a hand to collect and transmit the rents is generally all that is looked for. Whether that hand is pure is seldom inquired into." Writing in 1822 O'Driscoll put the case against absenteeism eloquently. He saw a satisfactory relationship between landlord and tenant as a potential cornerstone. "That we owe certain duties of care, personal example and superintendence to those from whose labours we derive our subsistence and rank, place and importance, cannot be doubted." Admitting that some great estate owners had immense lands to attend to elsewhere, he considers the careful choice of agent the next requisite and, as for the landlord himself, "to an occasional residence we think he is bound". He adds, "we might refer to Scotland upon this... to illustrate the duty of residence and to point out in its practice its good effects".

Throughout the country, a few humane and conscientious men tried to alleviate the problems they found around them. On their estates landowners found peasants living in huts constructed like birds' nests from mud and sticks, without any security of tenure on their land. Ireland had neither the security of the English Poor Laws, whatever their shortcomings, nor the Scottish parochial system. Those who failed to find employment, or any means by which to live, were abandoned to their own devices.

The 4th Earl of Kenmare was one of the exemplary landlords; in his notes on tenants kept between 1755–57[8] he makes a full commentary on each family, showing a remarkable humanitarian interest for the problems and weakness of each. Assessing every case individually, he pours scorn on those who prove to be habitually lazy and profligate, and praises highly those who are prompt with the rents, hard-working and who take advantage of the help he offers. His papers are full of ideas of founding villages and encouraging industry, awarding prizes on the lines of the Dublin Society, and he found often enough that his good nature and high principles were taken advantage of: one man defrauded him in the foundation of a linen centre — "seeing my public spirit and eagerness about this plan, laid me open to his designs", he ruefully commented.

Another of the best recorded instances of the benevolent landlord, well recorded because his daughter was the prolific novelist Maria Edgeworth, was R.L. Edgeworth. He was proprietor of the village of Edgeworthstown, four times married, a tireless inventor of gadgetry, both useful and useless, and an intelligent and liberal man. He had spent much of his life in England and elsewhere and when he came to live in Ireland in 1782, he brought back his experiences of a more humane society. Finding the tenants on his land in a state of abysmal poverty, he set out to improve the situation. In his daughter's contribution to his memoirs,[9] she wrote that in 1819 (the year of writing) it was hard to imagine the horror of the situation that they had been faced with forty years earlier. Edgeworth dispensed with agents, charged fair rent, and as Mr and Mrs S.C. Hall observed on their visit to the village,

> "all around us bore... the aspects of comfort, cheerfulness, good order, prosperity and their concomitants, contentment. There was no mistaking the fact that we were in the neighbourhood of a resident Irish family with minds to devise and hands to effect improvement everywhere within reach of their control."[10]

Arthur Young when travelling in Ireland in 1780 had heaped praise on Lord Kingsborough, who, although a young man just returned from a round of continental gaiety, had already begun to carry out improvements on his estate at Mitchelstown. Young had been employed by him so can be forgiven for his partisan approach, but he notes how Kingsborough was giving the tenant back his land at a fair rent, thus eliminating the middle man who had proved to be the scourge of the poor tenantry. Young felt that the expenditure of great sums of money on improvement could not be wasted, it would raise standards and as the full employment and relative prosperity became felt so "licentiousness will be less profitable and more odious", as he puts it. Certainly the principal monument today to Kingsborough's efforts is an imposing and flourishing town, Mitchelstown, which still bears the signs of the planning and distinguished architecture set in motion by an enlightened landowner.

Other travellers noted, because of their scarcity, the most exceptional landowners. Prince Pueckler-Muskau[11] remarked on Lord B. and Col. W., who on their respective estates near Bantry, although they were Protestants, were accorded by their Catholic tenantry "an obedience as boundless as it is voluntary and cordial. Col. W. indeed lives like a patriarch among them, as I learnt from the common people themselves and settles all their differences, so that not a penny is spent in the wiredrawings of the law." Against these men he set those Irish nobles who are so ill-equipped to administer their properties that they become objects of hate to their tenantry. Thackeray on his travels mentioned that "you hear promises of the Duke of Devonshire as a landlord, wherever you go among his vast estates; it is a pity that, with such a noble residence as this and with such a wonderful country round about it, his Grace should not inhabit it more". Many of

Tyrellspass, the most distinguished of Irish estate villages, with its great crescent-shaped green dominated by the church spire

the great Irish landowners had equally vast properties elsewhere and had genuine difficulties in sparing the time to investigate the administration of their estates. At this point the agent was the crucial figure and his personal qualities and capabilities determined the situation in which the tenants found themselves.

The work of the best landlords is well recorded, simply because it painted such an outstanding contrast to the normal state of affairs. If the situation in England was regarded as shocking by so many who travelled through the counties observing the poverty of accommodation and the misery of the labouring poor, the sight that met the traveller through Ireland obliterated every memory of bad conditions over the water. It was an easy escape route to blame the situation on inertia, congenital deficiencies, religious dogmatism and the rest, but exploitation, indifference and mismanagement were the root causes and too few were prepared to acknowledge that fact.

Lady Waterford's work in Ireland has already been mentioned. Maria Edgeworth herself had a great deal to do with the carrying out of her father's improvements, paying bills and bearing responsibility for a considerable amount of the administration of the estate. She also made a sizeable gesture of her own, giving the proceeds from one of her books to the Irish Poor Relief Fund. It was becoming traditional, as in England, for the women to take an active part in carrying through the social improvements on estates, although it was still regarded in the light of a permissible foible, reasonable enough if it was confined to the setting up of schools which could then carry out obeisances to their patroness. However, many English women who married into Anglo-Irish families were deeply and genuinely disturbed by what they found in Ireland, and attempted to make some attempt at remedying the situation.

One such was the Countess of Belvedere, whose memorial erected in the village church at Tyrellspass commemorates her in these ringing phrases:

"Gifted with a masculine understanding and most benevolent heart she employed the ample means with which it pleased providence to bless her as the wife and widow of George, Earl of Belvedere and afterwards Abraham Boyd in munificent acts of public and private charity thus conferring upon her peerage its best grace and exhibiting throughout her life a bright example of Christian principle and practice."

Such tributes adorn the drinking fountains in many village squares, carrying similar sentiments in appreciation of a benevolent landowner, or his wife. The Marquess of Downshire was a particularly conscientious administrator of his estates, which included numerous villages in Wicklow, Kilkenny and Kildare — at Blessington the fountain is inscribed "the water supplied at the cost of a kind and generous landlord for the benefit of his attached and loyal tenants". When an estate owner did make an effort to attend to the welfare and comfort of his tenants and employees, he was duly appreciated.

There was certainly nothing desultory about the Countess of Belvedere's efforts. Tyrellspass is one of the best examples of the planned village, in the English manner, in Ireland. The substantial detached houses stand around a crescent-shaped green. A church with an imposing spire and a pedimented courthouse flank each other and a neat single-storey schoolhouse is also included in the half circle. Trim pollarded trees interpose the houses and the large green sets off the scene. The Countess also established a Methodist chapel, savings bank, and set up a loan fund and a dispensary. She was helped in all this by a local vicar, and the work was reported to have met with such approval from the villagers themselves that they set about various improvements of their own, in addition. They levelled the green in order to show off the new church to best advantage, draining and planting it as they did so. They also founded an infant school, a centre for straw plaiting and a grain store, all three of which were situated in the office of the Loan Fund. A clock was added to the courthouse, and a public garden and footpaths were laid out. On her side, the Countess supplied an agronomist to teach the villagers more advanced methods of cultivation, proof that she considered the enterprise worthwhile. Such mutual trust was unfortunately rare in Ireland and there are few other estate villages with such evidence of a prosperous past.

Here and there architectural exercises were attempted, to enliven the aspect of a new foundation. One village, Bagenalstown, was to have been called Versailles, while another, Moy, was laid out on the plan of Marengo in Lombardy. If a man set out to create a new town or village, it was as well to do so with a flourish, rather than meanly or conventionally — and it usually commemorated its founder in the name. One of the finest of all

The forge at Enniskerry with a horseshoe entrance

such creations — though more town than village — was Westport, designed in its entirety by James Wyatt. At Adare the Earl of Dunraven built a Picturesque village outside the gates of his great Gothic mansion, Adare Manor. At the beginning of the nineteenth century, a dozen poor thatched cottages constituted the tiny hamlet of Adare,[12] but it soon grew into a sizeable village, the cottages complete with heavy thatched eaves, rustic verandahs and ornamental devices taken straight from P.F. Robinson's illustrations. This theme was imitated to good effect in the twentieth century, when Detmar Blow reused the verandahs and rustic posts on a number of houses he designed in the village. Enniskerry, the Powerscourt estate village, was built on the lines of many comparable English villages, in a restrained neo-Tudor style, together with the familiar stone horseshoe marking the doorway to the smithy. Similarly, Seaforde, a village in the North dating from 1820, was built with cottages and almshouses that might have come directly from Malton's pattern book. By the latter part of nineteenth century, estate owners were building standard cottages, just as in England, and entering competitions sponsored by the Board of Agriculture or the Dublin

The unimproved village street at Adare, as it was before 1810

Society for good design; both the Devonshire and Middleton estates were prizewinners.

But all this represented sporadic activity and a very late awakening to the poverty of conditions — far too late to be effective in any sense. At this stage housing could not be revolutionised to any marked extent, as it had been in England by the standardisation of design and the application of higher minimum requirements. The building of architectural set pieces was of little benefit to the population as a whole, and in any case was spasmodic and rare. The bulk of planned villages in Ireland were built in the traditional materials of the area, on basic plans, and the work was carried out by the tenants themselves on land rented to them for the purpose; in this respect the pattern was similar to that in Scotland, where nearly all villages conform to a standard.

In the area of more dramatic and novel attempts to better conditions, Ireland proved to be a suitable testing ground for utopian schemes; the land and the labour were available, though the suitable authoritarian figures were lacking. John Scott Vandeleur was a landowner who was prepared to direct his own experiment, on his own estates, and he instigated one of the initially most successful and carefully administered of all Owenite schemes. In the light of the general situation in 1830, with antagonism between the landed classes and their tenantry, the lack of resources and the intractibility of the Irish peasant, his achievements were all the more remarkable. Ralahine was a self-sufficient community where no money changed hands, no religious constraints hedged the members in, and the government was in the care of a democratically-appointed committee. Here were sown the seeds of a system with widely recognised repercussions, more clearly seen in Europe and America than in Britain. The history of the community was translated into French, German and Italian, and the man responsible for the translation of the French version was Godin, founder of the Familistère at Guise, the only bricks-and-mortar effort at realising Fourier's Phalanx in Europe.

The collapse of Ralahine was brought about by the gambling debts of Vandeleur, which meant the sale of the estate. In November 1833 the members of the settlement signed a motion which read: "We the undersigned members of the Ralahine Agricultural and Manufacturing Cooperative Association have experienced for the last two years contentment, peace and

The same street in Adare — now improved

happiness." There could hardly have been a more sincere tribute from its participants to an experiment which had worked against all the odds.

Owen's own efforts to found communities in Ireland met with less success than they did almost anywhere else. After his visit to Dublin in 1823 the only outcome was an anonymous pamphlet, "A letter containing some observations on the delusive nature of the system proposed by Robert Owen". The editor of the *Irish Observer*, O'Driscoll, dismissed him — "we are no advocates of the factitious system of Mr Owen, of Fellenberg and of numerous other contrivers".

One of Owen's followers, William Thompson, issued in 1830 his "Practical Directions" which outlined a scheme he hoped to found near Cork, a community for between 200 and 2,000 people. He spent the major part of his energy quibbling with Robert Owen over his dislike of the word village which, he felt, associated itself with poverty. The hairsplitting continued, which ensured that the community would never rise from the paper, but in 1831 William Thompson offered his own 600 acre estate at Carhoogardiff for another attempt at founding a settlement. The

Cottages at Adare by Detmar Blow: twentieth-century Picturesque estate housing

Cooperative Magazine made it a point to ignore his plans, but he received support from other quarters and produced a plan for a single block which was to be the centre point of the village. He managed to build a circular tower 100 feet high which was to be his private residence and headquarters of the operation, and was already envisaging a busy port. The first row of houses was being constructed when he died in 1833 and the plan went with him, only the tower remaining as a monument to his endeavours.

When genuine efforts to set up industry in country districts had failed, the results could be crueller still. The only area where industry consistently flourished was the linen area of Ulster, and Ireland as a whole presents a dismal picture of enormously over-ambitious schemes, many of which foundered from their inception, others which saw a brief era of extreme prosperity before a decline, and a very small number of which sustained some sort of growth. Other factors outside sheer ineptitude were often responsible — changes in world demand, changes within the industries themselves, and the fluctuating and unstable situation in a country where uprisings, famine and constant trouble undermined every attempt to set up new centres.

Thackeray, on his partisan journey around Ireland, pinpointed the basic problem after he had visited the great empty warehouses which lined the quayside at Westport:

> "These dismal mausoleums as vast as pyramids are the place where the dead trade of Westport lies buried — a trade that, in its lifetime, probably was about as big as a mouse. Nor is this the first nor the hundredth place to be seen in this country which sanguine builders have erected to accommodate an imaginary commerce. Mill-owners over-mill themselves, merchants over-warehouse themselves, squires over-castle themselves, little tradesmen about Dublin and the cities over-villa themselves and we hear sad tales about hereditary bondage and the accursed tyranny of England."

The ringing name of Prosperous bears witness to one such scheme. When Lewis's *Guide* reported on it the writer prevaricated by calling it "a town or a village" but in the dreams of its founder, Robert Brooke, it was to be very much a town. Set up in

Plan for building a new village presented by the Reverend Robert Rennie to the Highland Society in 1803

213

the late eighteenth century, the datestone on the central house is 1780. It was planned to be a cotton manufacturing centre, and within three years a town of 200 houses had risen; after granting £25,000 towards its continuation Parliament turned down a further request for finance in 1786 and in 1798 the struggling business was finally closed down. Now all that remains is a straggling and unexceptional village labouring under its resounding name, which it could not begin to justify.

New Birmingham did little better, and another foundation, Stratford-on-Slaney, presents even less evidence today of a formerly flourishing community.[13] Edward Stratford, later Earl of Aldborough (the same man who had been prominent in the planning of New Geneva), saw the advantages of the 10% import tax on calico and decided to set up a textile centre which he would then sell or let to a manufacturer. His aims were undoubtedly particularly philanthropic, and he lent considerable sums of money to interested parties. In 1786 it was said that "the noble

Datestone (1780) at Prosperous: a relic of unrealised hope

landlord gives every reasonable encouragement to this infant scheme", and in the following year it was advertised for sale with a considerable number of single- and double-storeyed cottages "just covered in slated, sashed and glazed", a church almost completed, and the first of the factory buildings in progress, although the bleaching house had been in production for three years already. The partnership who bought it, Orr Smith, spent another considerable sum on expanding the site and when Orr took over to run the firm alone he encouraged agricultural improvements in addition. At its height, Stratford-on-Slaney employed 1,000 workers, whose housing, church and chapel were situated around the great bleaching greens.

The Orrs were Presbyterians and had come over from Paisley, bringing many workers with them, and a benefit society and library were provided in the best Nonconformist philanthropic manner. By 1846 the entire enterprise had ceased, overtaken by the usual combination of economic, political and religious disruptions, and now the ruined mills and a tiny hamlet are all that mark the spot where a great textile centre existed in the late eighteenth and early nineteenth centuries.

Portlaw, the village which grew up around the Malcolmsons's cotton mill in 1825, was an altogether more successful venture.[14] The Malcolmsons were Quakers and Lewis's *Guide* compared the flourishing village against the scattered huts that had stood on the same spot twenty years earlier.

> "The health, education and morals of this newly created colony have been strictly attended to by its patrons, a dispensary for the benefit of the working people has been established under the care of the resident surgeon within the walls of the concern and a second dispensary is supported by the Marquess of Waterford. The formation of a Temperance Society has been so successful that its members are nearly five hundred in number."

But Waterford had not purchased peace with his dispensary. In the famine year of 1846 the people of Portlaw headed for Curraghmore, the Waterford demesne; when Waterford died he left behind him in Portlaw a church and police barracks, a combination of cajolery and law enforcement, the stick and the carrot, against further trouble. Yet the realities of the famine are best illustrated by the rent arrears recorded on the Kenmare estates: in 1845 rent arrears totalled £1,534, in 1850 they were

£27,806. It took more than a trail of public buildings to eradicate that deficit.

Succeeding generations of the Malcolmsons at Portlaw extended the mills, even at the time of the famine, and formed the village into a self-sufficient community to the extent that leather tokens were issued in place of money — a good security against those who strayed from the Temperance movement. A large proportion of the workforce was in fact English, and an entirely English section of the village was constructed on an island. The firm failed in 1874, and then carried on until 1904 when a new tariff on imported cotton raised the duty from 35% to 55%, dealing a body blow to the struggling company. By 1910, when an account of the village was published, the cottages had become pigsties and the place was in a state of collapse and abject poverty.

Another pioneering effort in founding a model industrial community (it should be remembered, contemporary with or even in advance of anything comparable in England) was at Bessbrook, in Ulster, by another Quaker, J.G. Richardson, in the famine year, 1846. Like the Malcolmsons or Titus Salt, Richardson's prime interest was in the Temperance Movement, and he made sure that the village was built without a pub, and for that matter, a pawnshop, police station or general shop. He made up for the lack of such facilities by providing a dispensary, with a company doctor, schools, evening classes and a community centre, and the village became widely recognised as a pioneer venture. The housing was high-quality, situated around greens and with gardens provided; it still exists intact, though much expanded.

The usual attitude towards Ireland, however, was the sort of infectious pessimism that one writer expressed, in 1844:

> "It will indeed be an epoch in the history of Ireland when a bale of cotton direct from New Orleans is spun and woven in Killaloe and in part returned as printed calicoes or muslins from Limerick to the States. The man who first accomplished that or any equivalent result will have effected a revolution."

Comparable gloom afflicted those who tried to think positively about Highland Scotland, where there were many similar obstacles.

Before the eighteenth century the village, in the English sense, was almost unknown in Scotland, outside a very limited area in the South East. Traditionally grouped around the nucleus of farm, church or castle, hamlets rarely became villages and certainly never functioned as such. Centres of trade and influence were the scattered market towns.

But from the eighteenth century onwards, and particularly after the '45 Rebellion, village building was taken up with missionary enthusiasm by landowners and reformers. It was abundantly clear that the only way in which to make a productive amenable body of the Scots was to develop an ordered pattern of settlement which would also form the framework for a stable economy.

The development of the villages in the Highlands and Lowlands met with two very different situations, but in each case the answer was reconstruction; the major part of the work in the Highlands was undertaken by official agencies, while in the Lowlands the rebuilding was in the hands of estate owners with a similar set of motives to those further south in England, even if in Scotland there was greater urgency.

In the early nineteenth century two accounts were published on the topic of village building and planning, one pure theory, the other based on observations of the actual situation. They both reflect the earnestly held belief that, given the right environment, the Scots would repay investment of time, energy and money — in marked contrast to the universally dim view taken of the Irish potential for similar development.

The first of the two publications was the prizewinning essay presented by the Reverend Robert Rennie to the Highland Society in 1803[15] — the same year that the Society was offering money to landowners to encourage village building. It is a plainly written, common sense account of how to choose a site, plan its layout and finance the exercise. Dry foundations, access to plentiful running water, coal and fuel supplies and availability of transport were all obvious points, and he laid enormous emphasis on fresh air, with which, as he puts it "the streets would almost wash themselves". A through current of air would keep the sewers running and blow away unpleasant fumes — presumably unless the wind direction changed. In spite of claiming to describe a small village, Rennie proposed a canal which would give the "easiest access to the Atlantic and German oceans and by them, to the whole world", and kept his options open by saying that, by keeping to a basic grid plan, "if the village would ever become a town, or a city, there will be no deformity".

217

What Rennie was in fact providing was a précis of other people's activities combined logically into a blueprint. In architectural terms he merely suggests the provision of materials and the size and height of the houses, pointing out that if single- and double-storeyed buildings are kept together, rather than alternated, a less muddled effect will be achieved. As was the usual custom, the cottages faced directly on to the street in his plan, and garden strips are provided behind, with access from a back lane. He ends his account, describing "the great desideratum for the original establishment, steady support and certain increase of a village which is trade or manufactures. Without this, men will not feu, or if they do, they cannot build; or if they build, it must soon prove a deserted village."

Added to this is an editorial note emphasising the importance of education in such a venture, the efficacy of offering prizes for good behaviour and of having a committee of respectable inhabitants to administer the affairs of the village and, to ensure success, the production of a certificate of character from each potential settler. He adds, "if these ideas should be objected to as utopian or beyond the powers of the founders or proprietors of most inland villages they are however such as do credit to the principles and intentions of the author". That such practical, workable and inevitably autocratic suggestions should be designated utopian is a reflection upon the standards obtaining in Scotland at this period, where the Highland turf hut and the Lowland shack still housed much of the population.

Added to Rennie's suggestions is a short critique by a practical village builder, Colonel Dirom of Brydekirk. His village plan shows a considerable sophistication, with more variety and certain practical improvements on Rennie's plan, such as front entry to the garden areas between every two houses, insistence on which type of materials to use, and the provision of sewers and effective guttering. He also suggested that a public house be provided only with the owners' approval, that noisier workshops and factories be situated out of the centre, that there be a common repair fund and that feu rights or ninety-nine-year leases be granted. In spite of his articulate approach to planning and the elegant plan he presented, Dirom's village never grew beyond a hamlet and the industrial village he had envisaged never materialised. The formal streets and great crescent are scarcely in evidence.

The second of the two influential publications, dating from a little later, 1825, was Sir John Sinclair's *Analysis*, in which he devoted a considerable section to the subject of village planning. He gave an outline history of such foundations. The earliest were set up to protect the landed interest "that they might have assistance near them, on any sudden emergency". The old villages, he continues, were often "absurd, irregular and inconvenient... erected in confused groups with a total want of taste. Dunghills, coalhills and peatstacks were put in front of the houses and often gutters filled with putrid water..." Having convinced his readers of the horrors of the past he turns to the present and future. His ideal, it is clear, is for plan and symmetry.

Unashamedly, Sinclair stated the real motives of the majority of village builders — among which he personally was numbered. "Villagers are in general contented and unambitious. They enjoy the pleasures of society and of frequent intercourse with strangers, which has the effect of exciting social affections and introducing urbanity among them." It is hard to imagine that he is writing of human beings at all. If a village really prospered trade might yet be found for "milliners and mantuamakers" (or would that make it a town?)

Villages directed along the right lines, according to Sinclair and his many supporters, can be among the "best nurseries of the human species". His practical suggestions include the inadvisability of building two rows of cottages confronting each other for "after toiling hard through the day, they return home to be involved in smoke". He argues the case forcibly for the mutual benefits to be gained from the foundation of villages, advantages for the proprietor being equal to those of the fortunate resident.

One of the most notable village improvement schemes was also one of the earliest. Ormiston was the creation of John Cockburn, the agricultural reformer, and was designed to be the market centre for his estates and also to become the thriving focus for rural industry in the locality. In spite of remaining much of the time in London — he did not retire north to his estates until 1744 — he began the work in 1734 contemporary with similar early schemes in England. The letters that passed between Cockburn and his gardener are famous in the social history of the period,[17] and he seems to have missed little even if he was living 350 miles to the south.

An alternative plan for building a village in Scotland presented by Colonel Dirom. Part of Brydekirk was built

Cockburn was an agricultural improver in the same mould as Coke at Holkham, and the building of a new village was only one limb of a massive programme of work. That Sinclair was writing nearly a century later shows how far in advance of his time were Cockburn's efforts.

A London civil engineer Lewis Gordon had laid out the village, feuars being granted timber and stone with which to build. It was ensured that there were to be no "paltry little houses" or any muddled mushrooming of cottages on every side. The plots were carefully planned out, and before the village had been built the foundations of the trades and manufactures which were to support the new village had been laid. In 1726 a brewery and distillery were founded and textile manufacture initiated, with an Irishman brought in to instruct the villagers in the techniques of bleaching. Other outsiders were imported to set the various industries under way, a Dutch lint-dresser, gardeners and an English innkeeper. Little was left to chance in Cockburn's village, and soon the people began to repay the efforts he had made, including setting up a flourishing Agricultural Club. Progress continued to be rapid until Cockburn's bankruptcy meant the sale of the estate in 1734. Gradually the impetus drained away and the village went back to an existence principally as an agricultural centre. Only the drinking houses prospered without any check; by 1845 they had increased to seven.

Most building, as in Ireland, was carried out in the local vernacular, using regional types of stone and tiling which tended, together with the absence of gardens on the street fronts of the houses, to make the proliferating symmetrical villages rather grey and drab. In the century after the '45 it has been calculated that well over 150 foundations were begun; some prospered, others failed or remained static. Sometimes a renewed lease of life came about through the introduction of a new industry or trade in the neighbourhood (the equivalent of North Sea oil today), or with the building of new roads or railways.

Eaglesham, a village planned on Picturesque lines for the industrial purpose of textile manufacture. Its wide central green was used for bleaching rather than recreation

Eaglesham

Sometimes, however, architectural innovation came into the building of a new village. Dirleton was a Picturesque village, and when Alexander Somerville passed it he noted the beauty of the cottages, surrounded by their flourishing gardens, which graced the entrance to the great house and which emphasised the tremendous disparity with those cottages less conspicuously placed, which were left to rot out of sight. This was, he felt, village building at its most meaningless, for it did not serve the general interests of the people, merely the fancies of the estate owner.

One very extravagant plan was that described by John Stuart to his friend, the architect John Soane,[18] which shows the aesthetic concerns of the period to good effect. The village was to be at Allenbank-by-Berwick, and in July 1782 Stuart wrote, "we are beginning to grant feus to build a village on top of the bank you remember where the rivers meet. Wish I could get a good plan, neat and plain. There is a public building necessary, which I would make appear like a castle with battlements. There must be a large square or green for the fairs etc. etc. A neat spire for a church high but not expensive." These comments are those of an architectural amateur thinking in line with current fashion. He had chosen a markedly Picturesque setting and by silhouetting the battlements and spire on the skyline was fulfilling the romantic imagery of the period. It was comparable with the ideas of a General Pearce, who, when building himself a house at Altadora, in Ireland, "affected to build it as a thatched cabin and erected a tower to make it look like a village with a church to it".

Another letter from Stuart later in the year mentions his plan being drawn out, though he favours an elliptical rather than the semi-circular layout given; it is not clear whether Soane was himself the author of this drawing, but Stuart's ideas were clear enough and he only needed technical assistance.

Most interesting is his insistence on a central feature for the ellipse, of a distinctly theatrical type; in the middle of the green he wanted "a high Gothic arch with a turret etc. for a clock and bells and at the same time constructed in such a manner that a church be added when wanted behind it, so as to make the entrance through the arch". This extraordinary *ad hoc* arrangement would certainly have been a notable feature of the Scottish architectural tour if anything more of it had materialised but, it seems, nothing did.

Many early nineteenth-century estate villages in Lowland Scotland were less original, though they echoed much that was being built in England. At Dunmore mullioned windows, overwhelming chimneys and even a horseshoe-shaped doorway for the smithy were all familiar from efforts elsewhere to keep in step with changing architectural fashions.

Villages such as Scone and Gifford were the product of emparking. Scone was nominated by Sir John Sinclair as an outstanding example of a newly planned agricultural village, and an anonymous writer praised the Earl of Mansfield's activities in these words: "everything which fortune, taste and patriotism can effect has been called forth to complete the embellishment of this spot so highly favoured by nature".

In the Highlands, activity was much more limited and there was little time for extravagance of style. The Duke of Argyll was one of the most conscientious landlords and created three centres: Inveraray was the principal one, but in addition he built Campbeltown, the site of an abortive whale-fishing centre, and Kenmore, where the displaced herring fishermen from Inveraray were resettled. The history of Inveraray has been well told,[19] and the first plans for its rebuilding date from well prior to the '45, and the subsequent rash of rebuilding. A constant succession of plans was then produced, including one from the Adam brothers' father William, and, finally, after the succession of the 5th Duke in 1770, work began in earnest to the plan of Robert Mylne.

The Marquess of Stafford, somewhat later, set up Helmsdale and Brora, and as one of the largest landowners in the Highlands, who had received a great deal of criticism during the period of the Clearances, he was doing little more than exonerating himself from further blame. He supported his claims by an apologia written by J. Loch,[20] which seems to protest too loudly for the good of the cause. Loch's whitewash job begins with a description of the ghastly huts in which the tenants were living, adding that "the great proportion of their time, when not in pursuit of game or of illegal distillation was spent in indolence and sloth". Certain considerations were kept in mind when erecting new cottages: the cottages must be in view from the road "so that they will not only be constantly under the eye of the local management, but will gradually acquire industrious habits from their being placed near the great lines of communication throughout the country". Badly built cottages, such as continued to be constructed, were due to poor materials, but Lady Stafford hoped to remedy this by the awarding of prizes for the four best cottages of 1819. Prize-giving, again whip and carrot, was judged effective encouragement. The Staffords also introduced skilled people to teach new trades, just as Cockburn had done earlier at Ormiston. At Brora a Dutch prisoner-of-war who had married a Sutherland girl taught herring fishing, and as a fearless boatman, was "teaching the people to go to sea in all weathers". Production of bricks and tiles was begun on the estate to facilitate building, and before long Helmsdale and Brora were flourishing centres.

Various bodies were formed to deal with the Highlanders.[21] They had been forbidden to carry arms or wear their traditional dress, and were rough human material for even the keenest of reformers. Many had refused to move from their homes, even the offer of more land and building materials failing to shift them, and such bodies as the Commissioners for Annexed Estates or the British Fisheries Society had a very tough challenge ahead. Much as colonists in Ireland had set up planned villages, so the Commissioners created a system of settlements around the

Highlands in areas which had scarcely boasted any inhabitants, and never in any concentration. The Annexed Estates were those forfeited by traitors during the '45 Rebellion; many were later sold off to pay creditors but thirteen became the property of the Crown by an Act of 1752. The commissioners, though humane men, took the gloomiest view of the Highlanders they had found on these lands, and resettlement seemed the only answer. They felt it necessary to "reclaim the inhabitants of these estates from their long habits of sloth and inactivity and reconcile them to the love of labour, industry and good order..." — the Highlanders then "may be better enabled to assist each other in agriculture and manufactures and in securing their property against theft and rapine..." Education was deemed the best weapon, and once out of their native dress, they began to seem more promising material. Just like the Irish, the people, despite their absolute poverty and deep-seated cultural differences, would be preached the positive virtues of hard work and given a certain, limited degree of literacy. Colonisation was afoot, and the villages were the medium through which it was to be carried out.

Owen's Institute for the Formation of Character, New Lanark, built in 1816

The attitude towards the Highlands, even from Lowland Scots, was aggravated by the fact that at this period the area was truly remote, and virtually unvisited. A tour such as Johnson and Boswell's was a real voyage of exploration, a daring adventure, and there was negligible contact between the English-influenced Lowland areas and the remote corners of the Highlands and Islands.

The British Fisheries Society was an organisation with more philanthropic than profiteering motives behind its creation. The first Governor was the Duke of Argyll and his deputy the Earl of Breadalbane, both tested adventurers into the tricky area of new foundations. Ullapool was the most notable of the Society's creations; the development began in 1788 and proposals were put forward by Telford to turn the village into a grandiose affair with a circus surrounded by an arcaded market building — not unlike Papworth's Hygiea, financed by the British entrepreneur William Bullock and to be built in Cincinnati. However, the plan that transpired at Ullapool was a conservative rectilinear layout. Other ventures initiated by the Society were Tobermory and Lochbay, on Skye. As time went on various factors conspired against the original economic intentions for these villages, and their fortunes vacillated. Lochbay became an agricultural settlement, rather than a fishing port. This was precisely what the governing body had hoped to avoid — one of the prime achievements of the new villages was to be a diversity of activities allowing for all contingencies, the failure of the herring catch, a bad agricultural season or any other possible problems. It says much for the optimism and energy of the governing body of the Fisheries Society that they should press on with plans to build Pultneytown (later known simply as Wick). This, in the event, was the most successful of their ventures and was financed and planned from 1806 onwards.

The geography of the Highlands obviously defeated the sort of regular village settlement that the Lowlands could support, so that fewer and larger villages were founded.

In the last resort emigration was always a remedy for a failure to absorb, house and employ the Highlanders. It was just such a boatload, from Skye, that David Dale diverted and made into his original workforce at New Lanark, the families who were to be the raw material for Robert Owen's experiments; proof, if it were needed, that correctly treated, the Scots were adaptable and amenable. At New Lanark they had become willing members of a community very foreign to their own within a comparatively short space of time.

New Lanark in its later form, as the testing ground for Robert Owen's ideas, has been dealt with in an earlier chapter, but David Dale had already provided more than merely basic accommodation, as at one of his other enterprises at Catrine. At Blantyre, Dale and Monteith founded a mill in 1785 where the workers "... living in one of the fairy neuks of creation, religious and moral, well fed and clothed and not overwrought... seem particularly happy as they ought to be". In later days New Lanark served to obscure the bad conditions which were the norm at the smaller establishments in Scotland — the excellence of its example was thought compensatory for much at fault elsewhere. However there were always some critics to be found, and a voice was raised against one of Owen's best-intended innovations, complaining that "they had got a number of dancing-masters, a fiddler, a band of music, that there were drills and exercises, and that they were dancing together till they were more fatigued than if they were working". Of course the basic complaint was of the strict organisation and rigid discipline, of which even the dancing was a part.

Housing at Deanston, Buchanan and Arkwright's mill village included the provision of gardens, and the housing was white-washed giving a "cleanly and cheerful aspect", while at Catrine, which later came into the hands of the same company, Finlays, the village was renowned for its supply of gas for lighting which was the best quality and most economically produced of any in Ayrshire, it was claimed. This seemed a great wonder to contemporary observers, greater than the existence of four separate libraries, two public, one philosophic and the fourth for the use of the Sunday School.

Catrine was also extremely generously provided with places of worship, including one elegant chapel placed prominently on the hillside above the village. On the orders of Dale and Claud Alexander the houses had to be built in a prescribed fashion; of two storeys and roofed in slate, meaning that the housing was solid and quite spacious. Of a pink stone, the cottages are in the vernacular of the area and are in fact considerably superior to the better industrial housing of the period in England. The Gregs' cottages at Styal, for instance, look flimsy by comparison.

The housing at Catrine, built of pink stone

Elsewhere in Scotland, Archibald Woodhouse was noted for his high quality housing for the workers at Crosslee, near Paisley, and the Crums of Thornliebank were also notably good employers in this respect. In general, though, the Scottish record was no better than that in the south and although different traditional styles prevailed, the single-storeyed cottage and the tenement, for mass accommodation, were the norm. New Lanark is in fact mostly tenement housing, and as such is considerably inferior to

228

Catrine. Other modifications came about, such as the double cottage consisting of two self-contained dwellings one above the other and entered from opposite sides, but in general the housing remained predictable and was innovatory more in terms of space and planning than style.

As in industrial settlements all over Britain, the overriding problem was the tremendous influx of workers to highly concentrated areas, where no provision had been made for their housing. Often time was the problem, the labour being needed immediately the mills became operational, and if housing was not provided in advance the situation rapidly became acute. As conditions became worse in Scotland, the Irish workers who were flooding in (most of the men at Catrine were Irish), together with the Highlanders, were blamed for the deterioration of conditions; but in reality it was a combination of all the usual factors, overcrowding, labour exploitation, the roughest of men and, on a wider front, an extremely slow-moving progress towards reform and a public consciousness of the existence of a human sewer, out of which the general prosperity of the country and many immense fortunes were being made.

Most of the activity in village building, rural and industrial, took place in the century succeeding the '45 Rebellion and was much on the lines of Rennie's plan — in effect Everyman's Guide to Village Building. There is always a touch of moralising in the accounts of any of the Scottish enterprises, a crusty tone which becomes increasingly familiar. However, it is certain that the bodies who set about the hardest task, the formation of settlements in the Highlands, were conscientious men — the Commissioners of the Annexed Estates, the British Fisheries Society and some of the large landowners all worked hopefully towards a goal which had less to do with personal gain and profit than with a general economic renewal of the country as a whole. That a number of their schemes, at least, succeeded — though not necessarily in the form in which they were designed — is something of a triumph.

Lord Gardenstone, who had built Laurencekirk, wrote: "I have tried in some measure a variety of the pleasures which mankind pursue, but never relished anything so much as the pleasure arising from the progress of a village." He spoke for many.

Notes

1. Articles in *Journal of the Waterford and South East Ireland Archaeological Society*, Vol. XV, 1912, and *Journal of the Royal Society of Antiquaries of Ireland*, 1947 (I owe these and other references for New Geneva to E. McParland).
2. MSS. in the British Museum.
3. *Irish Architectural Drawings*, catalogue R.I.B.A., 1965.
4. W.M. Thackeray (pseu. Titmarsh), *Irish Sketchbook*, 1843.
5. *Calcutta Journal*, 9 February 1819.
6. *Murray's Handbook to Ireland*, 1864.
7. Mr and Mrs S.C. Hall, *Ireland, Its Scenery and Character*, 3 vols., 1846.
8. E. McLysaght (ed.), *Kenmare Papers*, Dublin, 1942.
9. A. Hare (ed.), *Life and Letters of Maria Edgeworth*, 1894; *Memoirs of R.L. Edgeworth* (completed by M.E.), 1820.
10. Mr and Mrs S.C. Hall, *op. cit.*
11. Prince Pueckler-Muskau, *Tour in England*, 1832.
12. Countess Dunraven, *Memorials of Adare*, 1865.
13. *Journal of the Royal Society of Antiquaries of Ireland*, Vol. 75, part I, 1945.
14. *Journal of the Waterford and South East Ireland Archaeological Society*, Vol. 13, 1910.
15. The Rev. Robert Rennie, *Prize Essays and Transactions of the Highland Society of Scotland*, 2 vols., 1903.
16. Sir John Sinclair, *Analysis of the Statistical Account of Scotland*, 1825.
17. R. Mitchison, *Agricultural Sir John*, London, 1962.
18. Arthur Bolton, *Portrait of Sir John Soane*, London, 1927.
19. Mary Cosh and Ian G. Lindsay, *Inveraray and the Dukes of Argyll*, Edinburgh, 1973.
20. J. Loch, *Improvements on the Estates of the Marquess of Stafford*, 1820; also *Improvements... Sutherland*, 1815. A great number of volumes of allegation and counter-allegation were sparked off by the Clearances and the water has become a little muddied as a result.
21. A.J. Youngson, *After the '45,* Edinburgh, 1973.

Chapter 13

The Vision
of the Village

A very important contributory factor to the form which newly-built villages took was the literary and pictorial imagery of their time. Without going into regions far outside the scope of this book, it is essential to briefly consider the vision which writers were passing on to their readers, or painters to their audience.

The village, as a centre of rural existence, was the favourite setting in English fiction from Fielding onwards, and throughout the nineteenth century.[1] A village backdrop is a constant factor, its hierarchies, appearance and customs delineated with precise, myopic fascination. Often reality and fantasy compete to make up the picture — so that when fantasy becomes reality, as in the most far-fetched Picturesque villages, the circle has come around. The Picturesque village is surely the architectural expression of all the myths of rural life, and when suburban development sought to reproduce even that, then the area of absurdity had been reached. The village in its natural form was the starting-point, in architecture as in literature, but reality was rarely able to offer the total picture of the manufactured version.

Writers took many stands on the depiction of rural life. Some attempted to reveal reality through satire or reporting; others merely painted in the minutiae and let the picture as a whole resolve itself.

Whether viewed in its newly revealed[2] light as a depiction of a real village, or, as previously, as merely an account of a generalised situation, Goldsmith's *Deserted Village* was a committed statement against eighteenth-century despotism. He used the particular to illustrate the whole, using his authority and his literary skills to support the cause of the dispossessed country people who had no rights nor voice to plead their own case. Some

"The Wheelwright's Yard" photographed by Fox Talbot in 1843. At this early date photography represented the realities of country life

time later Crabbe in *The Village* told the same story — his observations were of the villagers in the 1780s around the Belvoir estates, where all lands had fallen into the ownership of the powerful landlord.

Other champions of country people — the country people of reality, not the pastoral images propped up in their stead — such as Cobbett or the Howitts, used more straightforward means, documentary reports of conditions, for the same ends: to reveal the grim realities and to break the stranglehold of idealisation.

Also, fact and fiction combined in satirical form were a potent mixture in clever hands, and in *The Age and its Architects* Edwin Paxton Hood introduces an apocryphal village with the apt name of Arcadia. We find all the figures that might be expected. At the head of the hierarchy, the Earl of Fitzham "looks on his villages as kennels where he keeps his dogs". At Humdrum, the neighbouring town, Lady Humdrum keeps herself busy, and her conscience placated, by establishing a school. This has as its objects the teaching of "a little reading and sewing but especially a proper reverence for the church, the state and the dignified family of Humdrum". The neighbouring village, glorying in the name of Drudgewell, exhibits architecture which is "altogether peculiar to our advanced state of civilisation in which is exhibited the graceful interblending of the rude hut of the Hottentot with the stone dwelling of the ancient Anglo-Saxon serf". The countryside, which belongs to the Duke of Driveover, has never received a visit from its landlord, whose policy it is to wait until the cottages fall apart, at which point the embarrassing poor can be removed. All the points are well made and the measured acidity and overstatement are certainly not uncalled for. Hood took issue with the evils of a system which allowed the rich to live at ease in their *cottages ornés* without any impingement upon their consciousness of the rural poor whose lot only seemed to worsen.

It is no surprise to discover, at the other end of the spectrum, that Ruskin enjoyed Miss Mitford's depiction of country life in *Our Village* (1819). For the man who could in all seriousness set a party of Oxford undergraduates to work remodelling a stretch of road into the image of what a country lane *should* be, such trivia was real enough. But when Anne Thackeray Ritchie, who wrote the introduction to one edition of the novel late in the nineteenth century, stepped off the train at Reading and into the waiting phaeton, she was in for a surprise.

"Was that all? I saw two or three commonplace houses skirting the dusty road... I had been expecting I knew not what: a spire, a pump, a green, a winding street: my preconceived village in the air had immediately to be swept into space and, in its stead, behold the inn with its sign-post, and these half-dozen brick tenements more or less cut to one square pattern! So this was all!"[3]

Brought up on a good Victorian diet of *papier-maché* villages and having avidly read the whimsy of Miss Mitford's pastoral life followed through the changing seasons, reality came hard on her. Yet *Our Village* is cleverly unspecific in every detail — what we are presented with is nature, some harmless beings and their animals, and the flimsiest of outlines. The rest the reader is left to construct unaided and it is this trap that we are meant to fall into, supplying our own preconceptions to pad out the outline. In *Our Village* nobody is touched by stronger emotion than being "much affected'; the rest is muted and well muffled, and the appearance of any of Jane Austen's characters would have shattered the windowpanes.

Just as Jane Austen's village society consists of busy, interesting and eminently recognisable people, so her background is no way coy and perfect, in no way idealised. It is a presumed location, picked out by specific landmarks and a general atmosphere — the atmosphere that a woman who had spent her youth in the centre of a Hampshire village, in the rectory to be precise, could so accurately depict.

The sort of imagery that Miss Mitford conjured up, however, is precisely that beloved of Uvedale Price — romantic, Picturesque and merely awaiting the addition of a group of bargeboarded and fantastic cottages with all their paraphernalia to complete the scene appropriately.[4]

Just as small town life was pinpointed for ever in *Middlemarch*, so in *Wives and Daughters* (1864–66) Mrs Gaskell delineated the subtle levels of village society with the greatest perception. The pyramid is topped by the family from the great mansion who spend the season in town, and only retreat to their country seat — with a feeling of anticlimax — in search of peace and recuperation, fulfilling their duties towards the village by giving an annual tea party. Contrasted against them is the Squire, a man far less sophisticated with his roots firmly planted in country soil, while his family are in their various ways altogether more admirable than the absent nobility. After these come the professional people (the doctor's daughter being the main figure of the novel), standing slightly apart from the good women of the village who knit the various strands and events together by holding gossip sessions with great regularity. Quite out of sight, except when occasionally spotted out blackberrying or on their sick-beds, are the labourers and their families.

A similar intricate social structure — as important an ingredient of village imagery as the physical form it might take — was noted by Flora Thompson at Candleford Green, from her observation point behind the counter at the Post Office, and by Raymond Unwin when he observed the fine mesh that made up village life. His training as an architect and planner did not obscure the details; he could see that "the landlord and tenants, parson and flock, tradesman and customers, master and servant, farmer and labourers, doctor and patients; all were in direct relation and share common interests forming a network of community life".[5] It was more important for a planner than a novelist to recognise this framework, and to work with it in mind. A carefully structured society had been built up for economic ends, and paternalism was an integral part of the whole. In her memoirs, Lady Carbery, daughter of the man who had built Childwick Green, a Hertfordshire model village, noted that "visiting the cottages was part of our lives from early years". The system was finely wrought, carefully observed, and seemingly eternal.

Flora Thompson's description of country life in hamlet, village and country town in *Lark Rise to Candleford* (1939) was one step further away from the synthetic creation of *Our Village*. Old and new are contrasted and there is little space for romanticism or illusion, reality providing its own charm. Laura — or Flora, as it is in reality autobiographical — moves from her birthplace, a very poor hamlet, to the relative affluence of the village where she takes up a job in the Post Office. Here, with the smithy next door, she finds herself at the centre of the community, and she observes the ritual and the relationships of the people as they come and go or stand and gossip in the shop. She was describing life at the end of the last century, but it could have been any point during the preceding hundred years, so little of the essentials had changed.

She also mentions a nearby village:

235

"It was what was called a model village, with three bedrooms in every house and a pump to supply water to each group of cottages. Only good people were allowed to live there, her father said. That was why so many were going to church. He seemed to speak seriously, but her mother clicked her tongue..."

Certainly romanticism, too great an emphasis on the prettiness of country life, its picturesqueness, bred its own reaction. When W.H. Hudson described his favourite village on the Salisbury Downs he emphasised its bleakness, its lack of creeper-hung cottages and its total absence of conventional attractions. He wrote this, in *A Shepherd's Life*, around 1910, and it demonstrates clearly how cloying some had begun to find these generally recognised standards of beauty and how devoid of the genuine interests and fascination of the countryside.

Now a more balanced attitude holds sway: the romanticism of *Cider With Rosie* can be taken as the opposite facet of the realities described in *Akenfield*; both are valid viewpoints, neither is quite the whole picture.

Rural life in fiction has usually been viewed in retrospect and thus invested with a golden haze; in fact it has been a standard practice to look nostalgically back at halcyon days when summers were longer, the countryside greener and life in general far closer to the ideal than in the present. To discover that Piers Plowman in the 1370s was recalling a better past[6] makes a perspective that can be followed without a break through the centuries until the novels that would have us believe that Edwardian summers were the last of the golden seasons.

In contrast with this idyllic pastoral vision, the city was treated on the principle that if the writer, and thus the reader, did not mention it, it might vanish from sight. The realities of city life were only described in the light of the evils — poverty and moral decline — which could, fairly enough, be attributed to urban existence in its worst aspects. Such reports as those offered by Dickens, Doré or Engels are merely the best known illustrations of the situation. It was always easier, however, to retreat into a glossed-over version of pastoral life, or even into fully fledged romantic utopianism. It was a rare moment then when Mrs Gaskell, in *North and South*, attempted to show realities of city and country, side by side. Disraeli had attempted the same, but *Sybil* achieves reality neither in the town nor in the country.

Typical Picturesque watercolour by Helen Allingham which conjures up the imaginary, or at least a heavily idealised, countryside which suburbia was attempting to recapture

Meanwhile, romantic utopianism had many subscribers. *News from Nowhere* was William Morris's version of the genre. In some senses its pictorial counterparts were the increasingly heavy-weight medieval offerings of his painter friends, and he showed in the novel a curious vision of a future England, whitewashed and permeated by a clinical medievalism denying modernity in any form. Rural and ancient charms placed against urban horror left little space for a middle path.

The two were placed directly side by side in Jules Verne's *The Begum's Fortune* of 1879.[7] Two cousins share a vast fortune and each decides to build a city with his wealth. One, the academic Dr Sarrasin, designs a modern city to be built in Oregon on land granted by the state. Verne did not embark on the description of his ideal city lightly; he was learned on the subject of town planning and had read a paper to a meeting on the subject of the "Ideal Township" in which he pointed to the advantages of well-lit wide streets and had expounded his ideas on colonisation.

He describes Franceville as being built with the most advanced principles of hygiene and construction in mind, with two-storeyed houses set in gardens. The community is run on the woolliest of lines: work and knowledge somehow render economics and government superfluous; it is enough for the purposes of the novel that the town be neat and clean, its people contented and wise. Its antithesis, the city of wickedness Stahlstadt, built by the other cousin, is a dingy pile of industrial monuments dedicated to the pursuit of wealth and governed despotically and inhumanely. The illustrations depict the two extremes clearly; they are oddly like Pugin's *Contrasts*, with the spires, pleasant prospects and cheery inhabitants of Franceville approximating the medieval city, while the brooding sequence of blackened buildings that is Stahlstadt could be Pugin's modern scene. The medieval has been overrun by the ugliness of industrial Britain.

Rural mythology was propagated as much by painters as by novelists. Uvedale Price, as has been seen, was moved by the milkmaids and urchins who populated Gainsborough's "fancy" pictures, while a bucolic peasantry, more typical of the Low Countries in the sixteenth century than England in the eighteenth, made their appearance and seemed accepted as in no way incongruous. Yet George Morland, a specialist in such scenes, could also remove himself totally from this fictional vision and paint with absolute clarity a group of workers in a stone quarry; he could pay lip-service to popular taste but retained his own clear view. Stubbs, too, applied a similarly analytic eye to the groups of country labourers he painted as they forked hay onto a cart or stacked the sheaves, as he did to his anatomical engravings of horses. We cannot see the warts in his view of the countryside, but the people are not unnaturally posed and simpering at us; yet such subjects were rare at this date.

It was the mid-Victorian narrative painters who began to emphasise credible people within credible scenes, and for them the village offered a perfect setting. Often this veracity was due to the fact that the painters actually lived in such small rural communities, for example the numerous artists already mentioned who lived around Cranbrook and Penshurst in Kent in the 1850s. No longer required to live close to the fringes of fashionable town society to obtain portrait commissions, they found their subject-matter around them, or even if the subjects were fictitious, then the models and background were real enough. Having then woven their neighbours, friends and countryside together in the form of a moral scene or vignette from a novel or poem, the results might be displayed upon the walls of the Royal Academy for the benefit of urban sophisticates. For those who could not stomach the historical idiocies of the costume dramas of the less proficient Victorian romantic painters, the homely little scenes of rustic life, at least superficially reflecting reality, were far more palatable.[8]

Every painting that showed the village forge and blacksmith, every book illustration that represented country folk loitering around their cottages, every photograph that portrayed an awkward besmocked labourer posing with embarrassed stiffness, reinforced Gilpin's view that "in the moral view the industrious mechanic is a more pleasing object than the loitering peasant. But in a picturesque light it is otherwise."

Photographers had immediately seized on the potential of recording country life in a quasi-documentary, quasi-sentimental way. Villages were recorded less for antiquarian interest than for associative qualities, and their inhabitants were treated in much the same way. P.H. Emerson photographed a country life that was marginally more literal than that painted in watercolours by Helen Allingham, where the banks of hollyhocks and the cottages tumbling under the weight of rambler roses threaten to suffocate the inhabitants. When a set of lithographs of Bedford Park was produced, it was depicted in exactly this light, emphasising the rural village qualities and virtually disguising its function as a commuter garden suburb.

The imagery of the thatched cottage, smiling rosy-cheeked residents and rioting garden was turning into a potent abstraction,

Queen Anne Gardens, Bedford Park by H.M. Paget; lithographs of the Suburb strove to emphasise its rural imagery

with its own mythology and an independent existence outside reality. Just as the *cottage orné* was a flimsy version of a cottage, so the picturesque village was a lightweight version of its traditional parent, and soon its people became equally insubstantial.

This imagery is still serving its purpose. To advertise the purity of brown bread or the natural origins of some pre-packaged frozen food, this insubstantial picture can prove extraordinarily potent. A ragged boy clambering up the cobbles at Clovelly bears a wholemeal loaf, the services of the bank are sold via the charms of a small country village where everyone is known to everyone else, even their bank manager; the advertising men have taken their cue from minor Victorian watercolourists and novelists and are feeding us the same diet.

Gradually we are introduced to a subtle distortion of reality. Hurtling cars, plastic carriage lamps and concrete lamp standards are focused out, and in their stead comes the church spire, the village green, the winding stream and the clustered cottages — no different from the Picturesque theorists' creation from almost two centuries earlier, but now we are attempting to preserve the picture, not to create it.

"A Garden End" by P.H. Emerson: country life without trimmings

Notes

1. Raymond Williams, *The Country and the City*, London, 1973, discusses the whole subject in depth.
2. Mavis Batey, "Nuneham Courtenay", reprinted from *Oxoniensia*, 33, 1968.
3. From the 1899 Macmillan edition.
4. E. Nesbit's *Harding's Luck* (1909), written for older children, uses the image of the Picturesque village — Lord Arden says, "I wish all

the cottages about here were like Beale's. It didn't cost so very much. If I could only buy back the rest of the land, I'd show some people what a model village is like." The children search for the lost treasure so that "the old cottages [could be] made pretty and good to live in".

5. Raymond Unwin, *Cottage Plans and Common Sense*, Buxton, 1902.
6. Raymond Williams, *op. cit.*
7. J. Chesneaux, *Practical and Social Ideas of Jules Verne*, London, 1972.
8. See discussion of obsession with detail and petty incident in Peter Conrad, *The Victorian Treasure-House*, London, 1973.

Chapter 14

The Private Sector
in a Public Age

The twentieth-century Picturesque village is not the anachronism it might at first seem. In fact it is the logical response to, and expression of, certain needs; the wish for an environment which represents historical continuity, visual significance and emotional appeal. These all constitute much underestimated desires.

The Picturesque village hinges on the core of a traditional village, emphasising all the necessary ingredients and paying respect to vernacular example. Uvedale Price had been acutely aware of this when he attacked the regimented lines of cottages at Nuneham Courtenay and Milton Abbas. From his point of view they might equally have been the rigid lines of Victorian working-class housing, the mean speculative suburban development of a later date or unimaginative council housing; all the categories of housing that offend us. Each type had effectively ignored the lessons learned over a long period, although careful siting of the housing, provision of gardens and the planting of trees in the streets, or intelligent use of building materials, would all have redeemed them from disaster.

Yet, in spite of the shift of emphasis from private to public areas of responsibility in housing which marked the early twentieth century, some villages were still being built privately. Here sufficient time and resources allowed for individual, non-doctrinaire responses to conditions; sometimes novel results were produced.

The Picturesque, in theory, lends itself to original, even bizarre, solutions. The combination of this flexibility of style with the esoteric produced two very distinct resort villages in the early years of this century. They were Thorpeness, on the Suffolk coast, a novel type of estate village, and Portmeirion in Wales

Portmeirion, a view of Clough Ellis' village, he being both patron and architect

which was a rare example of professional architect and client meeting in the same man, Clough Williams-Ellis.

The process by which the two villages came about, and the form they took, are very different, but a link lies in an architecture owing little to precedent beyond a licence to amuse. The variety and novelty which marks both is just that introduced earlier by men such as Boscawen or Ingilby, the result of marked independence of mind.

Clough Williams-Ellis, already an experienced cottage builder in more conventional circumstances,[1] followed this lead and gave to his creation an élitist wit well fitted to the situation. When Mr Milestone, the landscape gardener in Thomas Love Peacock's *Headlong Hall*, and his client, the bemused Squire, stood on a crag high above Tremadoc, it could almost have been Williams-Ellis' cliffside.

Portmeirion enjoys the perfect Picturesque setting.[2] It is seen over a vista of water, built up a steep hillside like an Italian fishing village (the similarity is intentional), with the bright colours of its miscellaneous architectural objects, relics and inventions evoking different countries and periods in the best Picturesque associative manner. The village is a folly, yet more practical: derivative, yet quite original. The colourwashed walls, turrets and domes reflected over the bay, in spite of reality (rain, grey skies, cracking plaster work and leaking pipes), manage to make the village a masterpiece of potent escapism. Portmeirion rekindled the flames of architectural eccentricity.[3]

Thorpeness, remote on the East Anglian coast, was less an exercise in self-indulgence than a fairy-tale paradise, principally for the children of wealthy parents. The village was described in an early brochure as "the Home of Peter Pan", and all the islands on the mere were named after characters from J.M. Barrie.

In 1910 work was begun on the Suffolk estate of the Stuart Ogilvies to build a holiday village around the central feature of a shallow lake or mere, only recently dredged. The architects were an obscure pair: Forbes Glennie undertook the greater part of the work, W.G. Wilson designed several of the later buildings, the church, almshouses and a club-house. On a desolate, flood-prone area of coast rose an extraordinarily varied group of housing, centred around the Kursaal, or Country Club.

Thorpeness was to be a village which gave "a well balanced picture with no back view".[4] Ironically, as the scheme was never carried out in full, the village has the air of a film set with elaborate fronts and nothing behind — more back view than front view in fact. Building, and the essential protective planting, went on from 1911 to 1914 and then continued, with interruptions, into the 1930s. The village is a curious amalgam of restrained weatherboarded and half-timbered housing laced with oddities. The two water towers, which provided essential fresh water for the houses, were masked, one by a great Norman keep, the other by a wooden cottage. The latter, known as the House in the Clouds, consisted of a superstructure (the tank) resembling a habitable cottage with the lower part (the metal structure supporting it) also having windows. In fact the lower part *was* a cottage, the upper part not. Like Portmeirion, it was part fake, part genuine, with the edges blurred. The idea for this form of disguise at Thorpeness came, appropriately, from a children's book authoress, Mrs Mason, who then became the first resident of the cottage.

The visual pranks continued with such buildings as the golf clubhouse, its four corner towers topped by, incredibly, vast golf tees, and the Swiss chalet decorated with a frieze of painted red and yellow tulips. While Clough Williams-Ellis scoured the countryside for shell-covered grottoes, the architects of Thorpeness reconstructed a windmill, built a new Country Club in an expert half-timbered style and built a passable neo-Norman church.

The resort, although in fact a private estate village, was run on the principle that the housing should be available only for seasonal letting, not for sale, in the hopes that families which had enjoyed the place one year would return each succeeding year; which, in many cases, they did. This meant that the village had an existence for less than half the year, the rest of the time it remained a ghost town with a scattering of estate workers to tend it. Remarkably, the venture was not designed to bring in great profits and was expected to do little more than cover its running costs.

Luxuriating "in the champagne atmosphere and exhilarating seaviews of the East Coast" accorded more with a life of ease before the First World War, yet the village has continued to flourish and still retains its sense of exclusivity and quirkish atmosphere.[5]*

Late Victorian and Edwardian estate villages were also potentially more original and various than ever before. While the last

*After various vicissitudes, the village and its amenities are reported to be in good shape (2007).

The school at Cornwell by Clough Williams-Ellis, built during the late 1930s

of the great country houses grew ever more extravagant, so too did their corollaries, the villages. Anything different was acceptable, and when W.H. Lever directed his architects to build him a country estate village, Thornton Hough, he was not asking for a line of John Birch's award-winning boxes. The village is interest-

Building in progress on a water tower at Thorpeness during the mid 1920s, with the object of turning it into the House in the Clouds...

ing as the rural counterpart to Port Sunlight; with its pleasant setting, the lack of formalism and the existence of some earlier buildings, the outcome is much happier.[6]

Joseph Hirst, a textile manufacturer, had already started work on an estate village there in the 1860s and 1870s and constructed a church with a fine spire and five clock faces (the fifth, such is the prerogative of the patron, enabling him to see the hour from his house), as well as a considerable amount of housing, including a row of cottages with a turreted shop on the corner. Lever's own plans originally centred on the restoration of some older cottages but, when this proved impracticable, he rebuilt the village. He had bought Thornton Manor for himself and encouraged his brother to buy Thornton House (which had been Hirst's home), while their father moved into Hesketh Grange, also in the village. With this family battery in residence, Lever could reasonably claim the place for his own, and he set about substantiating the fact.

He employed several of the architects from Port Sunlight, starting the rebuilding with the housing and then adding a club, primary school and a Norman church, the latter to complement the existing Gothic structure built by Hirst. The cottages compete with Port Sunlight in the range of their eclecticism; in the space of a single terrace styles and materials which include Dutch, Tudor, brick, plaster and half-timber fight to assert themselves on the various façades. Single-storeyed housing was provided, as well as larger two-storeyed housing grouped on three sides around a grass court. The village as a whole is set off by a

...the finished product

vast recreation ground cum village green, with a pavilion, beyond which stretches the open country.

Thornton Hough is the traditional country village, even down to its half-timbered smithy and chestnut tree, though it is entirely a creation of the late nineteenth century. Port Sunlight, by comparison, has a dour formalism, partly because of its grandiose plan, and its efforts at lightheartedness, in the form of "olde worlde-ness", seem to weigh it down. This type of evocative architecture is suited to randomness, and Lever at Thornton Hough had to tack his additions on to an existing plan and use the original house sites. With its view of the fields beyond, the village is at the furthest extreme from the claustrophobic exclusivity of Port Sunlight, which merely endorses the heavy paternalism of its foundation.

The Picturesque village continues to crop up repeatedly in the twentieth century. In 1900, 1917 and again in 1938 villages were built with far more reference to the words and ideas of Uvedale Price or Loudon than to any contemporary pundit.

Proving that the advent of a new century did not cow him into blind obedience to other men's rules, an architect called William Huckvale (whose other work was almost exclusively for the Rothschilds on their estates in Buckinghamshire and Hertfordshire) constructed a village for Charles de Rothschild at Ashton, near Oundle, in the purest Picturesque idiom.

Though the cottages are dateless in external details, the villagers benefited from the best in modern advances. The stone cottages, with deep-thatched roofs, clustering round the village green, were provided with modern bathrooms, and all the wiring was laid underground, thus eliminating one modern intrusion. A chapel and inn were also built to cement the new community together.

The village had come into being as a result of one of those whims that few but a Rothschild could afford to indulge. The area was the natural habitat of a particularly rare butterfly, the Chequered Skipper, and Rothschild, who was an entymologist of great note, bought the entire locality and presented the village to his bride as a wedding present. He extended the vernacular of the village to the boathouse, dovecotes and model farm which surrounded his new mansion, Ashton Wold.

In the period immediately after the First World War, two villages were built which established a continuity with villages such

Village Club at Thornton Hough, built for Lever

as Ashton and its earlier counterparts. One was in Dorset, where Sir Ernest Debenham (owner of the vast London department store) commissioned Halsey Ricardo and McDonald Gill to build a village at Briantspuddle and housing in the neighbouring Bladen Valley. The scheme centred on a model farm, which had been built to encourage rural repopulation at a time when much attention was being paid to the smallholding movement and the provision of economical housing. (The Ministry of Agriculture had built a number of cottages at Amesbury, in 1918–19, in order to experiment with different materials, but found that nothing could beat brick.)

The cottages at Briantspuddle were built in a full-blown Picturesque style, thatched and whitewashed, and grouped around a vast war memorial. A similar, and contemporary, village was built in Hertfordshire, at Ardeley, by the architect F.C. Eden, with cottages clustered around a village green and its spreading oak tree. Here no details were skimped to produce a satisfactory link with the traditional villages of the area, for Hertfordshire was falling victim to the grasping fingers of London and needed to reassert its regional identity before it was too late.

Ashton: Picturesque of 1900

Yet despite these schemes, and the cottages built to high standards by such architects as Lutyens,[7] the neo-Georgian was making inroads. At Dartington, new housing was constructed in traditional style and given an uncomfortable bedfellow — the International Modern style. This housing, with stark concrete walls and flat roofs, and a profusion of glass and metal, provided an odd contrast.

Turn-of-the-century developments did not, however, veer solely in the direction of starched neo-Georgian or thatched fantasy. The lessons of the Arts and Crafts movement led to such villages as Guy Dawber's at Sandon, in Staffordshire, where he was also asked to design a gymnasium, an innovation which was merely a further extension of the healthy gardening obsession. Much more hard to define was the scheme built by Charles Harrison Townsend at Blackheath (near Guildford). The architect (who also designed the Whitechapel Art Gallery) built a chapel, which with its great flattened entrance arch and steeply pitched roof emphasised structural essentials in a manner rarely attempted before. Beside this he also built a half-timbered village hall and a variety of cottages in much more conventional vernacular style.[8] In catering for a section of middle-class society who were moving into the "second home" bracket, he presumably decided to play safe. Yet in Surrey, home of the inglenook, even the isolated chapel is an extraordinary breath of fresh air, bringing to the Home Counties promise of work being carried out abroad.

As has already been noted, an area in which the village image was cultivated for its particular associations was the Cottage Homes movement which gathered strength in the Edwardian period. It received particular impetus from the foundation in 1907 of an entire village planned on these lines, Whiteley Village.[9]

The Mill Hill enclave of the Linen and Woollen Drapers' Homes founded by James Marshall, another store magnate with philanthropic leanings beyond the usual, was a series of one- and two-storeyed cottages, some in red brick, some half-timbered, ranged around a garden and a central institution; the club-house and offices were all under one roof. Taking this pattern as his model, and enlarging it, Frank Atkinson drew up the winning design for the competition for Whiteley Village. The foundation was made possible by a vast legacy left by William Whiteley, the "Universal Provider", founder of the Bayswater store, and which was freed by his premature death. (He was murdered by a man claiming to be his illegitimate son.)

The almshouse provided in its traditional form something approaching a microcosm of the village and its life, and thus its form was suitable for adaptation to a variety of different uses. The quadrangle of terraced housing, which, from medieval time onwards, had been the plan for such communities, influenced planning widely. The Cottage Homes were merely an extension of the same idea, with the accommodation provided by the employer or philanthropist rather than the parish or local landowner. The cottage form served to break down the connotations of institutional life, while single-storeyed housing was obviously practical for those immobilised by age or illness.

Whiteley's trustees bought nearly 300 acres of land in a carefully chosen part of Surrey, where the sandy soil and pine trees were felt to ensure a healthy environment. They appointed a consultant architect, Walter Cave, and set up a competition for its design. Atkinson, who also built Selfridges, laid out a central circular area which was to be left in its natural state with rhododendrons and wild flowers. This was enclosed by a road

Ardeley: Picturesque of 1917 with the village green seen through the lych-gate

flanked by curving blocks of cottages, mostly single-storey, and around this was a road which formed an octagon, with radiating access roads. The housing was carried out by seven architects who each took a portion of the octagon and working independently, produced subtly different cottages. They were restricted only by the fact that all had to use the same material, red brick. Housing was provided for 350 pensioners, though 800 had been the original aim. They were given living rooms with a sleeping lobby, the standard almshouse accommodation. Large porches were provided, and a village store with special heating, library, chapel, public hall and communal kitchens and restaurant were among the facilities.

As the leader of the group of architects who visited the village after its completion wistfully observed: "Those of us who for two years have been struggling with the cheeseparing details of modern housing schemes felt a real pleasure in seeing this example of 'pre-war' building, where genuine architectural materials have been properly used without any regard to expense." This was in 1921;[10] the first cottage had been ready for habitation in 1917. Despite these words, the original cottage, constructed as a

254

costing exercise, proved too expensive and could not be adopted as the representative standard.

Whiteley Village, the traditional almshouse taken into the twentieth century, provided a community where the elderly could escape the isolation of age by finding themselves in a situation where their needs were the sole consideration. Whiteley's statue, standing at the centre of the circus, commemorates the virtues of private enterprise and the inscription notes that his business career was prompted by a visit to the Great Exhibition of 1851.

The village continues successfully today. Each cottage is now modernised, and the estate is administered by a Trust which keeps the surrounding grounds immaculate, though each tenant is encouraged to cultivate a patch of individual garden if he or she wishes to. Tenants qualify if they are retired members of either the commercial or agricultural professions, and pay a minimal rent. The community centres on the clubhouse and its activities, and on the village shop, which faces the club across the centre of the village. Wooded grounds insulate the area from the surrounding exclusive closes and avenues, and make it visually entirely self-contained.

General view at Whiteley

The social centre of Whiteley, where the shop and social club form the centre of the village plan. Above and below

The human scale of the buildings emphasises the individual's place in the life of the community, while the overall planning reinforces the visual unity of the village. It is an extremely attractive example of architectural form and function happily integrated.

The Cottage Homes movement continued with the Haig Memorial Homes and the building of the British Legion Village, near Maidstone, where much of the accommodation consists of simple bungalows with verandahs and sizeable gardens, very like the Chartist cottages of the late 1840s. The post First World War "Homes for Heroes" movement[11] had attempted to whip up energy and resources to tackle the vast backlog of housing; the problem was to translate the enormous pre-war private enterprise effort, represented by the co-partnership schemes, into the general area of local authority and government housing. In some cases people continued to help themselves through housing trusts; one example was the Quaker garden village at Jordans.

Mass housing for the next twenty years was essentially the province of the speculators and private developers, who were rarely directed by any other motive than the financial potential of land.

Munitions estates showed that work could be carried out to remarkably high standards even under the most austere conditions and with the greatest urgency. At Gretna, Raymond Unwin was in charge, and another notable effort was that at Eltham, the Well Hall Estate, a scheme carried out in ten and a half months. The tenants were, and are, reminded of its origins by the naming of streets, for example, Shrapnel Road.

However, only war and its aftermath provided the impetus necessary to achieve results of this sort. The Tudor-Walters and Addison Reports gave official guidelines which were to influence local authority schemes, and Unwin's hand (he was the author of the Tudor-Walters Report) is frequently visible. Yet an accepted architecture based on confined spaces, finicky neo-Georgian at its worst, began to win the day, vying with an alternative, the "picturesque" neo-Tudor speculative villa, where misapplied and debased architectural details were tacked on to a standardised shell.

The chance for rebuilding that peacetime always brings, as much after the Napoleonic Wars or the Second World War as then, should have made way for the best of pre-war standards; either the generous spaces and simple design, both interior and exterior, of New Earswick, or, more traditionally, the Picturesque vernacular. Yet the open rooms and fitted furniture of the earlier cottages were diluted and split up into mean little

Plan showing the octagonal layout at Whiteley Village

compartments of Victorian dimensions.

On the other hand, the actual image of village life was being given a determined boost. Cottage Exhibitions and the small-holdings movement, together with publications on cheap country cottages, village halls and the other components of village life, all attest to the interest being paid to the rural community.[12] The village hall, by now recognised as the centre

Street view at Silver End

of the place, became as important a social expression as the church had been in Victorian times and illustrated the new self-determination of villagers even in the most "closed" of communities.

Although the increased provision of alternative housing made industrial housing less essential, some firms in the inter-war years took it upon themselves, for various reasons, to provide their own factory villages, though by now they were far from being cast in the mould of Port Sunlight under the omnipresent eye of its paternalistic founder.

At Stewartby, in Bedfordshire, the London Brick Company set up a new (brick) village for their workers, while at Kemsley, in Kent, Bowaters the paper manufacturers used the great acres of marsh around their mills to construct a village for their employees — conveniently situated only half a mile from their place of employment. Kemsley is built in a rather timid brick neo-Georgian style, despite the fact that Maxwell Fry, soon to be a leading figure in bringing the International Modern style to

Great Britain, was one of the partnership responsible, albeit early in his career.

Even in the twentieth century it was certainly expedient to be able to offer decent housing, close to the factory; the firms could thus ensure having a reliable workforce and, if properly administered, a village could promote goodwill between workers and their employers. F.H. Crittall was fully aware of the pitfalls of paternalism when he decided to build Silver End in Essex for the workers in his company.[13]

Crittalls had a direct connection with housing, since they produced the metal window frames with which most new houses of the period were being built. In the 1920s the firm was undergoing considerable expansion and in the necessity for expanding his works, Crittall saw the advantages of the situation. He saw a new community as a fresh start and the perfect way in which to express his ideals in practical form. A firm believer in land nationalisation, he also claimed to nurse a secret ambition to be a builder.

> "I saw a pleasant village of a new order... enjoying the amenities of a town life in a lovely rural setting rather than content ourselves with a few streets tacked upon a country town, perpetuating its errors and extending its shortcomings, should we not instead pioneer in pastures new and fashion for ourselves a completely new community?"

In the rare position of having land and the need to rehouse so many workers, Crittall commissioned various architects to work on the scheme for a brand-new company village. Building began in the late twenties. Crittall had already been sufficiently conscientious to provide a surgery and dental clinic for his workmen, and was a twentieth-century representative of that long line of Nonconformist enlightened employers which stretched back throughout the nineteenth century and beyond.

A company was set up in order that the employees could administer the village themselves, and the houses were planned with the best of facilities, including gardens and allotments. In the early stages of the operation they were being built at the rate of 100 a year, in various sizes and styles. Simplicity, light and space were Crittall's requirements, and before long the village, consisting mostly of flat-roofed International Modern housing, rose incongruously from the fields of Essex. Other housing was of

Picturesque c. 1938 at Freefolk

a plain neo-Georgian type, built of pale pinkish-grey brick, while the church, a barn converted by the editor of *Studio* magazine, struck an odd note, glorying in a thatched roof. There was also a village hall, hotel, bank, telephone exchange, shopping arcade, school and playing fields and a central public garden. The wide streets were planted with silver birch and poplars. Silver End did not take very long to achieve its aims, and the picture of self-sufficiency was emphasised by farms which produced fresh food, cutting out the middleman, and selling direct to the villagers. Like almost every model village builder, its founder claimed for it the highest birth rate and lowest death rate in the country, but whether or not that is proven, Silver End is a notable monument to well-employed capital and social vision.

Almost contemporary with this enterprise, Bata, the giant Czech shoe manufacturing concern, decided to build one of its company villages in England, at East Tilbury, on the Thames estuary in Essex. The design here was based on a prototype worked out all over the world, including seven towns built in Czechoslovakia and others in Europe, Canada and India. The company, founded by Thomas Bata in 1900 with ten employees, claimed to have a workforce of 27,000 by 1938. East Tilbury, though on a small scale, followed the pattern of the other settlements with its central hotel, the division of factory and housing by a green belt — here Lombardy poplars — and the use of advanced building techniques for its cottages in the International Modern style. The factory was built by revolutionary all-welded lightweight construction methods and attracted considerable notice for this feature. As at Silver End, all types of facilities were provided to knit the village, ready-made as it was, into a community, but of the two, Silver End was less overwhelmed by the presence of its *raison d'être*, the works.

On a wider front, for a brief period in the thirties the flat-roofed International Modern cottage was taken up by speculative builders as a cheap alternative to Tudoresque standard patterns, and in the "Village of Tomorrow" section at the Ideal Home Exhibition in 1934 it was allowed to flower briefly. The sales line made great play of the possibilities of the flat roof, where the surburban family was encouraged to take up an open-air existence, with summer evenings spent eating and sleeping among the chimney stacks.

In spite of this brief excursion into foreign fields, more familiar prototypes continued to appeal, and Freefolk in Hampshire, the estate village built for a wartime Minister of Works, Lord Portal, gives ample evidence of the continuing superior appeal of the Picturesque village over all alternatives.

The cottages, in a long curving terrace consisting of eighteen separate homes, employ the full complement of Picturesque tricks. They are reminiscent of the local vernacular, heavily thatched with some half-timbering; windows are mullioned and there are heavy, if not ornate, chimneys. Behind them rise the spire of the village church and a hillside thickly covered by woods, while in front of the cottages are a number of thatched wells and, finally, a thatched bus shelter.

Freefolk provoked a letter to a country magazine: "I should like to see a pretty photo of the village church of Freefolk. It is my dream village." Lord Portal himself had commented on his work in the village: "There is something very satisfying about seeing where you would like people to live and how you would like people to live."

Freefolk obviously satisfied the public and its builder alike and had little to do with changing fashion or contemporary pressures; it states, once again, the case for adapting the traditional form of the village to modern needs, which does not automatically give *carte blanche* to the worst excesses of "neo" and "pseudo" visions of the past.

In principle the area of public responsibility in the twentieth century was widening, to invalidate the efforts of individual companies or landlords. The examples quoted here are in many senses peripheral to the course of domestic building, isolated efforts with little connection with mass housing. Yet there were no signs that adequate housing was being provided by the public authorities to render such efforts superfluous. Political promises were still not matching performance, with the result that the great provider was still the developer-speculator, particularly in the 1930s when government housing programmes again fell below target.

Notes

1. Clough Williams-Ellis carried out cottage schemes at, for example, Cornwell, Oxfordshire, and Cushendun, County Antrim. There was also a proposal to build a model village for Daisy, Countess of Warwick, in the park at Easton Lodge. See *Architect Errant*, 1971.
2. Clough Williams-Ellis, *Portmeirion*, revised edition.
3. Baillie Scott drew up a scheme for a resort village at Pagham, Sussex, which he modelled closely on the image of the heaped rooftops of Portmeirion. It was never built. See the illustration in J.D. Kornwolf, *Baillie Scott*, Baltimore, 1972.
4. Various guides to Thorpeness were published, the first *c.* 1915.
5. Not for long. The estate is being broken up to pay death duties.
6. For a full architectural account see E. Hubbard and N. Pevsner, *Cheshire*, Buildings of England series, 1971.
7. Lutyens's cottage groups of importance were at Ashby St Ledgers, Upper Slaughter, Gloucestershire, Milton Abbott, on the Bedford estates in Devon, and plans for a scheme at Gidea Park (1909) and a resort at Rossall Beach, Blackpool (1901), of which only one house was built.
8. Horace Harrison Townsend, Studio, 1896. An article on artistic treatment of cottages, especially those built at Chilworth by Charles H. Townsend.
9. *The Architectural Review*, Vol. 56, 1924.
10. *Journal of the Royal Institute of British Architects*, 30 July 1921.
11. T.H. Mawson, *An Imperial Obligation Industrial Villages for Partially Disabled Soldiers and Sailors* (with introduction by Field-

Marshal Haig), 1917. The frontispiece shows a man on crutches against a scenic backdrop of village and church spire.

12. Clough Williams-Ellis was Superintending Architect at the Ministry of Agriculture in the period after the First World War.

13. F.H. Crittall, *Fifty Years of Work and Play*, 1934.

Chapter 15

No New Villages?

Villages today fall into various categories,[1] the carefully pre-served Conservation Area, the scattered village now probably pockmarked by "infilling", or its old centre bordered by a con-glomeration of estates, and the "urban village". The latter can be either part of a large city or a consciously created area within a new town. The obvious omission from this list is the newly built village.

Few have been planned since the Second World War, even fewer built. Everything seems to conspire against the foundation of new small-scale communities — or even against the satisfac-tory extension of old villages. Planning regulations and finance are the two biggest obstacles, despite the social advantages of a small, traditionally based community.

It is odd that in a period when a positive attitude to the countryside is general, bringing with it a genuine interest in the advantages and values of rural life and its traditions, so little is being done in practical terms to assist its furtherance. Worse, active deterrents are numerous and there are no adequate safe-guards, even at the stage when a project has been initiated, to ensure it being carried through. It is a common situation that plans are set in motion and then from economic or other factors collapse, either half executed or never begun.

Just after the war when Thomas Sharp put forward his plans for forestry villages, one might have imagined that time had stood still since the munitions village planned by Unwin at Gretna had heralded an important advance in quickly con-structed, adequate housing almost thirty years before.

Sharp had taken over from Guy Dawber the job of planning a considerable number of villages for the Forestry Commission, although of those designed, only three were built and in a very

265

reduced form at that.² Sharp, who was a leading planner and was knowledgeable on traditional village form, saw these as "enclosed" villages with tightly interconnecting terraces of housing. In the event, the stark rows of whitewashed cottages, providing a foil to the dark green of the newly planted evergreen forestry, were only rescued from a disastrously bleak appearance by the natural beauty of the countryside which even the military lines of conifers could not diminish. Each village had been planned to contain shops, but these were never built, so that occupants now depend on a travelling grocery van and children being educated at secondary level are forced to live in hostels far from home. On the positive side, community centres have been established in each village and primary schools in two of the three.

These villages, Kielder, Byrness and Stonehaven, isolated on the remote borders of Scotland and England, illustrate effectively the shortfall between the ideals of the most enlightened planners and the numerous intervening factors which can so easily invalidate the best of schemes. The details, such as the choice of whitewash to improve the aesthetics of the place, seem wasted effort set against the social realities. These are the sort of major problems threatening every village community in the country to a greater or lesser extent, and remain extraordinarily underestimated factors. As public transport, perversely, becomes less and less dependable, and employment opportunities become more and more centralised and distant, villages are rapidly becoming ghettoes of the elderly, the housebound and the wealthy and this not merely in the remoter corners of the country*.³

The catalogue of village schemes begun in the post-war years is very short, and of those that reached any state of completion, it is shorter still. Even when built, they cease to represent very closely the original intentions.

No better example is offered than that of New Ash Green, a private-enterprise model village in Kent dreamed up by Span (an unusually enlightened development company) and its architect-in-chief Eric Lyons. Bearing in mind experience gained from housing estates it had built earlier in South London, in 1965 Span put forward a scheme which it was hoped would provide a communal environment in the most positive sense. The

Since the first edition of this book, access to the internet and teleworking have helped reverse the situation

266

architecture was high quality, using good materials and carefully integrating housing and services, but most important was the attention paid to achieving a social mix and retaining a relatively stable population. In the London estates the housing was standardised, and people moved as their families expanded and outgrew their homes. New Ash Green was planned to overcome this by providing a variety of housing types, and the social mix was to be obtained by the understanding that the Greater London Council would be prepared to take one quarter of the total housing for its tenants. On the failure of the GLC to take up this option, one of the initial hopes of the scheme foundered and Span was forced to hand the development over to another firm, at which point the modifications began.

Span had fostered community spirit by making residents' groups responsible for the communal open spaces, and this sort of initiative seemed to have borne fruit when, in a survey carried out in 1969[4] on the 220 families then in residence, 81% were found to belong to one or other of the fifteen voluntary organisations that had been set up in the village. However, the residents were, inevitably, mostly middle-class and recently married — just the milieu for such societies.

The term used to describe New Ash Green was "urban village" — urban in the sense of a tightly-knit group and village in the communitarian sense. New Ash Green has only a primary school, no hospital, and because of planning restrictions, no industry; this presented less of a problem than might have been the case because of its proximity to urban areas, not least London.

From the same 1969 survey came the facts that the recreational and cultural facilities (even a theatre had been mooted) did not seem to have sufficient draw to solve the problem of a shifting population. Nearly half the residents thought that they would have moved within the next five years, the reasons they gave being career changes, family expansion, and, above all, the wish for greater privacy. This type of enclosed community benefits the mother with young children, the children themselves and the elderly, but suits less well the middle-aged generation or the teenager both of whom want more independence from others and a greater seclusion from the communal eye.

However, even the establishment of New Ash Green happened against the rule-book. It was supposedly the intervention, at ministerial level, of Richard Crossman that pushed the scheme through against planning objections on the grounds of the over-density of the South East. When the Greater London Council opted out in 1969 the Building Societies lost confidence in the project, and it was this factor that jeopardised the contribution of Span and caused it to sell out to Bovis.

As it now stands, the village centre has in its favour the intricately arranged spaces, excellent planting with imaginatively chosen shrubs and groundcover (for example, a bright yellow-green foliage is used as a foil for the dark-grey slated walls), and high-quality building materials. Against that are the lack of space and impossibility of privacy. The village has been enveloped by a spread of housing which takes the lowest common denominator of the original plans, in order to keep costs down, and is much diminished visually as a result.

The tale of New Ash Green was echoed, almost stage by stage, at Bar Hill Village, near Cambridge. It was originally to be one of a chain of "necklace" villages which would be built to ease the pressure of expansion in and immediately around the city of Cambridge. It was heralded in ecstatic, if none too accurate, terms as the first new village of the century, and the architect was quoted as regarding it as "more of a social than an architectural trial". The project for Bar Hill began in 1965, schemes for the other villages never getting under way.

The original plan was for a village of four thousand inhabitants, with their own shopping centre, social centre, primary school and light industrial estate — all to be planned on the Radburn system with pedestrian and traffic routes totally segregated.[5]

With the aim of securing a good social cross-section, the same idea as cherished by Span, 10% of the housing was sold to the Rural District Council, and administration was put into the hands of a Village Trust.

Nothing more serious ruffled the calm and optimism of the early stages than a slight altercation over the problem of whether to allow garden sheds, but after 100 houses (less than 10% of the total) had been built, the developers, Cubitts, sold the village and then followed the familiar tale of lower standards in the name of economy, loss of confidence and the disappearance of original ideas along the line. One problem here was that the housing existed in complete isolation in the absence of its projected centre, and it was only the building of a large hotel with some facilities that rescued the situation and prevented Bar Hill from becoming merely an unhappy housing estate in a particularly bleak area of East Anglia. The village people themselves had to raise funds for a hall for group activities, the ecumenical church being the only other centre provided.

Just as at New Ash Green, many early hopes were dashed by the eventual problems, principally financial, which changed policy and caused a reversal of direction. Neither was the social mixture so easily obtained — most residents were professional people connected with the University, though *The Times* managed to find what it quaintly termed "artisans" living there.

In the same area, on the fringes of Newmarket, is Studlands Village, a more successful attempt at a developers' village, designed by Ralph Erskine for Bovis. Prices have been kept very low and the one- and two-storeyed houses are plain in the extreme, with careful planning of space dividing the land into private gardens, semi-public play areas and a great central common green. Erskine's other "villages", Eaglestone (Milton Keynes) and the low-rise housing around the Byker Wall in Newcastle are sensitive to village qualities as is the local authority housing at Pershore by Darbourne and Darke where a Picturesque variety has been achieved.

However, in general the record of private enterprise villages, projects imbued by more than a mere wish for a quick return at any price, has been a depressing one.[6] Exigencies such as the general economic situation, which affects equally the fluctuating finances of the companies concerned and the house-buying market, the degree of involvement local authorities are prepared to enter into and finally, planning hurdles, are all able to overturn the most soundly based schemes at the last moment. Governmental interest in the founding of small-scale communities is minimal, despite the views of one former Minister of Housing, Lord Greenwood — speaking in a private capacity — who felt that on sites where a visual focus already existed, for example a deserted medieval church, a new village around a green could be effectively created on traditional lines. In this form, he felt, village building was to be encouraged and had great potential.[7] In a rather random fashion, this is happening at Papworth St Agnes, near Cambridge. A vestigial village is being rebuilt around the derelict church.

In fact it is a reflection on the very great distance between the decision-making levels and the general public they serve that, despite the attractions and advantages of the village — the need for more than mere housing estates, for proper communities — no positive general policy exists in this area. Argument number one is the cost of providing services to a site, lighting, water, drainage and so on. Yet, had a scheme succeeded to make developers contribute £150 to the relevant authority towards the cost of each house for the provision of this infrastructure, the situation might have been greatly eased, for inevitably, these costs in an isolated area are far higher than in an urban area or one close to extant services.

One recent attempt at suggesting an alternative form for new village housing, at Dartington in Devon, has met with opposition from the County Council despite strong local support, including that of the South Hams District Council. The idea put forward by Tom Hancock, architect-planner, is for cluster housing linked to extant villages but avoiding sprawl. It is felt this could operate on a joint private enterprise, local authority basis making the best use of developments in self-build and cooperative experiments in community building. Twenty to thirty houses, designed for maximum flexibility, would be grouped in a close around a workshop and nursery, some of the closeknit qualities of the street or traditional village centre being recreated in this way. Between the devil of continuous sprawl and the deep blue sea of key villages voraciously taking up all new activity in a neighbourhood, this scheme, a reduced scale version of the neighbourhood units of the New and Expanded towns, could represent an alternative path.[8]

No-one wants to see the countryside littered with pseudo-antique revival villages, nor with middle-class ghettoes, yet there are visual safeguards against the one and social means to preclude the other. A country such as Denmark, with a limited area, sees the foundation of new villages as an important part of planning policy, yet in Britain only with the slowness of the dinosaur are any of the obstacles in planning regulations eased or set to one side, even to allow thinking along these lines. New towns, with neighbourhood units, attempt to approximate village communities, yet the results are widely differing and though ostensibly "model" villages they are hardly a parallel to the traditional village. A new willingness to let some of the more restrictive of the bylaws lapse, leaving decision-making in the hands of the individual borough engineer and the outcome to his flexibility or obtuseness as the case may be, is a chink of light. If rigid rules on road widths or turning spaces can be waived then progress is being made.

270

Meanwhile some faintly daft solutions to the problem of building new villages have been dreamt up; none more so than the horrifying vertical village proposed, hopefully in a brainstorm, for Buckinghamshire in 1961.[9] It was to have been self-contained, the shops, community centre, primary school, clinic and garages all slotted in below the residential floors. Close beside it would be the church, for some reason the only building of human proportions in the complex. The ground saved by the scheme would be used for recreation. Theories of Le Corbusier were taken to their furthest limits and hopelessly misapplied.

The National Trust recognised the potential for the foundation of a new village — or more accurately, an extension of a village. The Trust sponsored a competition in 1965 for a twenty-eight acre site at Broadclyst in Devon and received sixteen entries.[10] The National Trust has in its care numerous traditional villages, as well as Blaise Hamlet, the epitome of the model village, and that it should consider the modern development of a village as a worthwhile object on which to devote time and money is perhaps more telling than the disinterested attitude given out elsewhere at official levels. In the event, lack of finance, in the form of potential developers, meant that the scheme foundered and Broadclyst never became a stick to beat about the heads of the intractable as it might have done.*

The one real estate village, in the traditional sense, built in recent years was that constructed for Lord Rothschild at Rushbrook, Suffolk. Here the cottages, built in whitewashed brick and with grey-tiled roofs, were in keeping with regional styles, yet expressed them in a novel way. The housing is grouped between the grounds of the great mansion (now burnt) and the model farm, the source of most of the employment for the village population. Just as at Nuneham Courtenay 200 years before, the cottages present neat frontages to the road, behind their grass verges and railings, while behind them lies an area for bicycle sheds, washing lines and all the paraphernalia of daily life.

The architects, Llewelyn-Davies and Weeks, used another ploy, the visual emphasis of a traditional feature, in this case a brick well-head. The old church also stands a short distance away and there are a few cottages nearby, the skeleton of an earlier community long dispersed.[11]

Now the National Trust is, with a national house-builder, developing a retirement community on 16 acres of its land at Cliveden.

271

The fourteen new cottages are served by a community hall, decorated by the Rothschild crest. Little difference exists — except in the roof lines and the interiors — from the line of whitewashed, grey-tiled cottages that Sir Robert Walpole had built in Norfolk 230 years earlier.

Landowners have made other such attempts, but usually in the role of developer — rather as the eighteenth-century owner of a great estate might find himself an industrialist overnight. The value of land has given a new dimension to the possession of mere acreage. Sir Francis Dashwood, in the mid-sixties, planned a village of 600 houses on his estate in Buckinghamshire, with a large provision made for single-storeyed cottage units for old people, which were to be the chief innovation of the plan. Again a historical continuity was kept, for his ancestor of the same name had owned, and built much of, the village of West Wycombe. For the modern scheme, however, the same fate awaited it as in so many other cases; planning permission was withdrawn and what had promised to be an interesting scheme in several respects faded out.*

Apart from the actual village building schemes that have been discussed briefly above, the imagery of the village is potent, and the word is employed in a wide variety of senses. Just as estate agents and developers in the 1930s delighted in misapplying the term Garden Village to mean housing schemes, now the implications of the word "village" are used to the full in every conceivable form of advertising. In a city it is the nostalgic connotation of rural life and tight community which are played upon; for example, when the residents of Tolmers Square in North London set up a body to fight the plans of developers to demolish the area, it became overnight Tolmers Village, while a large club formed to help lonely young people was called London Village.

For architects and planners too the term has a pleasing ring. The Reilly plan,[12] published immediately after the Second World War, advocated a seemingly simple device for linking areas of a town — treating each as a village centre, based on a green with the communal facilities at hand. The social advantages of this were the real point behind the Reilly plan, the advantages of the "neighbourhood unit" its American equivalent — or in its contemporary usage in the linked villages of the recent new

*See page 9, notes 2 and 3, for some more recent examples

272

towns, Washington, Milton Keynes and less happily, Telford. Washington New Town, County Durham, is planned on the system of nineteen new village units, each made distinct by employing different architects for each, and serviced by a central town area supplying the major services and industries; not so far from Ebenezer Howard, or in fact, from Robert Owen. The managers and planners of the New Towns have taken the place of the landowner/patron but it can be argued that the populations shuffled to and fro, now in their thousands rather than in their tens, are often as unwilling as the displaced villagers of the eighteenth century. The GLC overspill schemes to New and Expanded Towns, where families uprooted from traditionally urban backgrounds find themselves lost on the fringes of small country market towns encountered considerable setbacks and are now largely in the past.

Milton Keynes illustrates an interesting conundrum. The villages which are to be overtaken in the general development have lost their original function as farming communities (as, in a less dramatic way, have almost all rural settlements) and an inevitable rude disruption has followed. Older and more attractive buildings immediately take on a higher value, islands within the sea of new and mass-produced housing, and thus these village centres will become desirable and expensive housing for the managerial and professional classes. Precisely the same about-turn will occur as has been the case in countless villages around the fringes of the largest cities, where a desperate attempt is made to preserve a superficial resemblance to the country communities they once were. Usually they become grotesque over-statements of rural life, laden with sadly ill-chosen impedimenta of the countryside.

There is little cause for optimism in the future of the village. Although new local authorities with recently appointed staff and a renewed sense of regional identity are in a better position now to implement schemes in their areas than before, there are still discrepancies in thinking at official level and an inflexibility that it will take more than new boundaries to break down. At best the village can be preserved or subtly altered, at worst it can be destroyed or turned into a meaningless suburban creation, somehow much nastier than the whole-hearted artificiality of William Webb's conscientious efforts at Woodcote.

When it comes to new foundations the problem is usually based on a conflict of interests. The architect may have in mind a re-creation of certain elements, both visual and social, retaining the continuity of tradition within the dictates of modern living, transport and so on, but he or she meets with the objections of the developer, whose interests lie on the side of financial return, or those of the planners and engineers, who have to enforce a set of rigid standards. Thus as amendment after amendment pours down upon a scheme the original concept becomes quite lost and the end result a mockery of the earlier intentions, while architects despairingly watch the watering down of their ideas.[13] Development control, zoning and highway regulations are all part of the arsenal of the planners and other officials yet the cumulative effect of all these safety nets often gives a Janus-like aspect to their behaviour. The Design Guide controversy demonstrates this, where the guides are seen by their supporters as loose directives encouraging the waiving of certain regulations and, by their detractors, as restrictive interference. But just as Conservation Areas in villages and towns are only as effective as the available legislation so the Design Guides (the first of which was for Essex) are, at best, pointers not dictatorial statements.

It is argued that with increased job mobility, a general change of outlook towards the amount of time people are prepared to spend in their home communities, and the role they are prepared to play within these communities, most villages can only, at best, function as dormitory or commuter villages, serving the larger centres.

Yet as mobility threatens to become less and the prospect of reduced living standards becomes a certainty, when the 2.5 car-owning family may well find itself a one car family, with no public transport to remedy the loss, then perhaps the village proper can be allowed, and encouraged, to function closer to its original pattern which may well include the reintroduction of light industry. In this case, should it not be possible to create new villages to ease the pressure on the old?

The visual imagery of the village is immensely powerful,[14] but so too are its social connotations. Village life is a counterbalance to the blanket of anonymity offered by city life. There is constant potential for neighbourly contact in a village and each person can contribute to his community, according to his wishes. If the physical framework of the village disintegrates, so too does the social framework and that must be nothing short of disastrous.

As an ideal aspired to over centuries, the village, traditional or model, cannot suddenly be consigned to limbo, regarded as an irrelevancy and an ineffective solution to the problems of modern life. While we troop in hordes to visit the traditional beauty offered by the famed villages of Britain, aspire to a country cottage as first, or even second, home, and fall easy victims to advertising which uses every associative trick to conjure up rural utopias, we need to give evidence of faith in the village living and renewing itself — not merely in the village as a museum piece.

Notes

1. See the C.P.R.E. leaflet *The Future of the Village*, 1974.
2. *Town Planning Review*, October 1955; *The Guardian*, 23 August 1966.
3. *The Sunday Times*, 23 June 1974.
4. *Official Architecture*, June 1971.
5. See the publicity handout, *Spotlight on Bar Hill*, 1974.
6. Studlands Park outside Newmarket, designed by Ralph Erskine, is an altogether happier result, low-priced and ingeniously planned.
7. *The Surveyor*, 9 February 1973.
8. For full discussion of the "cluster" village idea see *Architects Journal*, 18 August 1976.
9. *The Times*, 7 November 1961.
10. Various reports of competition results in the architectural press, week of 14–16 July 1965.
11. Very primitive cottages stood on the site of the present new village: rebuilding was delayed while leases expired. The cottages were to be for older estate workers, rent free. Little resentment of this modern benevolent paternalism seems to exist — residents had no complaints.
12. Lawrence Wolfe, *The Reilly Plan. A New Way of Life*, London, 1945.
13. In addition, local authority restrictions applying to the provision of open spaces or tree planting often render well-landscaped schemes sterile; village greens become narrow grass verges, trees inadequately maintained soon die.
14. A Weybridge building firm is building a period-style village called The Old Meuse (see *The Sunday Times*, 21 February 1975). Said the director, "We are trying to recreate the sort of village scene that you can find in a place like Broadway in Worcestershire... but... we will build out all the disadvantages of previous centuries."

Gazetteer

The purpose of this gazetteer is to provide a comprehensive guide to post-seventeenth-century planned villages in England and Wales. It excludes the majority of ports, resorts, transport foundations (canal airport and railway towns), garden villages and suburbs, New Town neighbourhoods. Keeping always the "vision" of the title in mind, the listed places are, in principle, the product of social or architectural imagination.

Those marked by asterisks are discussed, and sometimes illustrated, in the text. Brackets indicate that the settlement is a housing scheme, rather than village or hamlet, of particular importance.

The list depends on published sources which are not infallible or exhaustive; they are to be found in the general bibliography, but chief among them is the series now published by Yale University Press; *The Buildings of England*, *The Buildings of Scotland*, *The Buildings of Wales* and *The Buildings of Ireland*.

In the case of Scotland and Ireland I have depended to a greater extent on information given personally: I have not attempted to be comprehensive in either case, and have made an arbitrary selection of villages of particular interest.

I have generally used the counties and regions, as followed by the "Pevsners" cited above. These do not always conform to current administrative boundaries.

England

Bedfordshire

Husborne Crawley: *Bedford estate housing in groups, red brick. (As at *Lidlington, Ridgmont, Willington* (yellow brick), *Woburn,* mostly C18). Estate noted for excellent housing, became model for others.

(*Cardington:* estate cottages built by John Howard, prison reformer, 1763–64.)

Melchbourne: Lord St John remodelled Melchbourne Park in 1741; row of thatched C18 estate cottages on The Street leading to church, rebuilt 1779.

Old Warden: Robert Henley, Lord Ongley remodelled church interior *c.* 1841. Contemporary Picturesque model village, thatched and highly decorative.

(*Podington:* terraced estate cottages *c.* 1773–75, for the Orlebars of Hinwick House.)

Shortstown: early C20 garden village built for Short Brothers' workers at Cardington airfield.

(*Southill:* simple vernacular type estate cottages, thatched and rendered, for Whitbreads of Southill, house remodelled by Henry Holland from 1796.)

Stewartby: garden village for the London Brick Company workers, 1927 onwards. Village Hall (1928–30) and Club (1933–34) by E. Vincent Harris.

Berkshire

Ardington [now Oxon]: model village for the Wantage estate, 1860s, as also *East Locking*. Tiled, half-timbered cottages.

Bearwood see *Sindlesham Green.*

Bourton: mid C19 Neo-Tudor estate village, school (1842) church (1860).

Buscot: Ernest George (architect of Buscot Park, 1889 on) rebuilt centre of village for Henderson family (Lords Faringdon) 1890s, village hall, well and estate housing, all in stone.

(*Coleshill:* Radnor estate housing, *c.* 1870.)

Leverton: hamlet of thatched cottages, with porches, *c.* 1800 for Chilton Foliat estate (Chilton Lodge, 1880 by W. Leverton), more added in C19 in same style.

Sindlesham Green: model village at gates of Bearwood, built by Robert Kerr for John Walter (proprietor of *The Times*) from 1864 on. Red diapered brick estate housing, school and inn contemporary.

(*Steventon:* Neo-Tudor railway cottages, built *c.* 1840 for the Great Western railway. Used for Board meetings as mid-way point between London and Bristol.)

(*Stockcross:* early C20 estate housing and shop, thatch and half timber.)

Sulham: scattered Picturesque estate cottages built for Rev. John

Wilder (squire and rector for fifty-six years).
Windsor (Great Park): estate housing by S.S. Teulon and garden suburb style village built for royal estate workers by S. Tatchell, 1930s.

Buckinghamshire

Aston Clinton: Sir Anthony de Rothschild bought mansion 1851. Schools, 1856 (demolished) and 1862 (by Gotto of Tring), extensive estate works (almost all demolished) by George Devey, 1874 onwards.
(*Bledlow:* courtyard group, brick, mono-pitched roofs, (1975–77, Aldington & Craig) for Lord Carrington.)
(*Cheddington:* 1870s estate cottages for Hannah de Rothschild (of Mentmore) by Devey, also railway hotel, The Rosebery Arms.)
Chenies: Bedford Estate property from early C16 until 1957; some housing of c. 1828–29, remainder, red brick, many semi-detached, built between 1840–70.
Dibdin Hill (Chalfont St Giles) P. H. J. Baume built short-lived socialist cottage colony, 1846 (two houses, ten cottages, some survive).
(*Eythrope:* see *Waddesdon*)
Gayhurst: sixteen houses and inn moved to road-side after George Wrighte emparked his estate at Gayhurst House, c. 1737. Surviving cottages, thatch and stone, dated 1738, 1739.
Halton: Baron Alfred de Rothschild built house, restored church and added to gardens, 1870 to mid 1880s.
Hulcott: Rothschild estate village. Much "Old English" work on cottages and older buildings by Devey also enlarged school (1860), rectory (1862) and manor house (1860–64).
Jordans: Quaker garden village around a grassed village square built by Jordans Village Ltd. around the original 1688 Friends' Meeting House, to protect it from encroachment. Designed Fred Rowntree, 1916 onwards, built 1919–26. Jordans Village Industries were to provide employment, on guild system (Guild Hall, 1919, now demolished). Closed 1923.
Medmenham: estate village largely rebuilt when split between the owner of Medmenham Abbey and the builder of Danesfield House, Robert Hudson, and Hudson Kearley (Lord Devonport) of Wittington House. Cottages for Hudson designed 1898 onwards by W. H. Romaine-Walker using local materials including chalk, as at Danesfield House (1899–1901). School (1900). Other contemporary work by Reginald Blomfield for Kearley.
Mentmore: house built by Sir Joseph Paxton for Baron Mayer Amschel de Rothschild (1850–55). Estate village built 1850s to late 1870s (latterly for Hannah de Rothschild, Lady Rosebery), successively by G.H. Stokes (Paxton's son-in-law), Devey and John Aspell. Cottages set around green, with almshouses and pumphouse disguised as lychgate. See also more Rothschild cottages, 1876–77, at *Wingrave*.
New Bradwell (Milton Keynes): railway village, additional to the railway town of New Wolverton. Church, vicarage, schools and church hall all by

G.E. Street 1857–60. Housing largely demolished but two terraces (1853) remain. Foremen, drivers etc. had three-storey end of terrace houses, others had back-extensions for workshops.

Waddesdon: estate bought by Baron Ferdinand de Rothschild, 1874. Waddesdon Manor built 1877 onwards and estate village, largely in half-timbered, "Old English" style, 1880s onwards, including club and reading room (1883), school, almshouses (rebuilt 1883). Further Rothschild lodges and estate buildings for Hannah de Rothschild by Aspell at *Eythrope.*

(*Wotton Underwood:* terrace of C18 cottages built after emparking. Victorian estate cottages around green.)

Cambridgeshire & former Huntingdonshire [H]

Chippenham: after emparking by Edward Russell 1st Earl of Orford of Chippenham Park, 1698–1702, village and roads realigned. School (converted from C17 house in *c.* 1708), three surviving cottages (of at least 14 built) in Badlingham Road (renamed New Street). The Tharp family bought Chippenham Park 1791-92, built more estate cottages, including New Row, late C18 or early C19, eight semi-detached colour-washed cottages, linked by outhouses, generous gardens.

Little Gidding [H]: ecumenical religious community founded by Nicholas Ferrar in the 1630s, surviving into the C20.

(*Great Staughton* [H]: group of C18 cottages at north entrance to Staughton House.)

(*New Wimpole:* stone, Neo-Tudor estate cottages, 1840s, replacing village near Wimpole Hall.)

Ramsey [H]: Fellowes estate housing around Abbey Green, 1863 etc., almshouses (1839) and school (1848).

Studlands Park (Newmarket): self-contained village development, Ralph Erskine for Bovis (1968 onwards). Road traffic kept to perimeter, shops, pub and village green.

Thorney [H]: Bedford estate village, much new building from 1848 by S.S. Teulon, initiated and supervised by 7th Duke's resident agent, Tycho Wing. Cottages built to specifications suggested by Society for the Improvement of Conditions of the Labouring Classes (President, Prince Albert). Gothic Revival Post Office and Relieving Office, including infirmary (1851), school (1850–51), tank yard and water tower (1855) supplying village with water, gas, even treating domestic sewage.

(*Toft:* Neo-Tudor cottages, 1845.)

Waresley [H]: model Victorian village around Butterfield church (1857).

Cheshire

Aldford: largest of Westminster estate villages, centred on Eaton Hall. Church (1866 John Douglas) for 2nd Marquess, also housing 1850s–60s. Rest of village later, for 1st Duke, including Grosvenor Arms, 1892.

Cottages and farms by Douglas, 1870s–90s. Other Westminster villages *Bruera, Dodleston, Eccleston* (most complete), *Lower Kinnerton, Pulford* (and hamlets *Belgrave, Poulton) Saighton and Waverton.*

Arley Green: built in grounds of Arley Hall (1833–41), including school and chaplain's cottage, William White 1854.

*Bollington: short-lived model industrial community set up around Lowerhouse Mill by Samuel Greg Jr. from 1832 until 1846, known as Happy Valley. Greg published his reforming ideas on factory communities in 1840.

*Bromborough Pool: model village founded 1853 for Price's Patent Candle Co. and built by George and James Wilson; expanded in 1870s and late 1890s. Laid out by Julian Hill, well planned, generous scaled housing with internal sanitation; village green with school 1858.

(Burton: estate cottages by H.S. Goodhart-Rendel for one of William Gladstone's sons who remodelled Burton Manor 1904).

Caldy: estate bought 1832 by Manchester merchant family. Village rebuilt and expanded 1830s–40s; R.B. Rampling for Richard Watson Barton. Further work in later C19 including school (became church later), 1868 by G.E. Street, and Reading Room, 1883.

Crewe Green: village for Crewe Hall estate; church 1857–58 by G.G. Scott, village mostly later; school, 1882. Some cottages by W. Eden Nesfield 1860–66. Other Crewe Hall estate work at *Barthomley.*

(Ellesmere Port: cottage estate for Wolverhampton Corrugated Iron Company by C.R. Ashbee, *c.* 1906–09.)

(Harthill: housing (1844) and farms (by James Harrison) for Bolesworth Castle estate.)

(Higher Walton: estate housing for Sir Gilbert Greenall, Warrington Brewer. Late C19, early C20, church 1885 by Paley & Austin.)

Marple: settlement around Mellor Mill, established in 1790 by Samuel Oldknow, cotton manufacturer. Church 1808–12, model farm, housing for apprentices.

Peckforton: Lord Tollemache's estate, around Peckforton Castle (1844–50, Anthony Salvin); later C19 built 55 farmhouses and many more cottages.

*Port Sunlight: begun 1888 for W.H. Lever's soapworks, moved from Warrington. With Bournville, earliest application of garden suburb planning to the industrial environment. Architect in chief William Owen; also J.J. Talbot, Grayson & Ould, Douglas & Fordham and many others. After 1910 J. Lomax-Simpson became company architect. Internationally admired and widely cited as a model.

(Rode: cottages for Wilbraham estate by William White *c.* 1854.)

(Rostherne: c. 1909 Tatton estate housing.)

(Sandiway: work in village by John Douglas (see *Alford, Port Sunlight,* above) who became Lord of the Manor. Church, 1902–03, cottages and other houses.)

*Styal: brick terraced housing for employees at Samuel Greg's Quarry Bank Mills (founded 1783), apprentice house 1790, cottages (with gardens) largely 1820s, also chapel (Baptist, then Unitarian) and school. Rents deducted from wages. (See also *Bollington,* above). Later

Manchester Guardians built cottage homes for children (1898, F.H. Overmann), 28 houses, chapel (became Styal Prison).

Thornton Hough: Port Sunlight's country cousin, initially built for Joseph Hirst, mid C19, (church, school, vicarage) then additions for W.H. Lever, architects as at Port Sunlight, including Congregational church 1906–07.

Warburton: estate village built by John Douglas for R.E. Egerton-Warburton, 1870s to 1890s.

Cornwall

Charlestown: Charles Rashleigh's diminutive port, c. 1800.

(*Duloe:* solid stone and slate Victorian estate housing.)

Halsetown: built c. 1832 by James Halse MP for St. Ives, to house employees in his tin mine. Stone cottages set in enough land to qualify the resident for a vote (thus, Halse supporters only).

Portreath: pocket-sized port founded by Francis Basset MP (later Lord de Dunstanville) for the benefit of his mining concerns, in particular copper. Pier begun 1760.

St Michael Penkevil: estate village for Tregothnan (much rebuilt 1845–48, Lewis Vulliamy), seat of the Boscawens, Earls of Falmouth. Constructed from elvan (local stone).

Treslothan: estate village built by the Pendarves family; church (1841), school, parsonage all by George Wightwick in pale granite. At *Troon*, industrial terracing (Pendarves Street) is laid out as a formal approach to Treslothan estate.

(*Veryan:* five circular whitewashed thatched cottages, Gothick detail, early C19 by local builder, Hugh Rowe of Lostwithiel.)

Cumbria

(*Greta Village* (Keswick): Derwentwater Tenants' Co-operative scheme, one of earliest in the country (1909 on, N.W. Hodgson). Initiated by local Quaker, A.B. Wilson.)

Harriston: colliery village (built after 1868) named after Joseph Harris, who provided cooperative store, school, Mission Hall and amenities. Demolished and rebuilt in mid 1970s; rendered vernacular style housing around green, single storey sheltered housing, remainder two storey terraced cottages, by Allerdale District Council (Wright, Johnston & MacKenzie).

Holker [formerly Lancs.]: village for Cavendish estate (Holker Hall remodelled 1840, rebuilt after fire, 1871, Paley & Austin).

Longtown: sizeable village on borders of England and Scotland. Developed in late C18 by Dr Robert Graham of Netherby Hall, largely to house home weavers supplying textile businesses in Carlisle. Graham also planned a port at *Sarkfoot*, on the Solway Firth.

Lowther: Lowther New Town c. 1683–84 built by Sir John Lowther to replace village in park (church remained, rebuilt 1686). In 1766, Robert

281

Adam designed another village further away from Sir James Lowther's projected Lowther Castle. The result, as built, was only a fragment of an ambitious scheme (a full circus and two Greek crosses), urban in form though rural in function, in a remote rural setting.

Maryport: developed 1748–49 by Humphrey Senhouse, named after his wife, as port for his coal mines. Planned on grid (like nearby Whitehaven) but did not grow. (Later expansion due to railway).

Nenthead: village built by Quaker-founded London Lead Mining Company, 1825 on. Cottages had running water, gardens and smallholdings. Company also rebuilt housing and contributed to schools etc. around mines at *Scordale, Hilton, Garrighill* and *Dufton.*

Silloth: small planned seaside resort, railhead and port, grid-iron plan. Scheme initiated by Carlisle businessmen, 1850s, but never fully developed.

Tebay: remote railway village, expanded after it became junction, 1861.

Vickerstown [formerly Lancs.]: Garden City-type development on Walney Island built by company estates office of Vickers Ltd. for workers at their shipyard at Barrow-in-Furness; late 1890s–1905 (W. Moss Settle). Strict allocation of various types of housing to workers of appropriate status, also restrictions on change to external appearance of houses (until mid 1930s). Further housing and amenities added postwar.

Derbyshire

(*Barrow Hill:* good quality housing for workers at Staveley Coal and Iron Co., 1850s on.)

(*Barlborough:* brick estate cottages with diamond-pane casements, *c.* 1840.)

Beeley: Chatsworth estate village (acquired from 1747 on) with housing by Joseph Paxton (1838–41), school and schoolhouse (1841), vicarage (1856), post office, Reading Room *c.* 1880 and inn (Devonshire Arms). Church heavily rebuilt 1882–84. Other Chatsworth estate villages, *Baslow, Edensor* (below), *Pilsley* (below).

*Belper: enlightened 1790s industrial housing built by the Strutts (first mill 1776) for workers, three storey cottage groups, some stone, some brick. Also larger houses for foremen. Unitarian Chapel (burial place of Jedediah Strutt) 1788. More at *Milford,* 1793–94.

Cressbrook: industrial village around Arkwright's late C18 cotton mill, rebuilt 1815. Housing of various periods, notably 1840s Neo-Tudor cottages on hillside above, school.

*Creswell: model colliery village, 1896–1900 by Percy B. Houfton for Bolsover & Creswell Colliery Co. Recently extensively rehabilitated.

*Cromford: settlement around cotton mills, founded by Richard Arkwright, *c.* 1771. North Street, 1771–76, three storeyed stone terrace, mullioned windows; enlarged attic windows, for weaving. Later housing in village and school (1832), built for Richard Arkwright II.

Darley Abbey (Derby): workers' housing around Walter Evans' cotton mills, early C19 brick terraces, school 1826, church 1818–19.

Edensor: rebuilt Chatsworth estate village, sited by Joseph Paxton out of sight of house; in 1838 6th Duke of Devonshire bought ten eclectic house designs from John Robertson; built in stone along winding, rising lane. Completed 1842. Church, G.G. Scott (1867).

Great Rowsley: estate village belonging to Duke of Rutland, C17 and C18 stone cottages.

Higham: estate village, late C19 improvements by Turbutts of Ogston Hall.

Ironville: brick workers' housing for Butterley Iron Company 1834–50; school 1841, church 1852. (Also at *Golden Valley* earlier stone housing for same company, 1797–1813).

Kedleston: village rebuilt for Curzon estate after emparking, 1758–68. Housing, inn, model farm.

New Bolsover: model colliery village, 1883–93 for the Bolsover & Creswell Colliery Co.. Three storeyed houses stepped around large green, school, managers' detached houses.

Ockbrook: small Moravian settlement, chapel (1751–52) and brick houses.

(*Osmaston:* numerous Picturesque estate cottages, church 1845.)

Pilsley: Chatsworth estate village, C18 and C19 work including housing (1838–39) and school (1849) by Joseph Paxton, inn (The Devonshire Arms). Chatsworth Farm Shop.

(*Pleasley:* mid C19 company housing and amenities around Hollins textile mills.)

Riddings: cottages, school, model farm, *c.* 1880 built by ironmasters, Oakes.

Shardlow: inland port for the Trent and Mersey Canal. Warehouses, cottages, mills, 1780s on.

Sudbury: one street estate village, brick houses. Vernon Arms 1671, school 1831.

Tissington: Fitzherbert estate village, Picturesque Neo-Tudor housing, church restored 1854.

Devonshire

Ashprington: estate village for Sharpham. Picturesque cottages with bargeboards, gables and latticed windows, village school; church restored 1845.

(*Beer:* Rolle flint and brick estate buildings including cottages with porches, gables (some dated 1873). From 1850s on extensive Rolle estate building at *Bicton, Exmouth, Otterton, St. Giles in the Wood, Stevenstone, Woodbury*.)

(*Bolham* (Tiverton): decorative C19 housing for Knightshayes estate).

(*Churston Ferrers:* some C19 Yarde estate housing; also private estate of flat-roofed, rendered houses, with sun terraces and corner windows, by William Lescaze 1933–34. Landscape by Beatrice Farrand.)

(*Clovelly:* village in ownership of Cary, then Hamlyn families. Most improvements 1914–25.)

Dartington: Trustees of the Dartington estate (Elmhirst family) commissioned numerous buildings including groups of cottages in styles ranging from Arts and Crafts to International Modern, late 1920s to late 1930s. Housing by Louis de Soissons (*Huxhams Cross* and *Broom Park*, 1932) and W. Lescaze (1934–38), later work by Leonard Manasseh Partnership 1968–75.

Huntsham: estate village improved by Arthur Acland Troyte, 1852 onwards. Church restored 1854 on by Benjamin Ferrey, architect of Huntsham Court, 1868–70. Stone cottages, smithy, school and schoolteacher's house.

Membland: estate bought by Edward Baring *c.* 1877. Quirky Picturesque lodges, cottages, farm buildings (possibly by George Devey who rebuilt house). Also cottages at *Noss Mayo.*

Milton Abbot: estate buildings around Duke of Bedford's Endsleigh Cottage, 1810 (Sir Jeffry Wyatville); school 1820 (Wyatville), village hall 1840, mid C19 model farms. Cottage group (1909) by Sir Edwin Lutyens, two others in similar style.

Morwellham: abortive port development, some Bedford estate cottages, 1856 (c.f. Tavistock).

Newton St Cyres: C18 estate village, partially lost by road widening scheme but replaced by careful local authority rebuilding in 1960s, one and two storey cottages around village green.

(*Poltimore:* C19 Bampfylde estate cottages.)

(*Rewe:* late C19 estate buildings, fire engine house, cottages (one with shop), model farm.)

(*Tavistock:* 1840s to 1860s, Bedford Estate built some 300 model cottages for miners as well as ten blocks of flats in various parts of town, all designed by Theophilus Jones.)

Tiverton: planned industrial settlement around lace factory, founded by John Heathcoat 1816. Plain three storey housing (separate upper storey lodgings, c.f. *Halstead,* Essex), school (1841), working men's institute (1876). Also inter-war neo-Georgian terraces with lawns.

(*Upottery:* early Victorian estate housing and school built by Lord Sidmouth.)

(*Wood* (South Tawton) *c.* 1900, gabled and roughcast roadside cottages by Daniel Gibson.)

Dorset

*Briantspuddle: estate cottages and model farm, 1919 onwards, for Sir Ernest Debenham. Nearby *Bladen Valley,* emulating *Blaise Hamlet,* around Eric Gill War Memorial (1916–18), architects Halsey Ricardo and MacDonald Gill (sculptor Eric's brother).

Canford Magna: model village for Sir John Guest, south Wales ironmaster, possibly by Sir Charles Barry, (Canford Manor 1847 onwards).

(*Durweston:* C19 housing for Portman estate.)

(*East Lulworth:* thatched, late C18 estate housing, beyond Lulworth Castle park.)

284

Frampton: built as model estate village by Browne family to either side of road, one side demolished *c.* 1840.

Hilton (Lower Ansty): group of pub, farm and cottages, all mid C19.

Iwerne Minster: late C19 estate village built by 2nd Lord Wolverton of Glyn, Mills banking family, builder of Clayesmore (Alfred Waterhouse, 1878) school 1884.

Little Bredy: model village inspired by Blaise Hamlet, irregular green. Picturesque pattern book author and architect, P.F. Robinson, worked nearby in 1830s.

*Milton Abbas: model estate village *par excellence* built (to residents' dismay) to replace Middleton, by 1st Earl of Dorchester (formerly Joseph Damer, then Lord Milton). Town removed to provide a lake and park, setting for rebuilt Milton Abbey (1771–74) by Sir William Chambers. Valley site and planting (chestnut trees) by Capability Brown (1773), cottages designed by Chambers. Each detached cottage housed four families; church 1786 by James Wyatt, almshouses rebuilt 1779, vicarage *c.* 1780.

Newtown (More Crichel): new village built following emparking of Crichel House, when Humphrey Sturt rebuilt house after 1765. All but one house now demolished.

Poundbury (Dorchester): "village" for Duchy of Cornwall estate described as "autonomous new extension" to Dorchester. Leon Krier appointed master-planner by Prince of Wales (Duke of Cornwall) in 1988; first phase 1993 onwards, 18.5 acres, 20% social housing. Second phase 2 began 1999, 35% social housing. Vernacular materials and forms, emphasis on pedestrian movement.

(*Wimborne St Giles:* C18 and C19 estate cottages.)

County Durham

Bournmoor: "sadly decaying" (Buildings of England, 1985) Lambton Castle estate village (built 1795 on, further building in C19 after family coal mines led to subsidence); church (1867–68), chapel, school, cottages and lodges in yellow brick with red patterns.

Brancepeth: Brancepeth Castle rebuilt early C19 by John Paterson for the Russells, with coal mining fortune. Georgian cottages with mid C19 additions, also school and schoolhouse, station house, smithy (horseshoe doorway) — perfect estate village setting.

Castle Eden: Rowland Burdon II built workers' housing and amenities, cotton (later sailcloth) factory *c.* 1792. Later housing after railway arrived (1835), station, post office and hotel.

Hunstanworth: entire village rebuilt 1862–63 by Rev Daniel Capper of Newbiggin Hall, architect S.S. Teulon. Church, vicarage, school and cottages, stone in varied shades, two-tone patterned slate on roofs. More Teulon estate cottages and school at *Townfield,* nearby.

Masterman Place (Middleton-in-Teesdale): mining village for Quaker enterprise, London Lead Company (c.f. *Nenthead,* Cumbria). From 1815 on, cottages, school (1819); then 1823–24, Ignatius Bonomi designed "chaste and appropriate" cottages, set in sizeable gardens, for twenty-five miners and two overseers — approached through classical archway. Village had amenities but temperance. From 1880 became headquarters of company.

Seaham Harbour: port, designed by John Dobson for Lord Londonderry in 1823, harbour for coal from Sunderland and Durham mines. Original design had housing for various grades of employees, managers to artisans. Some sea front housing survives and stuccoed hotel.

Thorpe Thewles: estate village to Wynyard Park, for 3rd Marquess of Londonderry 1822 on.

Tudhoe Grange (Spennymoor) exemplary coal miners' housing built by Marmaduke Salvin (of Burn Hall) 1865–70; parallel streets, semi-detached cottages set in quarter acre gardens.

Essex

Audley End: two rows of terraced cottages built after emparking by Lord Braybrooke, after 1764 (incorporating some earlier structures). Later estate buildings and numerous lodges, mostly Neo-Jacobean, 1830s-40s.

Barkingside [Greater London]: Barnado's Village Home: first ten cottages developed by Thomas Barnado in 1875–76, designer Ebenezer Gregg, novel institutional form (replacing barrack-like buildings), for girls only. Eventually planned around three greens; 60 cottages, church (1892, Gregg), hospital and schools. 17 cottages survive (model for the society's Victorian collecting box). Boys' village (now demolished) at *Woodford Bridge*.

(*Braintree:* semi-detached, flat roofed housing for Crittall workers at Cressing Road and Clockhouse Way, 1918–20 by C.H.B. Quennell and W.F. Crittall, the first example of the International Modern style in England. Pioneering cheap modern housing, concrete with steel casement windows, now replaced. Precursor of Silver End, see below.)

(*Bocking:* C19 and C20 housing and amenities for workers at Samuel Courtauld & Co, including cottage hospital (converted from cottages, 1871), semi-detached "mechanics" cottages by John Birch (1872), see *Gosfield* below. Nearby *High Garrett* has many Courtauld estate cottages of 1870s and 1880s with latticed glazing and decorative features.)

(*Earls Colne:* workers' housing for Atlas Iron Works (1856–1988), 1870s and *c.* 1905–12.)

East Tilbury: factory village built from 1933 onwards for the British Bata Shoe Co.; designed by company architects from the parent town, Zlin in the Czech Republic. Company hotel with shops below, factories, hostels and semi-detached houses: all flat roofed, concrete and steel construction with brick infill, Crittall windows. Cinema 1938.

(*Gidea Park* (Romford) [Greater London]: garden suburb conceived in 1909, probably planned by Parker & Unwin and built as competition, two categories, £500 houses and £375 cottages. Resulting exhibition opened 1911, no communal focus, merely housing estate with interesting architecture. Initially 140 houses by more than 100 architects. Expanded by 1934 "Modern Homes" exhibition.)

Gosfield: village largely built by Samuel Courtauld (of Gosfield Hall). School 1858, Reading and Coffee Room, numerous pairs of estate cottages, including some probably by John Birch (1875), one incorporating village bakehouse.

(*Halstead:* much building related to the silk works established here by Samuel Courtauld in 1825, extending to new (traditional) housing and amenities from the 1920s and 30s, largely by E.W. Coldwell; two three storeyed terraces on Factory Lane East, by John Birch (1872), provided additional top floor lodgings for weekly workers; cottages on the Causeway, 1882–83 by Sherrin, with Dutch gables.)

Mistley: in the 1770s Richard Rigby II whose father had laid out *Mistley Thorn* with a wharf and kilns beside the river, built a village centred on Fountain Square, designed by Robert Adam who also transformed the (largely demolished) church in 1776.

Radwinter: after a fire in 1874, rebuilt by William Eden Nesfield and Temple Moore. Nesfield designed the shops and cottages, 1874–75, Moore the almshouses and Reading Room.

Silver End: Francis Crittall's model industrial village, designed on a Garden City plan, for employees in the Crittall window factory; begun 1926, designed by architects working in both International Modern (see *Braintree,* above) and more traditional styles. Detached houses for managers, semi-detached or terraced for workers, by 1932 almost 500 houses built, with shops, village hall, hotel, two churches (one a converted barn), and factory for disabled ex-servicemen. Regardless of style, all buildings had Crittall windows.

(*Stisted:* village largely rebuilt 1853–78, in Picturesque style, for Onley Savill-Onley.)

Gloucestershire

Beverston: model village built after 1842 by Robert Holford (heir of New River Company fortune), architect Lewis Vulliamy. Simple stone terraces, gables, porches. Church rebuilt 1844–45 by Vulliamy, also built several model farms. Matching Holford estate village at *Westonbirt,* semi-detached cottages, school (1870–71, Vulliamy) built to replace the older village, emparked before 1856. Vulliamy built Westonbirt House, from 1864.

(*Eastleach:* estate housing, almshouses (1871, William Wilkinson), cottages with clock tower (1869, H.A. Darbishire), model farms, all for Bazley of *Hatherop,* see below.)

(*Forthampton:* estate cottages, some in patterned brick by William Burges (*c.* 1865) who restored church and built Yorke almshouses, 1863–64).

(*Haresfield:* estate buildings for (and by) the Niblett family, rectors, squires and architects.)

Hatherop: C19 estate village, improved by W.F.S. Ponsonby (Baron de Mauley) and then, from 1867, by Sir Thomas Bazley, Lancashire cotton magnate. Architects as at *Eastleach*.

Highnam: Thomas Gambier Parry's estate from 1837; church built by Henry Woodyer (1849–51), school and teacher's house, (Woodyer, 1850), many estate cottages, including pair by Sidney Gambier Parry, *c.* 1887, architect of Parish Hall, 1904.

Great Badminton: estate village, mostly rendered and lime washed, buildings of many dates, 1700s onwards, for succeeding Dukes of Beaufort. Notably, several mid C18 *cottages ornés* by Thomas Wright, also work by early C18 estate surveyor (William Killigrew) and mid Victorian clerk of works, John Tait.

*Lowbands (Redmarley d'Abitot): second of Feargus O'Connor's sites for the Chartist Cooperative Land Company, bought October 1846. More than forty cottages built in six months; standard design, single storey, with pediment gable, rendered rubble; kitchen in centre, living and bed room to either side, outbuildings in yard to rear. Water supply and privy. All set in 3–4 acres. Firewood, seed and manure provided for each new settler.

Rendcomb: estate bought 1864 by Sir Francis Goldsmid QC, MP. Rendcomb House rebuilt (P.C. Hardwick 1867), stone cottages, village pump, Village Hall.

Sherborne: east part of village rebuilt by 2nd Lord Sherborne in 1830s, cottage terraces and almshouses. Stone, slightly Neo-Tudor.

*Snigs End (Corse and Staunton): fourth of O'Connor's Chartist land schemes (see *Lowbands*, above), founded June 1847. At least eighty cottages built to usual pattern. Brick school (now Prince of Wales Inn). Some housing laid out in crescents. Estate sold in 1857.

Tibberton: estate cottages and farms, in patterned polychrome brick, 1860s and 70s. Built by James Medland, rebuilt Tibberton Court 1852–53 for W.P. Price of the Midland Railway.

(Toddington (New Town) roadside estate cottages, for Hanbury-Tracy family, (Lords Sudeley), heirs to Pontypool Ironworks.)

Tortworth: largely rebuilt C19 estate village for Earls of Ducie of Tortworth Court (S.S. Teulon 1849–53); scattered cottages by Teulon, 1850s, increasingly Picturesque, others by George Devey *c.* 1879. Also at *Avening Green*, hamlet of gabled cottages 1846–47.

*Westonbirt see *Beverston*, above.

Warmley: in 1746 the Quaker metallurgist, William Champion, established integrated works for metallic zinc, brass and copper production. Built terraced housing (from basalt slag, factory by-product) nearby for workers (2000 by the 1760s). All cottages demolished by 1970.

*Whiteway Colony: Tolstoyan self-sufficient community founded 1898, an offshoot of the Purleigh Colony in Essex. Village hall, shop and bakery, small workshops, self built housing. Still in existence.

(Woodmancote (North Cerney) C19 estate cottages, including some by Hardwick (1865) for Goldsmid of *Rendcomb*, above.)

(Yanworth: Eldon estate cottages *c.* 1860.)

Hampshire & Isle of Wight

Blackmoor: Sir Roundell Palmer (later 1st Earl Selborne, Gladstone's Lord Chancellor) built Blackmoor House, 1869–73, architect Alfred Waterhouse. Church (1868), vicarage, school (became Reading Room) and cottages, larger schoolroom (1871) all by Waterhouse.

(Bramley: school, 1848, Picturesque Brocas estate housing, gabled, tile-hung, fancy glazing.)

*Bucklers Hard: single broad street village to waterside, mid 1770s on. Only remnant of port planned by the 2nd Duke of Montagu.

(Chalton: Victorian housing for Idsworth estate, Idsworth House (William Burn 1852)

(Crawley: estate cottages with timber framed gables on village street.)

Eastleigh: 1840s railway village (station built 1839) on line to Gosport; later much expanded.

*East Stratton: five pairs of brick cottages, built by George Dance the younger, c. 1806 for Francis Baring of Stratton Park (Dance 1803) who also added to Micheldever church, 1808.

East Tisted: estate village of "enterprising and entertaining" *(Buildings of England)* cottages from 1820s onwards; Rotherfield Park 1815–21 by J.T. Parkinson, church rebuilt 1846.

Elvetham: estate village to Lord Calthorpe's house, Elvetham Hall built by S.S. Teulon 1859–60, also water tower, school and cottages.

(Fawley: early Victorian Cadland estate cottages in yellow brick, barge-boards etc.)

*Freefolk (Laverstoke) curved crescent of thatched cottages, late 1930s, built by Major Mort for Lord Portal: wells and bus stop also thatched. (Victorian red brick housing for Portal's paper-mill workers in *Laverstoke.)*

(Hursley: Neo-Tudor Heathcote estate cottages with latticed glazing.)

(Lee: estate housing for Broadlands, Lord Palmerston's seat, some possibly by Eden Nesfield; chapel, 1862.)

*Talbot Village (Bournemouth): philanthropic model village on heathland, built by Georgina Charlotte and Mary Anne Talbot, from 1835 onwards. Cottages, farms, schools (1860) almshouses (1862) and church (1868–70).

Whippingham (Isle of Wight); scattered village for Osborne House, many estate buildings, farms, lodges and cottages designed under Prince Albert's aegis (1848 onwards), with John Blandford, royal estate Clerk of Works and A.J. Humbert, (latter remodelled church 1854–62). School (1863–4), Victoria and Albert almshouses (1875–6). Also scattered cottages and post office.

Herefordshire

Eastnor: village of Picturesque cottages built by Somers family (of Somerstown, North London). Church and rectory by G.G. Scott 1849–50. Lady Henry Somerset (see also *Duxhurst*, Surrey) active local philanthropist. Drinking fountain with decorative terracotta panels on green, stone school and stores with ornament, post office thatched.

Hertfordshire

(*Abbots Langley* (Bedmond): pair of model cottages designed by Henry Roberts for Prince Albert at the 1851 Exhibition, see also *Cowbridge*, below, and Kennington, south London.)

Ardeley: Picturesque model village (1917), white thatched cottages around green with pond, Village Hall and brick well; designed by F.C. Eden.

(*Barkway* (near Newsells Park): hamlet of thatched C17 estate cottages.)

Bentley Heath: church (1865 by S.S. Teulon), row of cottages 1864 built by 2nd Earl of Stratford.

Childwick Bury: estate bought by H.H. Toulmin in 1854; built model village around green with decorative well-head as focal feature. Next owner, Sir John Blundell Maple (the furniture maker) added to it in late C19.

(*Cowbridge:* replica of Henry Roberts cottage for the 1851 Exhibition.)

Heronsgate (Chorleywood): originally called O'Connorville, first of Feargus O'Connor's Chartist Cooperative Land Company settlements (1846). Planned school and 35 cottages, each with two to four acres of land. Only Chartist village with two storey houses.

(*Kings Walden Bury:* estate cottages, late C19 gabled, brick and half-timbering.)

(*Knebworth:* various cottages, c. 1896–1910, designed by Edwin Lutyens on the estate of his parents-in-law, the Lyttons.)

Letchworth Garden City: self sufficient town dreamed up and founded by Ebenezer Howard, planned and built by Raymond Unwin and Barry Parker. Inspiration for the international garden village movement, establishing planning principles and architectural forms for innumerable new settlements in the early 20th century (See *Hampstead Garden Suburb, New Earswick* etc.)

(*Stanstead Abbots:* several 1870s estate cottages probably by Alfred Waterhouse, who built Easneye (1868–69) for Buxton family.)

(*Tring:* much estate work for the 1st Lord Rothschild of Tring Park in and around town, including Louisa Cottages 1893 and 1901, by William Huckvale.)

Isle of Man

Cronkbourne (Tromode): site of Moore family sailcloth works, set up 1790. Place name an invention; "cronk" being Manx for hill and "bourne" English for river. Hamlet built in late 1840s for employees. Two rows of single storey housing with green between, schoolroom and chapel and a handful of larger houses for skilled workers.

Kent

Allhallows-on-Sea: post WWI holiday resort, served by Southern Railway station and pub (The British Pilot) built in the 1930s; never achieved its objectives and became caravan park.

Aylesham: planned colliery town for Snowdown Colliery, 1926–27. Beaux-Arts scheme with central grassed square, designers included Patrick Abercrombie. Intended to house 15,000 but failed to expand.

Barns Cray (Crayford), (LB of Bexley): garden village for Vickers munitions workers, 1914; designs (1919) for expansion.

(*Betteshanger:* estate cottages by George Devey (who enlarged Betteshanger House for Lord Northbourne, *c.* 1856), also cottage hospital.)

Birchington: seaside resort of bungalows around the Bungalow Hotel, built by John Taylor in late 1860s on land owned by J.P. Seddon, who later continued the development, employing the Indian style, low sweeping roofs and verandahs, *c.* 1880.

(*Birling:* Nevill estate housing.)

*British Legion Village (Aylesford): wooden bungalows with verandahs and large gardens, some dated 1923.

Calverley Park (Tunbridge Wells): Decimus Burton following Nash's Regent's Park. Planned 1828 onwards; very early example of the villa estate, built around pleasure ground, church, shops, hotel and market.

(*Chevening:* red brick estate housing, C18 and C19, for Earls Stanhope.)

(*Fordcombe:* C19 estate housing around green, for Lord Hardinge. Church 1847.)

(*Goodnestone:* C19 housing for Dering estate (as at *Pluckley*, school 1849) all with Sir Edward Cholmley Dering's "lucky windows", special arched window lights.)

Great Chart: housing, school (1845), almshouses (1833) all marked by signature shaped gables of the Toke estate of Godinton (also at *Little Chart*).

Hersden: planned village for miners at Chislet Colliery, planned by G.J. Skipper pre 1927.

Hever: a Neo-Tudor "village" built for William Waldorf Astor to extend accommodation at Hever Castle; guest rooms, servants' quarters and offices, architect E. L. Pearson 1903–06.

*Horton Kirby (Farningham): Home for Little Boys, pioneer philanthropic cottage home for 300 (and up to 500) "destitute" boys, with chapel, station, workshops and eleven houses for 30 to 40 children. Opened 1867 (moved from Tottenham), closed 1961. Site largely redeveloped, but main building survives within Southdown Retirement Village.

Kemsley: model village, housing and social centre, on the marshes near Bowater paper mill. Formal plan, 1925–26 by Adams, Thomson & Fry (Maxwell Fry).

*Leigh: large village with much estate work by both Ernest George and George Devey for Samuel Morley MP of Hall Place (built 1871–76 by Devey).

Linton: C19 estate village with almshouses, village hall all built of local ragstone (1887).

(*Lympne:* cottages by Sir Robert Lorimer 1906–12 for F.J. Tennant.)

Mereworth: John Fane, the Earl of Westmorland, destroyed hamlet and church when creating park; new church and housing *c.* 1746.

291

New Ash Green: planned by former architects turned developers, Span Developments, with Eric Lyons as consultant. Begun 1965. Financial and other problems diluted architecture and plan. Best neighbourhoods have typical austere Span ingredients, short terraces, tile-hung or weather boarded, mono-pitch roofs, often with skylights. High density around quality landscaping by Ivor Cunningham; road traffic and garaging segregated. Small shops, primary school, pub and village hall.

(*Nonington:* several large estate cottages by George Devey.)

Patrixbourne: early C19 Picturesque village, some cottages dated later, built for Marquess Conyngham of Bifrons (demolished).

Penshurst: Picturesque group of cottages at approach to church, George Devey for Lord de L'Isle, *c.* 1850, later more ornate additions. (At *Redleaf,* William Wells cottages, 1825–26).

(*Riverhead:* C19 Amherst estate housing.)

(*Shipbourne:* 1880s housing, restored church and "jolly" pub, for Edward Cazalet of Fairlawne.)

Lancashire

Aigburth (Liverpool), St Michael's Hamlet built by John Cragg, of the Mersey Iron Foundry, using cast iron from his works: church (1813–15), five villas pre 1840.

Alkrington Garden Village (Middleton): initial plan 1909 by Thomas Adams of Letchworth.

Aspull see *Haig* below.

Barrow Bridge (Bolton): Robert Gardner and Robert Bazley founded their cotton business at Dean Mills in 1831; built model village for workers. Stone terraced cottages with gardens and allotments, water and gas. Institute (1846), cooperative shop, larger houses for managers nearby. No church or inn.

Burnage Garden Village: Co-partnership Tenants Ltd. scheme of 1911, 136 houses, with tennis and bowling club. Raymond Unwin consulted on form of plan.

(*Calder Vale:* terraced housing around cotton mill, built 1835 by Quaker brothers, Richard and Jonathan Jackson. Church and school built 1863.)

Eagley Mills (Egerton): workers' housing for Ashworths (cotton magnates) mostly 1830s and 1840s, stone cottages around gardens, some larger houses for managers.

Fairfield (Droylsden): Moravian self sufficient settlement, third and most complete in England. Founded 1785, plan and designs by young Benjamin Henry Latrobe. Church (with cupola), brick housing sited around a square within a square, single men and women's houses became boarding schools. Brethren House still a school, Sisters' House now community centre. Wooded graveyard with flat gravestones, sundial. Nearby, Fairfield Tenants Ltd. housing, 1913–22, Edgar Wood & Henry Sellers, land leased from Moravians.

Fazakerley (Liverpool): small model estate built for workers at William

292

Hartley's jam factory. Competition for housing held 1888. Won by William Sugden & Son; gardens and 3% mortgages. Health care, near equal pay for women and profit-sharing from 1889. Also at Fazakerley, *New Hall:* reformist cottage home "village" for deprived children, on the Swiss and German model. 1887–89, Charles H. Lancaster; all amenities on site, including farm. Houses laid out along broad street with Hall as focal point.

Haig: estate around Haig Hall (1827 onwards, built by 7th Earl of Balcarres, amateur architect) and foundry (set up 1788); school (1845, also by the Earl) cottages (1821, 1854 etc.) model farm (1853). More Balcarres housing at *Aspull*, miners' cottages, some C18 (for 6th Earl).

Halliwell (Bolton): church, schools and housing (all 1847, James Greenhalgh) for John Horrocks Ainsworth (family fortune from bleach-works), modelled on (unspecified) village in south of England.

Holker: estate housing (Holker Hall remodelled 1840, again after fire, 1871, Paley & Austin)

Howe Bridge (Atherton): model mining village of 1870s for Fletcher, Burrows & Co. by J. Medland & Henry Taylor. Brick terraces, shops, village club (1875), baths (1873), church (1875–77, Paley & Austin), schools. Also gardens, sporting facilities.

Oldham Garden Suburb, Hollins Green: result of the "Beautiful Oldham" movement of 1902 set up by two exceptional women, Mary Higgs (first woman to take the Natural Science Tripos at Cambridge, later social worker in Oldham) and Dame Sarah Lees (suffragist, first woman mayor of Oldham). Ebenezer Howard at opening in 1909. Plan and first phase by Heywood & Ogden in Arts and Crafts style. Post-war phase, houses smaller and cheaper.

(*Ravenhead* (St. Helens): remnant of original 1770s housing for the British Plate Glass Company Works, Factory Row.)

Reddish: model industrial village around Houldsworth Mill (1865, A.H. Stott). Working Men's Club (1874, Stott). School (1876) church and vicarage (1882–83, Alfred Waterhouse).

Singleton: estate village owned by Horrocks Miller family (textile manufacturers), whitewashed housing with gabled porches, post office, church (1861), Hall (1871), Picturesque fire station.

(*Turton:* mid C19 model estate.)

Vulcan Village (Wargrave): Vulcan Foundry manufactured locomotives from 1832–1970 (Robert Stephenson a partner). Terraced company housing, 1833–38, laid out around triangular central area, with pub and school in centre. After long decline, major housing association renovation took place in 1990s.

(*Walton* (Warrington); includes late C19, early C20 estate village for Walton Hall, owned by Greenall family (Greenall, Whitley & Co, brewers) in various styles and materials.)

Worsley: 1760s terraces, for canal workers and boat builders employed by the Duke of Bridgewater's enterprise. Other estate cottages *c.* 1800. Factories and works relocated in 1903, further Arts and Crafts style housing, (1904–10, Douglas & Minshull).

Leicestershire

(*Buckminster:* Dysart estate housing of several periods.)

(*Braunstone:* brick estate cottages, 1858–59 by William Butterfield for Winstanleys of Braunston Hall, see *Kirby Muxloe* below.)

(*Elmesthorpe:* Wentworth Arms and Wortley Terrace, roughcast, slate-roofed cottages by C.F.A. Voysey for Lord Lovelace, 1895–6.)

Horninghold: one street planned village begun by Thomas Hardcastle of Blaston Hall. Post Office and cottages 1882–85, Goddard & Paget. Later Hardcastles and Goddards enlarged it, 1903–14.

Hungarton: village rebuilt by Shukburgh Ashby in red and yellow chequered brick, 1766–75, following "a principle laudable and truely disinterested".

(*Kirby Muxloe:* terrace of farm workers' cottages in Main Street, Butterfield 1859 for J.B. Winstanley.)

Knipton: Belvoir estate village; school 1854, cottages mostly 1890s.

Stapleford: village razed *c.* 1500, not rebuilt until late C18; church (in park) 1782, bedehouses made Picturesque in early C19, rest of village scattered beyond park.

(*Swithland:* much C19 estate building using local Swithland slate.)

(*Theddingworth:* Patterned brick estate cottages for the 4th Earl Spencer, 1860–61; also range from 1851 by Samuel Beazley.)

Welham: hamlet built *c.* 1720 by Francis Edwards, Lord of the Manor. Coaching inn was to have been central feature, on re-routed turnpike. No more than 13 houses built.

Lincolnshire

Appleby: village largely rebuilt in 1870s for the Winn family, 14 pairs of semi-detached cottages in local limestone with red and yellow brick details.

Aswarby: Neo-Tudor estate village for Whichcote family, cottages dated 1845, 1851. Model farms, 1848, 1852.

*Belton: outstandingly complete model village built for Brownlows, mostly stone. First phase by Jeffry Wyatville, Waterloo Cottages and pump (disguised as obelisk). Remainder largely Tudor and Jacobean revival cottages, many by Anthony Salvin. Rebuilt almshouses (1827), smithy with horseshoe over doorway (1838), school (1838), inn (altered 1839). More Brownlow estate cottages at *Londonthorpe* and *Manthorpe*, below.

Blankney: stone Tudor style model village laid out by W.A. Nicholson in 1830s and 1840s for the Chaplin family of Blankney Hall.

Brocklesby: the Lords Yarborough of Brocklesby Hall were largest landowners in Lincolnshire. In Victorian period, they built estate cottages in 27 parishes, centred on Brocklesby and *Great Limber*. Picturesque cottages with elaborate bargeboards and distinctive brickwork, numerous schools and grand Jacobean railway station at Brocklesby 1848–49.

Denton: homogenous ironstone estate village for Welby family, C19 and C20.

Easton: C19 estate village for Easton Park, no church.

(Edenham: village on Grimsthorpe estate, with much C19 rebuilding and long row of late Victorian cottages, Elm Terrace.)

Gedney Dawsmere: estate village became an ecclesiastical parish in 1855, date of neat estate cottages set in ample gardens. Church (1869) and vicarage (1871) by Ewan Christian.

(Greetham: includes row of early C19 Gothick estate cottages.)

(Hainton: Heneage estate cottages by William Danby 1836, church and school rebuilt by E.J. Wilson, 1846–47.)

*Harlaxton: existing village rebuilt by George de Ligne Gregory 1790–1820 (hence initials G.D.G.) before being further ornamented in an eccentric Picturesque style by Gregory Gregory in the 1830s. Described by J.C. Loudon in his *Encyclopaedia of Cottage, Farm and Villa Architecture and Furniture* (1840).

Holton-le-Moor: created by Dixon family, 1870s onwards, cottages with decorative name plaques. Early C20 almshouses, school and half-timbered Moot Hall with plaster panels recording events in British history.

Manthorpe (near Grantham): complete Neo-Tudor Victorian estate village for Brownlows, built in red brick and stone between 1849–65, including church (1847–48), school and conduit.

New Bolingbroke: nucleus of planned industrial village for John Parkinson's crepe and bombazine weavers. The Crescent, 1823, and terraces nearby. Methodist Chapel 1825.

Nocton: stone estate village built by 1st Earl of Ripon of Nocton Hall. Gothic revival cottages and terraces, one *c.* 1860 by Sir G.G. Scott (who designed both church, 1860–65, and school).

Normanby: village rebuilt outside gates of Normanby Park in early C19. Further rebuilding and additions for Sheffield family, late C19 and early C20.

Redbourne: village improved in 1770s by Rev. Robert Carter Thewall who built pair of pedimented terraces and smithy in form of classical temple.

Revesby: 1850s estate village for Banks family of Revesby Abbey, rebuilt 1844 by William Burn. Red brick semi-detached cottages, perhaps by Burn, with bargeboards and gables, laid out around large village green. School (1858), almshouses rebuilt 1862 (and late 1980s).

(Scawby: C18 and C19 estate cottages, latter with elaborated chimney stacks. School 1854.)

South Rauceby: late Victorian village to Rauceby Hall (William Burn 1842), cottages 1884.

Stoke Rochford: Neo-Tudor 1840s stone estate village belonging to Turnors. By William Burn, as Stoke Rochford Hall (1841–43). Almshouses 1850–51, school.

Woodhall Spa: wooded, sandy area developed as a miniature resort, especially from the 1890s onwards, consisting of pump room and spa, tea rooms, hotels and detached housing. The tennis pavilion became the Kinema in the Woods (1922).

London *for Greater London. see also Essex, Middlesex, Kent, Surrey*

Holly Village, Highgate (LB of Camden): Picturesque hamlet of eight decorative, stock brick cottages with Gothic details set around green. Built by wealthy philanthropist, Angela Burdett-Coutts, architect Henry Darbishire, 1865.

Park Villages East and West (LB of Camden): laid out by John Nash, 1824 onwards, completed by James Pennethorne. Miniature villa estate in various styles on winding road, precursor of *Edensor*, Derbyshire and suburban schemes everywhere in the 1830s and 40s.

Well Hall Eltham (LB of Greenwich): munitions estate, designed from 1915 by Frank Baines; built in under a year. (See also *Roe Green Village*, Middlesex).

Middlesex

Bedford Park (London Boroughs of Hounslow & Ealing): estate of 24 acres bought by Jonathan Carr in 1875 to develop estate which would attract artistic folk (and artists). Picturesque principle applied to garden suburb; E.W. Godwin, then Norman Shaw dictated the overall "Queen Anne" style. Church (Maurice Adams, 1887), Tabard Inn (1880).

Brentham Garden Estate (LB of Ealing): expanded from Ealing Tenants Ltd.'s co-partnership scheme (1901) with Raymond Unwin's 1906 plan. By 1914, 650 houses built. Henry Vivian MP, promoter of scheme, emphasised importance of communal focus; hence Institute 1911, playing fields, allotments. Other co-operative housing ventures followed this example, eg. Sevenoaks Tenants Society.

Hampstead Garden Suburb (LB of Barnet): novel concept. Dame Henrietta Barnett, founder, envisaged socially integrated "village" served by newly established suburban railway lines. Prospectus 1905. Architect planners Raymond Unwin and Barry Parker, also Edwin Lutyens. 1907 onwards. Central square, two churches, Institute, school. Much early housing promoted by co-partnership companies, thus ensuring co-ownership and management control at outset.

Mill Hill (LB of Barnet): two garden village groups, Linen and Woollen Drapers Cottage Homes. Marshall Estate (1897) established by son of founder of Marshall & Snelgrove, architect George Hornblower. 61 cottages and Central Institute and Clubhouse, Reading Room extension (1901), on part of family estate. Another group, Chalet Estate, 1927 onwards.

Roe Green Village: (LB of Brent) 270 flats and houses built for aircraft workers, designed 1916 by Frank Baines, principal architect Office of Works, built from 1918. Five classes of accommodation, some with bath in scullery. Closely based on Woolwich Garden Suburb (*Well Hall*) built for the Arsenal, 1915, also Baines.

Norfolk

(*Beachamwell:* pairs of two-storeyed estate cottages around green, *c.* 1815–20; gault brick, cast iron windows. Built by John Motteux.)

Brettenham: estate village for Shadwell Park (remodelled 1856–60, S.S. Teulon), church (1852, Teulon).

Glandford: flint and brick model village built for Sir Alfred Jodrell (of Bayfield Hall). Church (1899–1906, Hicks & Charlewood), cottages with "Dutch" shaped gables 1890s.

*Holkham: enormous volume of estate building for Coke family, from 1780s (Samuel Wyatt) onwards. Among it all Wyatt built 14 cottages in a half circle, Longlands village, 1799. (Rebuilt 1910 as New Holkham.) Village rebuilt from 1780s until late C19, almshouses (1851–55, William Burn), school (1837 and later); elsewhere Holkham estate work at *Egmere,* novel shuttered concrete cottages 1878–80, and *Wighton,* houses of various dates including flint cottages with brick dressings (1834) and more concrete cottages.

*New Houghton: following enclosure of parkland in the 1720s, replacement village begun July 1729, continuing line of avenue in park. Detached, two storey houses (forming multiple dwellings), single storey almshouse, two farmhouses. All whitewashed brick, black glazed pantiles.

Melton Constable: 1880s village built for railway workers.

*West Newton: scattered estate village for Sandringham House, built from local ginger coloured carstone, from 1862; Alexandra Cottages (1864), club (1873), church (restored 1881, Arthur Blomfield) school (1881).

(*Woodbastwick:* estate housing for Cators, early C18.)

Northamptonshire

Apethorpe: village remodelled after 1904 by Sir Reginald Blowfield for Leonard Brassey.

(*Ashby St. Ledgers:* cottages, thatch, buttresses and heavy chimneys, Edwin Lutyens 1908–09.)

Ashley: village rebuilt in mid C19 by Rev. Richard Pulteney (rector as well as squire); church (1867) school (1858) and schoolhouse (1865) by G.G. Scott; also estate houses.

*Ashton: Picturesque stone-built, thatched village (including inn) rebuilt 1900 for the Hon. Charles Rothschild by William Huckvale. All electricity wires underground, cottages with indoor bathrooms.

Chapel Brampton: Althorp estate village (for Spencers), Neo-Tudor ironstone cottages, designed by Edward Blore, 1848. Also at *Church Brampton,* Spencer estate cottages and almshouses (1858); *Harlestone,* similar estate housing, school (George Devey); *Little Brington,* cottages (Blore, 1848), school (1850, P.C. Hardwick) and almshouses 1851.

Edgcote: village lost after 1750s emparking; church rebuilt in park, 1747 (Smith of Warwick), cottages and farms rebuilt beyond.

Finedon: estate village with cottages, almshouses, town hall and inn

(1872) mostly in William Mackworth-Dolben's "peculiar Gothic taste" (*Buildings of England*).

Grafton Regis: c. 1840 estate village with several model farms for Duke of Grafton's estate. Also *Potterspury*, cottages of c. 1850.

Hulcote: hamlet built for 3rd Earl of Pomfret of Easton Neston, c. 1800–20 to replace earlier village lost by emparking. Eight cottages and school (1816) with chequered brickwork and Gothick windows, third storey tucked into gable.

(*Lamport:* polychrome brick estate cottages, 1854, contemporary with William Burn's work at Lamport Hall for the Ishams.)

Laxton: village rebuilt (after C18 emparking) by George Freke Evans, Picturesque gabled stone cottages and a village green. Possibly by J.A. Repton (rebuilt Laxton Hall c. 1811).

(*Orlingbury:* mid C19 housing for Mr Young "after his own plans", architect R.C. Hussey.)

(*Overstone:* village removed from park to nearby roadside. Estate cottages, 1821.)

(*Thorpe Achurch:* line of estate cottages on main road, c. 1830–40.)

(*Watford:* C19 estate cottages, Watford Court rebuilt 1854 onwards.)

Northumberland

*Belsay: old village demolished c. 1816 replaced by single arcaded stone terrace in Italianate style, probably contemporary with Sir Charles Monck's house, Belsay Hall, built to his own Greek Revival design, completed 1817. Inn 1836, school 1841.

Blanchland: planned village built by Crewe Trustees, mid C18 onwards. Central square follows form of ruined outer courtyard of Blanchland Abbey.

Bothal: estate cottages remodelled in Picturesque style in 1885. Village Hall 1895.

*Byrness: Forestry Commission village (for Kielder Forest) by Dr Thomas Sharp, 1950s. See also *Stonehaugh*.

Cambo: terraced estate village built for Sir Walter Blackett of Wallington, probably by Daniel Garrett, c. 1750. Inn closed in 1840s by temperance reformer Sir Walter Trevelyan; village remodelled by Sir Charles Trevelyan in 1880s.

Capheaton: model village at gates to house, late C18 for Swinburne family (see *Stamfordham* below); single storey terraces in local stone.

(*Chatton:* mid C19 Tudor revival cottages on Duke of Northumberland's estate. Similar cottages at *Denwick*.)

Chillingham: estate village to Chillingham Castle, rebuilt 1830s in two-storeyed blocks of four by architect Edward Blore for 5th Earl of Tankerville.

Creswell: Neo-Tudor estate cottages and school, contemporary with church, mid 1830s.

Etal: estate village to Etal Castle, largely rebuilt post 1907 by Lord Joicey.

*Ford: model village built by widowed Louisa, Marchioness of Waterford,

1860 on; further housing for Lord Joicey c. 1914. Former school, Waterford Hall, decorated with biblical scenes (in watercolour) by Lady Waterford, 1861–62. Smithy, 1863, with horse-shoe doorway.
Howick: Early Victorian hamlet replaced earlier village. Tudor style cottages dated 1841.
Longhirst: early C19 estate village, remodelled c. 1880.
Matfen: Tudor revival estate village, built to complement Sir Edward Blackett's Elizabethan style Matfen Hall of 1828–30. Landowner also designed church, 1841–42.
Rock: mid C19 Tudor revival estate cottages built by Bosanquet family. Sunday School (later Village Hall) 1855.
(*Rothbury:* Addycombe Cottages, two terraces in Tyrolean style, built 1873 by Norman Shaw for Lord Armstrong's retired staff from Cragside. Designed as flats.)
Simonburn: Allgood family estate village, around green with C18 and early C19 whitewashed cottages.
Stamfordham: large Swinburne estate village of many periods.
Stonehaugh: Forestry Commission village of terraced housing for workers in Kielder Forest. 1951 by Dr Thomas Sharp.
Swarland: settlement built 1934–39 to house unemployed craftsmen from Tyneside. 77 brick and rendered houses (of varied types) with community buildings; architect Miss M.P. Reavell.

Nottinghamshire

Bothamsall: late C19 estate housing for Duke of Newcastle (see *Hardwick-in-Clumber*).
Bradmore: early C18 estate village rebuilt (following 1706 fire) by Sir Thomas Parkyns (the "wrestling baronet") to his own designs (also *Costock* and *East Leake*, see *Bunny* below).
Budby: model village built by William Wilkins Jr. for 1st Earl Manvers of Thoresby, c.1807–12. Two storey, stucco cottages with Gothick windows, eaves, porches (others at *Holme Pierrepont, Cotgrave, Radcliffe-on-Trent*).
Bunny: Parkyns' own house, Bunny Hall c. 1717–25, school and almshouses, 1700, old vicarage, c. 1701, home farm (demolished), 1739.
Gonalston: estate village, church rebuilt (1853), smithy with horseshoe-shaped doorway (1854). Further late C19 improvements by Francklin family.
*Hardwick-in-Clumbe*r: late C19 estate village, farm and cottages.
Harworth: colliery village built as garden suburb with central boulevard, Fred Hopkinson of Worksop.
Holbeck: estate village at gates of Welbeck Abbey; much cottage improvement by 6th Duke of Portland, c. 1900, church 1913–16, and at Welbeck (largely by 5th Duke, including about fifty Neo-Tudor lodges).
Kingston-on-Soar: estate village of semi-detached cottages around village green, for Edward Strutt, later Lord Belper, of Kingston Hall (Edward Blore 1842–6).

Moorgreen (Greasley): estate hamlet for 7th Earl Cowper by E.W. Godwin (1872–7), also designer of the Manse (1873) and Cowper's seat, Beauvale House (1871).

(*Perlethorpe:* Manvers estate housing (and half timbered almshouses) sited in parkland surrounding Thoresby Hall, by W.O. Hickson, c 1890; church by Anthony Salvin 1876.)

Sherwood Energy Village (New Ollerton): Energy efficient village conceived in 1994 and now under construction on fomer colliery site, with offices, industry and freehold houses and flats, to meet high ecological and environmental standards.

(*Strelley:* late C18 brick estate cottages for Edge family, built as street after emparking.)

Thrumpton: estate village of gabled brick cottages *c.* 1700–45 for John Emerton of Thrumpton Hall; also more work in C19.

(*Wiseton:* late C18 buildings by owner of Wiseton Hall, Jonathan Acklom, amateur architect.)

Oxfordshire

(*Bletchingdon:* terrace of stone cottages, 1794 for estate of Earl of Anglesey.)

(*Broughton:* Neo-Tudor terraced cottages, 1841, almshouses 1859.)

Burcot: roadside estate cottages. gabled brick, *c.* 1860. Combined church and school, G.G. Scott, 1869.

*Charterville (Minster Lovell): at 300 acres, largest of Feargus O'Connor's National Land Company colonies and third to be set up. 78 small holdings and model cottages, school, all on established pattern.

*Cornwell: largely rebuilt in "stagey" manner by Clough Williams-Ellis, late 1930s, with Village Hall created from former school.

*Great Tew: estate village for Lucius Carey, Viscount Falkland; given early C19 Picturesque treatment and planting, perhaps influenced by J.C. Loudon who managed the estate 1809–11.

Heythrop: village rebuilt by Albert Brassey (son of Thomas, railway magnate), 1870s. School, with schoolhouse (1873) church (1880 A.W. Blomfield).

Middleton Stoney: village much improved *c.* 1820 by Lady Jersey, with allotments, cooperative shop and enlarged schools. Later work included Village Reading Room 1884.

Mixbury: model village created 1874 by order of Court of Chancery.

*Nuneham Courtenay: Lord Harcourt's rebuilt roadside model village of 1760s, replacing Newnham Courtenay, commemorated in Goldsmith's *The Deserted Village*. Harcourt himself designed the 19 double cottages, forge, curate's house and inn.

(*Rotherfield Peppard:* estate of Edward Hermon, cotton magnate; built Wyfold Court, (1872–28, G. Somers Clarke), cottages etc. same date, same architect.)

Rutland

Ashwell: ornamental brick estate cottages and estate buildings for Viscount Downe (see also *Baldersby St James*, N. Yorks.) by William

Butterfield, who restored the church in 1851.

(*Exton:* slate roofed estate cottages, some contemporary with Exton Hall, extended by Henry Roberts (1851–53).)

Hambleton: 1892 estate cottages, Post Office. Early 20th century planned new village; unexecuted.

(*Normanton:* previous village removed in mid 18th century emparking; population moved to Empingham. Rutland Water (made 1970 onwards) stranded the rebuilt church (which had been a feature of the park). New Cottages, plain stone with eaves detail.)

Tinwell: Cecil estate village, cottages with variations on Tudor Revival 1830s to 1850. Smithy with stone horseshoe arch, bakehouse.

Shropshire

Acton Burnell: village has "something of the estate village about it" (*Buildings of England*), with half timbered decoration painted onto Picturesque cottages to match the genuine article.

Atcham: estate village to Attingham (1783, George Steuart, additions by John Nash). Cottages on main road all that was built of Nash's Picturesque scheme *c.* 1800 for 2nd Lord Berwick (drawings in house), designed a decade before *Blaise Hamlet*.

Calverhall: church rebuilt in two stages in 1870s by W. Eden Nesfield for Liverpool banker, John Pemberton Heywood (and then for his widow) of Cloverley Hall, Ightfield (Nesfield 1864–70). Also lychgate *c.* 1878, village hall 1875. Estate cottages with gabled porches, post office, inn and ornamental timber bus shelter.

(*Coalbrookdale* (Telford): some brick C18 workers' terraces close to the Iron Bridge and works of Quaker ironmasters, Abraham Darby I, II and III, eg Carpenters Row, 1780s.)

Harlescott, Chatwood Village: designed on garden city principles, W.G. Green 1925–57 for skilled employees relocated to Shrewsbury from Bolton by Hall Engineering (safe manufacturers). Each garden had 6 fruit trees provided. Only 44 of 124 houses built. (See also *Burton Manor Village*, Stafford). Nearby, Sentinel Gardens, 1920–24, similar development for employees of Sentinel Wagon Works (steam lorry manufacturers); marked by 40 foot water tower for failed district heating system.

Lightmoor (Telford): site of 1980s self built hamlet. Nearby joint venture by English Partnerships (national regeneration agency) and the Bournville Village Trust (providing management). Second phase underway (2007) proposed sustainable mixed community (up to 800 houses), with 25% affordable housing. Centre will include primary school and shops.

(*Quatt:* stone and half-timbered roadside cottages for Wolryche-Whitmore estate, of Dudmaston Hall. Each block of three cottages designed to look like a pair, *c.* 1871.)

Somerset

Barrow Gurney: much of village restored and rebuilt in 1880s by H.M. Gibbs, church rebuilt 1889 by Henry Woodyer.

Blaise Hamlet (Henbury): built 1810–12 by John Nash for John Scandrett Harford, Quaker banker and industrialist. Picturesque cottages, irregularly sited around generous green, for elderly retainers from Blaise Castle estate. Spawned many imitators. National Trust owned.

(*Charleton Horethorne* (Waterloo Crescent) and *Compton Pauncefoot:* unornamented, urban crescents. Built to swell electorate for the Pagets, pre Reform Act.)

Lympsham: owned for a century by rectors and Lords of the Manor, Stephenson father and son, rebuilt church 1820s–40s, rectory, Gothicised cottages and inscribed cross.

Newtown (Milborne Port): built from 1819 by Earl of Darlington to increase his vote.

(*Porlock:* cottages by C.F.A. Voysey (1936) at Anstey Combe, Lord Lovelace's estate.)

Selworthy Green: group of Picturesque cottages for estate pensioners around green, rebuilt by Sir Thomas Acland *c.* 1828 on model of *Blaise Hamlet*. Possibly inspired by P.F. Robinson's *Rural Architecture* (1823), Acland's copy was heavily annotated.

Street: model factory village built around works by philanthropic Quaker leather manufacturers, C. & J. Clark, from 1829. Factory extended 1857 and later (ceased production 1993). Quaker Meeting House 1850, Institute (Crispin Hall) by G.T. Skipper (1894–95) also Bear Inn 1894 (despite the Clark's temperance ideals). Much high quality plain stone housing. Clark family built library, outdoor swimming pool and theatre, emphasised education.

Staffordshire

Barlaston: factory and housing built in park setting for Wedgwoods (formerly of Etruria), Keith Murray 1938–40; rest of village plan curtailed by war.

Burton Manor Village (Stafford): mid 1920s garden village for employees of British Reinforced Concrete (relocated from Bolton) for owners Hall Engineering (see also *Harlescott*, Chatwood Village, Shropshire). 200 houses, church, cinema and school. Architect W.G. Green. Only 70 houses built.

(*Drayton Bassett:* Gothic estate housing, *c.* 1820s -30s, for textile magnate Sir Robert Peel, father of Prime Minister. Peel built industrial housing at *Fazeley*.)

Fallings Park (Wolverhampton): early Co-partnership garden village, set up by Sir Arthur Paget (landowner) from 1907. Tenants were shareholders in enterprise. Radial streets from central circus with small public buildings. Architects, Thomas Adams, Pepler & Blow.

(*Forton:* housing emulating style of Forton Hall, datestone 1665.)

Ilam: Picturesque model village, close to Dovedale, built by Watts Russell family (fortunes made in soap, beer and City finance). Cottages and school, 1854, with steep roofs and tile-handing, possibly by G.G. Scott who rebuilt church, 1855–56. 1840 version of an Eleanor Cross in memory of Mary Watts Russell.

Sandon: estate village of Earls of Harrowby (statesmen); cottages, inn, Village Club, E. Guy Dawber *c.* 1905 in Arts and Crafts style, contemporary with work for 5th Earl on Sandon Park.

Stoke on Trent, Hartshill Road: Herbert Minton, potter, commissioned G.G. Scott to build church (1842), school, parsonage. Group of Gothic patterned brick houses opposite, pre 1858.

(*Tean Hall Mills, Upper Tean:* terraced cottages, with octagonal privies, for employees of Philips, linen tape weavers; mid C18).

(*Wednesfield, Amos Lane:* Board of Guardians' Cottage Homes, 1889–90 by G.H. Stanger; cf. *Styal*, Cheshire).

Weston under Lizard: roadside estate village (after emparking of Weston Park) for the Earls of Bradford. Red brick cottages with rustic porches, some with light Gothic detail.

Suffolk

(*Culford and Culford Heath:* estate building by early C19 squire cum rector, Rev. E.R. Benyon; 1840 mission hall and school. Additions *c.* 1889, by his successor, 5th Earl Cadogan.)

Easton: Picturesque village rebuilt in late C19 by Duke of Hamilton, racing stud was here.

(*Elveden:* late C19 estate cottages, red brick and timbered gables, for Lord Iveagh.)

(*Eriswell:* chapel, 1848, terrace of cottages, 1852, erected on land long owned by the Company for the Propagation of the Gospel in New England and Parts Adjacent.)

Euston: estate village grew up after emparking of Lord Arlington's (later Dukes of Grafton) Euston Hall. Some cottages thatched, some flint walled.

(*Fornham St Genevieve:* 1780s cottages at park gate to replace earlier village.)

(*Newbourn:* 1930 government smallholding scheme for unemployed miners. Small brick cottages with glasshouses and land.)

*Rushbrooke: model village built for Lord Rothschild, Llewelyn-Davies & Weeks, 1955–63. White painted brick, monopitch roofs. Cottages and club-house centred on old well-head.

*Somerleyton: Picturesque model village *c.* 1850 built around a large central green for Samuel Morton Peto (railway magnate and local MP) by John Thomas, inspired by *Blaise Hamlet*. Twenty-eight cottages, school, wooden chapel (demolished late 1970s).

*Thorpeness: resort village built on land belonging to Stuart Ogilvie family. Architects F. Forbes Glennie and W.G. Wilson; cottages, almshouses, inn, church, club house, mere etc., 1910–30s. Plan never fully executed.

Woolverstone: village rebuilt after William Berners' Woolverstone Hall (1776, John Johnson). Victorian cottages, 1869 etc., along roadside.

Surrey

Addlestone: Princess Mary Village Homes for Girls opened 1872 (preceding Barnado's at *Barkingside*, Essex); 17 cottages around green, church, schools, laundry. Demolished 1980.

(*Albury:* group of cottages in village street with immense brick chimneys. Original village destroyed for park, *c.* 1810 (earlier church became disused in 1842). Probable involvement of A.W.N. Pugin who remodelled Albury Park 1846–52 and helped design Irvingite church (1840) for banker and politician Henry Drummond.)

*Blackheath: squatter colony largely rebuilt by Charles Harrison Townsend for W.C. Roberts-Austin and Henry Prescott; pump (1889), church (1892–95), chapel (1901–02), village hall (1896–97) and several detached houses 1896–1907).

(*Brockham:* tile-hung estate cottages in long row, 1871.)

Chipstead: Victorian model village at crossroads, with pond.

(*Dippenhall* (Farnham): eccentric group of nine houses built by Harold Falkner, 1921 to 1963, in "whimsical free Tudor vernacular".)

(*Dormansland:* roughcast terraced cottages for the Ford estate, F.C. Eden, 1920.)

(*Downside* (Cobham): large green surrounded by C19 model cottages, schools (1867).)

*Duxhurst: Lady Henry Somerset's Colony, founded 1895, on 180 acres leased by the British Women's Temperance Association. Grouped Picturesque single storey thatched cottages around green, one, "the Nest", for children, wooden church. All except Lady Somerset's own cottage demolished 1960s. (From 1923 became Princess Marie Louise Village for Gentlefolk and then housed Italian prisoners-of-war in WWII).

East Horsley: village largely remodelled by 1st Earl of Lovelace (Byron's son-in-law), enthusiastic architectural amateur; everything of flint, patterned brick (from his brickworks), often battlements and arrow slit windows; all 1855–67. Similar work in *Ockham.*

(*Merton Park Estate* (LB of Merton): local squire, John Innes, developed estate on lines of Bedford Park; 1870s, H.G. Quartermain.)

(*Newlands Corner* (Harrowhill Copse): group of cheap, experimental cottages designed by Clough Williams-Ellis, Arnold Mitchell and St. Loe Strachey, *c.* 1920).

Ranmore Common: church (1859), schools and rectory, all by G.G. Scott for the builder Thomas Cubitt's son.

(*Shamley Green:* at Lordshill Common, modest cottages built by Nonconformist sect, the Society of Dependents (known as the Cokelers) founded by John Sirgood, *c.* 1850. Chapels elsewhere in Sussex, including *Northchapel*, with shops and housing above for Dependents.)

(*West Clandon:* cottages, 1884 George & Peto, for Onslow estate.)

*Whiteley Village: octagonal symmetrical village for "thrifty" retired members of the agricultural and commercial trades. 225 acres bought in 1911 with William Whiteley's Trust fund. Competition for plan won by Frank Atkinson; architects Reginald Blomfield, Walter Cave, Mervyn

Macartney, Ernest Newton, Aston Webb, Ernest George and Atkinson himself. Brick cottages, communal kitchen, shop and post office, around central open area, wrapped by woods and commonland. Church Walter Tapper, village hall by Webb. 1914–21. Extension by Robert Adam Architects, 2004.

Woodcote Village ("Garden First") (LB of Sutton): garden suburb designed according to William Webb's principles (later published). Business man and horticulturalist, Webb ordained that gardens be laid out before houses built (1901–20).

Sussex

(*Ashburnham:* estate buildings ranging from late Georgian to Victorian.)
Easebourne: Cowdray estate village (as *Cocking,* see *Midhurst* below) with many cottages rebuilt or added in C19. Painted in rich yellow estate "livery".
(*East Lavant:* numerous mid C19 estate cottages.)
(*Eridge:* Picturesque estate cottages near church, only reminder of Eridge Castle, built for the 2nd Earl of Abergavenny in 1787, demolished in the late 1930s.)
(*Fletching:* much half-timbered, late C19 housing for Sheffield estate).
(*Flimwell:* estate cottages for the Goschen family of Seacox (1871, Slater & Carpenter); gabled, Neo-Gothic with half-timbering, barge-boards and tile-hanging.)
(*Goodwood:* among James Wyatt's many estate buildings are late C18 cottages.)
Lindfield: Pelham Place and Little Pelham represent the Quaker William Allen's land colony for distressed labourers on 100 acres, cottages self-built 1823–33. Allen had advanced educational and social ideas; village included school, printing works and workshops.
(*Midhurst:* many Cowdray estate cottages, including by E.C. Lee, tile-hung, late C19.)
Oving: village improved by Miss Woods of Sopwyke, designs by John Elliott (illustrated by Loudon); almshouses and school (1839).
(*Sedlescombe:* Pestalozzi Village at Oaklands by Casson, Conder. Work stopped 1963).
Tillington: Petworth estate village, church rebuilt 1807; almshouses 1840, schools 1835.
(*Walberton* (Stoughton); cottages, drawn by Thomas Little, 1850–1.)

Warwickshire

Bournville (Birmingham): first industrial garden village. 1879 George Cadbury (Quaker cocoa and chocolate manufacturer) relocated factory to rural site, first houses for key workers. 1893 bought 120 acres and developed estate (not just for company employees), architect W. Alexander Harvey. Mortgages were made available to home owners. By 1900, when Bournville Village Trust founded, 313 houses built. Cottage almshouses, schools and community facilities 1890s–1900s. Emphasis on health and outdoor recreation, especially gardening. Enormous influence on city-planning ideas and international Garden City movement. Bournville Village Trust continued to buy land and expand settlement.

Combrook: stone Neo-Tudor estate village for Compton Verney (Willoughby de Broke). Church (1866) and school, John Gibson.

(*Hampton-in-Arden:* row of jettied, pargetted cottages with massive chimney stacks (1868) by Eden Nesfield, architect of Hampton Manor House, *c.* 1870–73.)

Preston-on-Stour: Alscot model estate village for Roberts-West family, gabled red brick housing with diamond-paned windows, 1852, school 1848. (More Alscot housing, 1858–59, *Alderminster* and *Wimpstone*).

(*Radford* (N of Coventry): three storey weavers' houses of 1857 built as model dwellings for workers at Cash's name-tapes factory.)

(*Sherbourne:* mid C19 housing for Ryland estate; church by G.G. Scott 1862–64.)

Walton: estate village for Mordaunts of Walton Hall (G.G. Scott, 1858–62). Polychrome brick cottages (one dated 1867), school.

Wormleighton: Spencer estate village, largely remodelled mid C19. Large Elizabethan style stone cottages with drip moulds, mullioned windows. Post Office, school and teachers house.

Wiltshire

Alderton: estate village built by Joseph Neeld MP (of Grittleton), with gabled cottages, church by J. Thompson (1845), probably responsible for vicarage also. Picturesque school with tower (1844–45). Neeld estate buildings at *Leigh Delamere* included parsonage and almshouses; at *Sevington*, school (1847) and estate cottages with bay windows.

Bowood: village lost during emparking. C19 Neo-Tudor estate village built outside gates with inn, Lansdowne Arms.

(*Britford:* plain grey brick estate cottages, early 1800s, for Longford Castle.)

(*Burcombe:* flint and brick Wilton estate cottages, on main road. See *Netherhampton* below.)

Erlestoke: estate village made Picturesque with architectural ornaments and fragments, perhaps from the house preceding Joshua Smith's Erlestoke Park (1786–91).

(*Fonthill Gifford:* Victorian estate cottages built for Marquess of Westminster)

Hilmarton: sizeable village for Poynder estate; plain stone cottages 1832–35, gabled cottages *c.* 1874–77. Church restored by G.E. Street 1879, school (1851), almshouses (1878).

Little Bedwyn: 1860s patterned brick estate cottages, some gabled. John Birch illustrates those at *Great Bedwyn* in his *Country Architecture* (1874).

(*Netherhampton:* C19 stone cottages for Wilton Estate, Neo-Tudor model farm.)

(*Oare:* cottage terrace, white stucco with giant pilasters and pediment, Clough Williams-Ellis who worked at Oare House 1921, 1925 and built Cold Blow, 1922.)

(*Sandy Lane:* thatched village housing for Spye estate.)

Swindon New Town: rectilinear model industrial village built for railway workers, possibly by Sir Matthew Digby Wyatt, from c. 1850. 243 stone cottages and other amenities erected by 1853. Mechanics Institution (1853–54) by Edward Roberts, school (1845) and lodging-house (1840s). Cambria Place, 1860s housing for Welsh workers with Baptist chapel.

Worcestershire

Great Dodford: the fifth and last Chartist settlement, set up by Feargus O'Connor's renamed National Land Company. Only site close to industrialised areas. 44 single storey cottages and school (c.f. *Snigs End*, Oxon), 36 tenants paid deposits and were chosen by ballot in June 1849. Sold by spring 1850, reverted to conventional smallholdings.

(*Ombersley:* Sandys estate village of various periods; cottages c. 1840, church by Thomas Rickman 1825–29.)

(*Overbury:* late Victorian additions to village, mostly by Norman Shaw (work at Overbury Court, 1895). Village Hall (1895–96), cottage improvements.)

East Riding of Yorkshire

Birdsall: estate village for Willoughby family, Lords Middleton; old village was near church and Birdsall House (remodelled several times, finally 1871–5, Anthony Salvin). Replacement village largely C19 — first the Square, stone and pantile cottages, then school and schoolhouse, 1871, home farm 1868, scattered estate cottages.

Bishop Burton: set around two greens and large pond, whitewashed cottages, embellished by rustic porches and half- timbering, for Hall-Watt family. Late 1880s until 1914.

Escrick: estate village for Thompson family, Lords Wenlock. Emparking after 1781 saw village relocated. Early C20 improvements to existing housing by agent, Claude W. Thompson, for 3rd Lord Wenlock "a beloved and respected Landlord" (nephew of Duke of Westminster, see *Aldford,* etc. Cheshire). Built club house, almshouses and shop, (latter for village Co-operative Society founded by his father).

(*Howsham:* emparking, 1750s–70s; much of village removed leaving ironstone cottages on one side of street.)

Hull Garden Village: model industrial village for Quaker starch manufacturer James Reckitt. 1907 onwards, Percy T. Runton & William E. Barry; by 1913 over 500 houses on site. Many semi-detached, generous gardens with back lanes for access (once for manure, now for cars). Amenities included the Oval, a central green with half-timbered village hall (demolished), also parade of shops and three sets of almshouses.

(*Langton:* stone estate village, cottage datestones from 1814 to 1857; (old) school, 1841.)

Londesborough: of two dates, the bottom street C18 for Lord Burlington, the "father" of English Palladianism, the top street late C19 for Lord Londesborough, pairs of houses and large former estate laundry, now Concert Hall, built for visit of Prince of Wales in 1880.

Settrington: estate village for the Masterman Sykes, mostly rebuilt *c.* 1795–1810.

Sledmere: village cleared from park in two stages, 1750 and 1770s by Sykes family; present village largely created by Sir Tatton Sykes II, Victorian landowner and most active builder of his family. School and schoolhouse (1874–75 by G.E. Street), cottage pairs, (mid 1870s, John Birch) also post office and other estate buildings by Birch, 1890s.

South Dalton: village closed up by Hotham family in early C19; built estate housing in 1870s, almshouses in 1874 and half-timbered reading room in 1896.

Sunk Island: Crown property, with much C19 work by S.S. Teulon — farmhouses, cottages, school and schoolhouse (1857). From 1917, part of area taken for resettlement of soldiers on small holdings; Crown Colony consisted of 20 pairs of cottages, designer Gordon Allen.

Thixendale: Tatton Sykes (see *Sledmere*) built church, school, vicarage (1860s–76, G.E. Street). The same at *Wansford* where there are remnants of terraced cottages for Christopher Sykes's 1789 carpet works.

Warter: estate village belonging to Lords Muncaster, then Hull shipping magnate Charles Wilson (Lord Nunburnholme), rebuilding began 1858. After 1879, Smith & Brodrick employed, more decorated cottages and village shop. Thatched cottages of 1930.

West Ella: village transformed by Richard Sykes on inheriting estate in 1832 until his death in 1870. Picturesque whitewashed cottages with Gothic details.

North Riding of Yorkshire

*Baldersby St James: complete village group, church, lychgate, school, vicarage and cottages, all in red brick Gothic with an unusual touch of relaxed Georgian, too, built by William Butterfield for 7th Viscount Downe, 1856–58. Some estate cottages also at *Baldersby*.

Brandsby: church and Brandsby Hall built by Thomas Atkinson, *c.* 1767 for Cholmeley estate, also rows of estate housing, replacing earlier village lost by emparking.

Bulmer: dignified Castle Howard estate housing.

Coneysthorpe: main estate village for Castle Howard, oblong green with cottages on three sides. Church, 1835. Two versions of plan for circular model village drawn by George London *c.* 1699 to replace Henderskelfe, which lay within new park. Earliest scheme for an architecturally sophisticated planned village (unexecuted).

East Witton: estate village for Earl of Ailesbury. Cottages around large green, vicarage, church (H.H. Seward), all *c.* 1809.

Hackness: estate village for Hackness Hall (1791, Peter Atkinson) for Lord Derwent, expanded in mid C19, school, post office, agent's house.

(*Kirby Misperton:* estate housing dating from 1868–77.)

(*Newby Wiske:* C18 and C19 estate housing.)

New Earswick (York): model industrial village near cocoa works. Site purchased by Joseph Rowntree 1902, building started 1903. Joseph Rowntree Village Trust founded 1904 to pursue project. Planned by Raymond Unwin and Barry Parker; cottages with gardens, simple, light, informally grouped. Folk Hall (1907), managed by village council school, 1912. Village not aimed solely at Rowntree company employees. The Joseph Rowntree Housing Trust actively continues work begun over a century ago. Model "Continuing Care Retirement Community", Hartrigg Oaks, opened on 21 acres at New Earswick in 1998.

North Ormesby: planned from 1860 on grid system. Later absorbed by Middlesbrough.

Ripley: model stone village built at gates of castle by Ingilby family, *c.* 1780–1860; modest variants on Neo-Tudor detail. Grandiose Hôtel de Ville, 1854 (c.f. gatehouse to castle, inscribed "Parlez au Suisse")

(*Rosedale:* C19 estate housing, school 1822, church by Vulliamy 1839.)

East Rounton: village developed for industrialist family, Lowthian Bells (amongst whom Gertrude Bell), around Rounton Grange (Philip Webb, 1872–76), school (1876, Webb) and later work by George Jack, Village Hall, 1906.

Thirkleby: Frankland-Russell estate village, work by Edward Lamb including church (1850).

Wilton: estate owned by Lowthers, became resident landlords from 1802. Begun possibly by Robert Smirke (Wilton Castle, *c.* 1810); extended *c.* 1850, including school and schoolhouse.

West Riding of Yorkshire

Akroydon (Boothtown, Halifax); founded by Edward Akroyd of Haley Hill Mills, 1859 (see *Copley,* below). G.G. Scott plan, church (1856–59). 350 houses by W.H. Crossland, 1861–68; stone, gas lit, in rows around square, simple Gothic Revival detail (different sizes mingled workers and supervisors), large central green, market cross, penny bank, cooperative shops. Akroyd's expenditure initially underwritten by Halifax Permanent Building Society.

(*Carlton-in-Balne:* gabled brick estate cottages by J.F. Bentley, who worked on Carlton Towers for Lord Beaumont, *c.* 1875.)

Copley: model mill village for Edward Akroyd. Copley Mill 1847 onwards; nearby in rural location, built 112 back-to-back cottages, 1849–53. Second phase *c.* 1865 two terraces (24 houses) built as "throughs" with gas lighting. Horticultural society to encourage gardening.

(*Elsecar:* row of 1799 mineworkers' cottages by John Carr for estate of Earls Fitzwilliam (of Wentworth Woodhouse); also Reform Row.)

(*Ferham Estate* (Rotherham): laid out by William Flockton, *c.* 1840.)

*Fulneck (Pudsey): first Moravian settlement in England. Land given to community in 1742, soon after built chapel and adjoining houses for single brethren and sisters; after 1755, more houses (one for widows), school added. B.H. Latrobe's birthplace.

*Harewood: rebuilt by Edwin Lascelles at gate of Harewood House, designs by John Carr 1760. Terraced houses, classical forms and varied height (some for professional classes, doctor, agent etc.). Inn (Harewood Arms), ribbon factory (converted to cottages later). Church remained in park.

Lydgate, Robinwood Terrace (Todmorden): Robinwood Mill (1835, William Fairbairn) bought by philanthropic cotton manufacturers, Fielden Brothers, 1843. John Fielden MP born Quaker, became radical Unitarian and Chartist sympathiser, architect of Ten Hour Act; built terraced houses and manager's house. Piped water, three heated bedrooms.

(*Penistone (Cubley Garden Village):* designed by Herbert Baker for steelworkers. 1921–22, gabled grouped cottages, concrete construction.)

*Saltaire (Shipley): Sir Titus Salt's creation, most ambitious of all model industrial villages. Italianate mill for alpaca worsted cloth, 1853 William Fairbairn; by 1860, 450 cottages built by Lockwood & Mawson and laid out on grid, larger houses for foremen etc. set on ends of terraces. Piped water, also communal wash-houses and drying rooms, public baths. Riverside park, cricket, croquet and bowling green, full range of amenities, Institute, almshouses, chapel. By Salt's death (1876), 820 houses built.

*West Hill Park (Halifax): competition winning model estate (by Paull & Aycliffe, 1864) for Crossleys, carpet manufacturers of Dean Clough Mills. Finance underwritten by Halifax Permanent Building Society. Stipulated no houses to be "back-to-back", emphasised ventilation, cavity wall construction, more bedrooms (to segregate male and female children), more privacy (entrance hallway), earth on (private) privy roofs for extra garden space.

(*Whitwood:* terrace of miners' cottages and Institute (later Rising Sun Inn), 1905, C.F.A. Voysey for Briggs Colliery).

(*Wincobank* (Sheffield): result of model cottage exhibition, 1907, planned by W. Alex Harvey (of *Bournville*) and A. McKewan.)

Woodlands (Doncaster): large colliery village for Brodsworth Main Colliery Co., 1907–12; planned by Percy B. Houfton, effective use of landscape and mature trees. Simple white-washed, rendered cottages.

Scotland

Aberdeen & Moray

Archiestown (originally called Ballintomb): founded by Sir Archibald Grant (see *Monymusk*) in 1761, to house weavers. Partly burned in 1783. Still consists of little more than houses along a single street, with attractive, tree-lined central square.

Findhorn: community founded in 1962 based upon notion of spiritual retreat; Findhorn Foundation set up 1972. Since 1981 a growing eco-village, with facilities and employment on site, houses and flats for residents and thousands of annual visitors.

Fochabers: estate village built to replace village displaced for an extension to 4th Duke of Gordon's castle. Laid out 1776 by John Baxter, William Adam's mason, around large market square; church 1798 by Baxter.

Monymusk: rebuilt by Sir Archibald Grant, lawyer, MP and agricultural reformer who was appointed his father's estate factor in 1716, aged 20. Set up lint mill (1749), lapidary workshop for polishing granite and greatly increased employment. Further rebuilding 1826 around church, new school; more late C19, early C20.

Argyll & Bute

Bowmore (Islay): developed from 1768 by Daniel Campbell II to replace razed village of Kilarrow. Gridiron plan focused on Main Street, by 1790s 500 residents. Stone built, slate roofed houses. Parish church (1767 Thomas Sparrow).

Ellenabeich and *Easdale:* pair of slate workers' villages, twin harbours c. 1826. Rows of single storeyed cottages.

Furnace: 1788 planned village drawn up by George Langlands, for Craleckan Ironworks (1754 onwards). Nearby, on Loch Fyne, *Kenmore* village, two parallel cottage rows for fishermen, 1771–72, by surveyor William Douglas for 5th Duke of Argyll.

Kerrycroy (Bute): hamlet laid out from 1803 by the 2nd Marquess of Bute's wife at north gates of Mount Stuart House.

*Tobermory (Mull): founded 1787 by British Fisheries Society (see also *Ullapool, Lochbay, Pultneytown*), Governor 5th Duke of Argyll, supervised by his agent James Maxwell who drew up master plan for new upper "town" in 1790, still in evidence despite later expansion with building of Caledonian Canal.

Ayrshire & Arran

*Catrine: Claud Alexander of Ballochmyle (former East India company paymaster) and David Dale built mill in 1786 (demolished). Provided

housing, workers' smallholdings, built school and provided medical care and sickness payments. James Finlay & Co bought works in 1801 (see also *Deanston*, Stirling).

Straiton: main road village originally *c.* 1760 built for Thomas, Earl of Cassilis. Rebuilt *c.* 1900 by Hunter Blair family of Blaiquhan Castle (1824).

Borders

(*Abbey St Bathan:* Turnbull estate housing, mid C19 cottages forming a square).

(*Eddleston:* rows of one and two-storey cottages built for Black Barony estate, 1780).

Foulden: late C18, early C19 terrace improved 1850–52 "in imitation of English cottages", with bay windows and brick ornament, by John Lessels (schoolroom, 1865) for John Wilkie of Foulden House.

Galashiels: Lucy Sanderson Cottage Homes, sheltered housing for retired Sanderson mill workers. Site of 7 acres, 1930–33 by Mears & Carus-Wilson. Cottages grouped around green, gabled hall (with clock tower and interior murals), rest house, wash house and laundry.

Greenlaw: planned as county town of Berwickshire, never grew. Mid C18 regulations laid down by 3rd Earl of Marchmont ordained all new housing be two storeyed.

(*Hawick:* early industrial housing for millworkers *c.* 1800 Slitrig Crescent. Also *Wellogate*, post 1880s development for Hawick Working Men's Building & Investment Company, with various house types.)

Newcastleton: laid out from 1793 by 3rd Duke of Buccleuch to his own (gridiron) plan, to house handloom weavers; by 1800, over 200 houses built by tenants, held on 99 year leases.

(*Peebles: Elliot's Park*, cottage scheme built on garden suburb principles by J.D. Cairns for the Scottish Veterans Garden City Association. Nearby, *c.* 1934 Mears & Carus-Wilson scheme on Connor Street for Association for the Preservation of Rural Scotland.)

Sinclairshill: early C19 cottages for the Bonars of Kimmergame House, made Picturesque in mid century with ornament, gables, porches and smithy with horseshoe motif. Old schoolhouse *c.* 1825, more housing around mill.

Sprouston: cottages, schoolroom and master's house around green, mid C19, smithy 1876.

Swinton: estate village enlarged by Lord Swinton in 1799, then cottages remodelled and roofs changed from thatch to slate in late C19, primary school 1876, former library and reading room set up post 1888.

Walkerburn: grew from 1855 onward, around Ballantyne's Tweedvale Mill (1859), into industrial settlement. Sir Henry Ballantyne, chairman of Royal Commission on industrial housing in Scotland (Ballantyne Report, 1917) inspired Park Avenue, 1919 onwards, garden city development.

Dumfries & Galloway

(*Beattock:* mid C19 estate housing with bargeboards and deep eaves.)

*Brydekirk: 1800 planned village, on gridiron pattern, set up by Colonel Dirom of Mount Annan, but only Bridge Street followed his outline.

Carronbridge: early to mid C19 estate village, school 1844, several outlying architect designed farmhouses and steadings of same period, all for Nithsdale estate of Dukes of Buccleuch & Queensbury.

Cummertrees: Queensberry Terrace (*c.* 1900, F.J.C. Carruthers) "piece of seaside fun" (*Buildings of Scotland*), first phase of (failed) holiday village projected by General Brook of Kinmouth.

Eastriggs: munitions village for workers at cordite factory built 1916–18, plan by Raymond Unwin. Church (1917, C.M. Crickmer). *Gretna* was an enlarged version.

Gatehouse of Fleet: 1760s planned village for James Murray of Broughton. Additional industry brought workers' housing, especially after cotton mill built 1785.

Parton: Picturesque estate hamlet, one and a half storey cottages, octagonal communal lavatory, laundry 1901 for B. Rigby Murry of Parton House (demolished). Village Hall 1908 bears motto *floreat partona.*

Fife

Coaltown of Wemyss: estate village for Wemyss Castle, after 1890 became Picturesque miners' settlement, some with rustic tree trunk porches. Primary school (1896–97, Alexander Tod), Miners' Welfare Institute and war memorial (1924–25, A. Stewart Tod).

Methil: miners' housing as garden village, for Wemyss Coal Co. (1924–26, A. Stewart Tod).

Highlands & Islands

Beauly: planned around a central square by the Frasers of Lovat, from *c.* 1805. Further Victorian estate building.

*Brora: coal mines reopened in 1811 by Elizabeth, Countess of Sutherland; "Brora New Town" on gridiron plan 1814; sluggish growth until railway arrived, 1871.

Grantown-on-Spey: founded by Sir Ludovick Grant 1765; laid out around elongated square.

*Helmsdale: laid out from 1818 by Countess of Sutherland (see Brora) as fishing port. She had already (in 1805) planned *Golspie*, close to Dunrobin Castle, the Sutherlands' seat, for fishermen and others.

Kingussie: laid out from 1799 on land which had belonged to Duke of Gordon.

Kyleakin: 1810 foundation, designed by James Gillespie Graham, on urban pattern of crescents and formal layout. Failed.

Portree: village planned by Sir Alexander Macdonald from 1739; by 1763,

313

21 houses with an acre each constituted Sir James Macdonald's intended "compleat City". Thomas Telford's harbour 1818–20 encouraged growth into small town.

Strathpeffer: planned as spa, based on its sulphurated waters, from 1800 onwards. Sporadic expansion after George Devey's plan of 1860.

Tomich: picturesque gabled model village built to rehouse (reluctantly) crofters on Lord Tweedmouth's Guisachan estate, bought in 1854.

*Ullapool: early British Fishery Society foundation, see also *Tobermory*, *Lochbay* (1788 on) and *Pultneytown* (1803 on, plan Thomas Telford, rapid expansion to town). Grid plan (1788); collapse of herring industry soon stymied growth. Revival from mid C19.

Lanark & Renfrew

Blantyre (Low Blantyre): "neat and cleanly little village" on the Clyde, founded 1785 around cotton works of David Dale and James Monteith. Second mill built 1791, then dyeworks in 1806. Laid out formally. By the 1850s "quite a model of a manufacturing village; everything in apple-pie order" with chapel (used as schoolhouse in the week), laundry and drying green.

*Eaglesham: founded 1769 by Boswell's friend, Alexander, 10th Earl of Eglinton, for workers at his cotton manufactory. Two rows of houses, laid out in a proprietorial figure "A" to either side of central stream with generous green (originally bleach grounds), church 1788. Factory burned down 1876.

*New Lanark: mills founded 1783 by David Dale, in 1800 his son-in-law Robert Owen became manager. Terraced tenements around mill built late 1798 onwards. Owen built model amenities to encourage his community of enlightened workers and their children; nursery, 1809, Institute 1816, school, 1817. Now World Heritage Site.

*Thornliebank: village built to house textile workers at linen, then calico printing and dyeing business, bought by John Crum (friend of David Dale of New Lanark); works expanded enormously in C19. Gas, water, baths, gardens and community hall; described having "aspect of cheerfulness and prosperity'.

Lothian

*Dirleton: Picturesque estate village, housing of various dates around large village green, church remodelled 1836.

*Gifford: "first and grandest estate village" of Lothian, built for the Marquesses of Tweeddale of Yester House (1701 onwards, James Smith) and named after Giffords, Norman builders of original Yester Castle. Boundaries adjusted 1708–10, church completed 1710, J. Smith. Small holdings and cottages around large green — laid out more formally in C19. Tweeddales also introduced industries, tiles (for land drains), linen and paper-making.

Ormiston: from 1735 planned by John Cockburn as industrial and market centre, set regulations for housing, planted trees. Sold on to Earl of Hopetoun 1747, industries faded out but remained estate village for agricultural workers.

Ratho: on Union Canal (1822) close to John Bonar's Ratho Park (1824 William Burn); schoolhouse 1840, New Inn and early C19 cottages.

Tyninghame: "the very model of an estate village" (*Buildings of Scotland*). Built for the Earls of Haddington, largely by Thomas Hannan, mason; school 1836, widows' row 1841, more cottages dated 1854, post office etc.

Perth & Kinross

Baledgarno: C18 village for Kinnaird family's Rossie Priory estate; housing and school.

Birnam: Atholl estate village linked to Dunkeld by Thomas Telford bridge. Early Victorian.

(*Blair Atholl: Garryside Cottage Community*, cottages and hotel, 1856 by R. & R. Dickson.)

Fortingall: Garth Castle estate purchased by Sir Donald Currie (founder of the Union and Castle shipping line), 1880. Thatched village built 1890 onwards by pioneer Scottish Arts and Crafts architect J.M. Maclaren with Dunn & Watson.

Gartmore: estate village for Gartmore House, built by William Adam for the Graham family, bought by Cayzers c.1900.

Inchture: rebuilt in C19 when road moved. Neo-Tudor cottages, hotel and church for Rossie Priory estate (see *Baledgarno*, above).

Kenmore: village rebuilt late C18 by 3rd Earl of Breadalbane, a Campbell. When Taymouth Castle was extended in 1842, Kenmore given Picturesque remodelling. Village round central square, with post office, reading rooms and church. Castellated gateway for Taymouth Castle.

Scone (formerly New Scone): estate village and church rebuilt by the 3rd Earl of Mansfield, 1805, who had razed the old village, too close to Scone Palace (1802, William Atkinson). Village became a suburb of Perth.

Stanley: in 1784 4th Duke of Atholl contacted Sir Richard Arkwright and advanced £2,000 towards an industrial village for textile workers at Bell Mill (1787), designed by Arkwright. By 1795, village housed 350. Two more cotton mills built and working by c. 1800. The Duke's factor helped design tunnels for water system as well as gridiron layout of village, consisting of neat two-storeyed houses of stone and brick.

Stirling & central Scotland

(*Callander:* Veterans' Houses (1919–20, Stewart & Paterson) fragment of unbuilt garden village which was to centre around a farm, greenhouses, workshops and community hall.)

Deanston: cotton mill built 1785 by the Buchanans to Arkwright's design, taken over (after serious fire) by James Finlay & Co, 1808. Parts of weaving shed survive in modern distillery. Workers' housing in flatted two storey cottages, mostly early C19.

Dunmore: stone, Neo-Tudor estate village begun *c.* 1840, 3–sided plan with 4th side open to River Forth. At the centre, Gothic Revival pump inscribed "the school and village of Dunmore together with this well built by Catherine Herbert Countess of Dunmore were completed A.D. 1879." Former forge with stone horseshoe doorway.

Kennet: single storey miners' hamlet, originally roofed in dark blue pantiles, built *c.* 1800.

Muirhouses: estate village built by Admiral Sir James Johnstone Hope of Carriden; school, 1866, cottages mid C19.

Wales

Caernarvonshire

Llandwrog: estate village for Glynllifon, house rebuilt for Lord Newborough (Wynn) after 1836 fire. Church (1860 Henry Kennedy), Gothic Revival stone cottages, probably contemporary.

Llandygai/Llandegai: estate village for Penrhyn Castle built near existing parish church. Picturesque Tudor style stone cottages with bargeboards. Also mid C19 housing for slate quarry workers at Bethesda, and elsewhere on Penrhyn estate.

*Tremadoc: found by William Madocks (Tre = town) on poor land bought 1798. Village founded c. 1805. Formal plan published by Loudon who advised on landscape. Central square with market hall, school and stone housing, all early C19.

Carmarthenshire

Golden Grove/ Gelli Aur: estate village for 1st Earl of Cawdor (minerals magnate); mansion built by Jeffrey Wyatville, 1826–34; church (G.G. Scott, 1849) school (Henry Ashton 1848) almshouses (Wyatville, c. 1840) and stone Neo-Tudor cottages.

Ceredigion

Haford: estate of Thomas Johnes bought by 4th Duke of Newcastle 1833. School (1837–39) and cottages in *Cwmystwyth.*

Llandygwydd: village for Blaenpant and Penylan estates, mid C19 Picturesque. Schoolrooms 1846, 1856 (latter became parish church after demolition), other estate buildings and cottages.

Llanerchaeron: house built by John Nash c. 1793–95 for Col. William Lewis, scattered estate cottages including at least one by Nash.

Tresaith: 1852 J.S. Harford proposed new resort, architect R.K. Penson. Unexecuted.

Tre Taliesin: lead mines, terraced housing 1860s–70s, schools 1856, 1873.

Clwyd (Denbigh, Flint)

Bersham: Plas Power estate village, church (1873, John Gibson), estate cottages (1859, Gibson) but also site of Wilkinson brothers' C18 ironworks (also as *Brymbo*, workers' cottages, 1815) with remains of single storey workers' barracks (1775) and other buildings including early C19 cottages. Production ended 1820s.

317

(*Chirk:* Halton Low Barracks and Halton High Barracks, late C18 or early C19 miners' back to back housing.)

*Marford: Gothick village for the Boscawen family's Trevalyn estate. Some were thatched, some of pisé (mud), ogee windows with cast-iron casements, brick dentil courses: building in progress 1813–15. More similar cottages beyond village centre. John Boydell, George Boscawen's agent (and nephew of engraver) possibly responsible.

Glamorgan

Butetown (Rhymney): unfinished model village for workers at Union Iron Company, *c.* 1802–04, apparently on initiative of works' manager R. Johnson. Handsome two storey classical stone terraces, central section rising to three storeys (perhaps lodgings for single men) set in three parallel rows (with foundations of a fourth). 2nd Marquess of Bute bought company in mid 1820s and built Egyptian-style works 1828 (demolished).

(*Gilfach Goch:* 1910–14 first work by Welsh Garden Cities Ltd.; *Fernhill Garden Village*, Abercwmboi followed, 1913 on, W. Beddoe Rees.)

(*Glyn-Cory Garden Village* (or Wyndham Park): set up by John and Reginald Cory, coal magnates, from 1909. Amphitheatre plan by Thomas Adams, landscape consultant T.H. Mawson. Only 22 of the 1,000 houses built by 1914.)

(*Mayhill* (Townhill, Swansea): site of 1910 South Wales Cottage Exhibition, with prototype cottages set onto a plan much influenced by Raymond Unwin.)

Melingriffith (Whitchurch): major tinplate works, founded 1760 and *c.* 1800 taken over by Harfords of Bristol (see *Blaise*, Somerset) who set up school (1807), provided medical care, friendly society and built two ranges of split level terraced housing (demolished).

Merthyr Mawr: estate village improved at various dates, for Merthyr Mawr House (1806–08, Henry Wood of Bath) for lawyer, Sir John Nicholl.

Rhiwbina Garden Village (Cardiff): 1912 Raymond Unwin plan for Cardiff Workers' Cooperative Garden Village Society Ltd.. First phase by A.H. Mottram 1912–13. Some set around a green; village continued to develop to early 1920s. Largely unspoiled.

Treherbert: formally planned mining village, largely built in 1870s, on the estate of Marquess of Bute. Welsh Baptist chapel, 1870; English Baptist chapel, 1873.

Gwent/Monmouthshire

*Blackwood: John Hodder Moggridge of Woodfield Park, colliery and landowner and admirer of Robert Owen, set up colony for miners, 1820. Initially to be called Tremoggridge (Moggridge Town). Leased plots to encourage them to build own houses and cultivate land. Provided shops,

workshops school and market house. Further similar colonies nearby at *Ynysddu* and Trelyn (renamed *Fleur-de-Lys*). By 1829 the combined population of these villages was 2000.

Hardwick Village (Chepstow): built for shipyard workers according to modern principles (the approach road is, tellingly, called Garden City Way), *c.* 1915–19 by Dunn, Watson & Curtis. Gabled housing in small groups.

Llanover (Tre Elidyr): part of an existing estate village (owned by Sir Benjamin Hall, later Lord Llanover, of Big Ben fame). Extended in early C20 to celebrate Lady Llanover's Victorian campaign to revive Welsh language and harp playing. Built *c.* 1925 for Lord Treowen by Arts and Crafts architect Alfred H. Powell. Welsh school inscribed "Ysgol, Haddwch Gwlad" (Schooling, Beauty, Country), war memorial, cluster of rendered, slate roofed cottages around a green.

Llanwern: village institute and cottages built 1906–13 by Oswald P. Milne (Lutyens's assistant) for Lord Rhondda of Llanwern Park.

Oakdale: 1910–11 competition held for a model village for miners at Oakdale Colliery but Oakdale as built was designed by architect brother-in-law of the company's managing director, A.F. Webb. Very symmetrical formalised plan on garden city lines.

Merioneth

Maentwrog: village rebuilt *c.* 1830 for William Oakley, slate magnate. Stone cottages with rustic porches, lychgate incorporating clock.

Morriston: built on regular plan, *c.* 1768, by W. Edwards for Sir John Morris, colliery and copper workers.

Penrhyndeudraeth: similar to *Tremadoc*, neat plan by brother of Madocks' agent.

(*Pentrebach:* The Triangle: three terraces of two-storey cottages around green, 1840–52. Demolished 1970s.)

**Portmeirion:* resort village founded and built by Clough Williams-Ellis in 1920s. Picturesque mixture of colour-washed new and reconstructed Italianate cottages clustered on steep site, design gives emphasis to silhouette and reflection over bay.

Pembroke

(*Newchapel/Capel Newydd:* estate work for Saunders-Davies family of Pentre. Also at *Boncath*, 1885 cottage row by George Morgan for Fanny Saunders-Davies.)

Powys

Berriew: village restored in 1880s for Vaynor estate, with plenty of Picturesque trim, bargeboards and ornate chimneys.

Elan Village: built 1906–09 above the new reservoir for maintenance staff; stone cottages along river valley, school slightly above. Architects Buckland, Haywood & Farmer. (Earlier timber built settlement, frontier style, for army of navvies (and families) working on first dam, 1890s to 1904.)

(*Tregynon:* innovatory estate work for 4th Lord Sudeley at Gregynog estate in 1870s; cottages, school, schoolmaster's house and farmhouses of concrete, but without reinforcement.)

Ireland

Antrim

Bessbrook: Quaker industrial settlement, founded 1846 by J.G. Richardson, textile manufacturer. Emphasis on education and recreation; cottages with gardens around two large squares.

Cushendun: resort village built for Lord Cushendun, (1912–25 Clough Williams-Ellis).

Gracehill: Moravian settlement, founded by John Cennick and Benjamin Latrobe before 1755 and laid out around the church (1765), houses for single brethren and sisters, schools, inn grouped around square and burial ground. (First designated Conservation Area in Northern Ireland.)

Armagh

Moy: 1760s estate village built by 1st Earl of Charlemont, around long narrow square.

Carlow

Bagenalstown (modern Muinebheag): late C18 foundation ("New Versailles") by Sir Walter Bagenal of Dunleckney Manor. Grid layout.

Clare

Rahaline: landowner John Scott Vandeleur rented 600 acres to cooperative community, managed by Owenite from Lancashire, Thomas Craig. Built cottages, school, library. Lasted just two years; Vandeleur gambled away the land in 1833 and fled. Nevertheless, members declared their "contentment, peace and happiness... under the arrangements introduced by Mr. Vandeleur and Mr Craig and which through no fault of the Association was now at an end.'

Down

Seaforde: Colonel Forde rebuilt his mansion in the family demesne, 1819. Cottages, smith, shop and almshouse combining courthouse (1828) followed.

Kildare

Ballitore: founded by Yorkshire Quaker, Abraham Shackleton, school 1726. Burial ground opened c. 1745; existing Meeting House c. 1770; village expanded around main square, with Market House c. 1770.

Johnstown: founded by Bourke family, Earls of Mayo, of Palmerstown demesne and improved in early C19. Described as "peculiarly neat" with an inn and girls' school, founded by the Countess of Mayo. Also flour mills.

Prosperous: c. 1780 Robert Brooke established "Manchester Mills" for cotton and machinery manufacture and built workers' housing, with "the flattering prospect of success... the town rather prematurely derived its name" (Lewis); by 1786 it was failing.

Robertstown: settlement on Grand Canal, with large hotel (*c.* 1800), cottages.

Kilkenny

Inistioge: laid out around square by Tighe family of Woodstock.

Laois

Abbeyleix: built after 1770 by 2nd Viscount de Vesci (Vesey) who razed the previous settlement. Established around textile mills.

Stradbally: rebuilt into substantial late C18 settlement by Cosby family (who also founded *Timahoe*). Plan was for six-pointed star, with circular market house and ruin as focal point; not built in this form.

Limerick

*Adare: estate village made Picturesque by the 2nd Earl and Countess of Dunraven, early 1800s, cottages with thatch, trelliswork and rustic ornament. Further early 20th century work by Detmar Blow.

Mayo

*Achill Island: Rev. Nangle's failed attempt to assure conversion by building an improved settlement, 1830s.

*Westport: original plan by James Wyatt *c.* 1780 for 1st Marquess of Sligo. Focal point the Mall.

North Leinster

Ardagh: Picturesque Victorian model village, (1862–63, J. Rawson Carroll) a memorial to Sir George Fetherston erected by his nephew and heir. Grouped around triangular green, mostly detached cottages, steep roofs with gables, bargeboards, ornamental chimneys and mullioned windows. 1863 clock tower marks Sir George Fetherston's "life-long devotion to the moral and social improvement of his tenantry".

Castlebellingham: Picturesque Bellingham estate village around green; Widows' houses 1826–30, cottage group, half timbered, oriel windows with lattice panes (William Vitruvius Morrison?), Presbyterian meeting house 1840.

Castlepollard: improved by two separate landowners, Pollards of Kinturk House (extended 1821, C.R. Cockerell) and Earls of Longford of Tullynally Castle. Estate village in Regency style, houses around green with fanlights, sash windows and bracketed eaves.

Collon: estate village developed by Foster family, statesmen and churchmen, whose Collon House stands at crossroads in the centre. Estate housing early C19, two-storey with bargeboards and porches.

Dunleer: ambitious village improvements around two interlocking crescents, planned by Richard Bellew of Barmeath (1830s–40s, William Deane Butler). Scheme unexecuted.

*Edgeworthstown: considerable C18 improvements by the Edgeworths whose patronage was "unambitious'; row of two-storey houses, market house (1829, James Bell).

Moynalty: estate village built by John Farrell of Moynalty Lodge (1820s), cottages colour-washed with dormer windows, 1826–37.

Slane: formal estate village centred on four large houses "the Square" (actually octagonal) at crossroads, laid out by Conyngham family 1760s onwards. Two streets of terraced two-storeyed houses, limestone or render.

*Tyrellspass: Rochfort estate village of C18 and C19. Village green and crescent, consisting of school, courthouse (both of the 1820s), parish church and two storey houses (completed 1818) laid out by Jane, Countess of Belvedere (c.f. *Dunleer*, above).

North West Ulster

Burton Port: harbour and fishing village developed in tandem with *Rutland Island* (below). Hotel and C18 grain store survived.

Rutland Island: 1783 fishing company supported by Marquess Conyngham, grant from Irish Parliament to develop. Ten years later buried in sand dunes, ruins of housing still evident.

Sion Mills: model industrial settlement around linen spinning mill, exhibiting "a fine moral system". Developed by Herdmans of Belfast from 1835 onwards; most existing housing later.

Offaly

Tullamore: village (now town) set up by the Earls of Charleville, largely rebuilt after fire in 1785 caused by hot air balloon crash. Market House, 1789.

Roscommon

Strokestown: grandiose plan based upon 2nd Lord Hartland's wish for the village street of his foundation to emulate the thoroughfares of Vienna.

Sligo

Ballymote: single street village built by Sir Robert Gore Booth of Lissadell House, C19 resident landlord and improver.

Tipperary

New Birmingham: "town" founded 1801 by Sir Vere Hunt to attract English manufacturers who would initially live rent-free and benefit from unexploited resources of local coal. By 1817 it had foundered (Hunt died 1818).

Waterford

Curraghmore: Marquess of Waterford's desmesne with ranges of cottages, c. 1860, for estate employees.

*New Geneva: a late C18 scheme to bring Swiss skilled tradesmen to Ireland; 2000 acres offered and substantial financial backing (about £55,000) from English parliament and others. Circular fortified town planned.

*Portlaw: model industrial settlement around cotton mills, founded by

Quaker, David Williamson, from 1825. Factory doubled in late 1830s, population over 3,500 by 1841. 1850s–60s village replanned for Joseph Malcolmson by John Skipton Mulvany; formal axial layout centred on the Square. 50 two-storey and 250 single-storey houses, all uniform; rubble built with distinctive "Portlaw" roofs of tarred calico. Ornamental bargeboards around eaves. Health and morals kept in check with dispensaries, various denominations of places of worship and temperance. Business failed in 1870s.

Villierstown: C18 settlement built by John Villiers, 1st Earl of Grandison for linen workers; village improved by Villiers Stuart family.

Wicklow

Blessington: village founded by Michael Boyle (last ecclesiastical Chancellor of Ireland), 1667; later improved by Downshire estate, after 1778. Simple stone vernacular cottages, inscribed drinking fountain. Typical main road estate village.

Coollattin: estate owned by Fitzwilliam family (of Wentworth, Yorkshire); village improved and rebuilt mid C19.

Enniskerry: estate village for Powerscourt; improved by the Londonderry family, early 19th century cottages and school (1818), later cottages in Tudor revival style, mid C19, including smithy with horseshoe arch.

Stratford-on-Slaney: Edward Stratford, 2nd Earl of Aldborough (connected with *New Geneva*, see above) founded model village for agricultural and textile workers, Protestants brought from Paisley. Failed.

Bibliography (revised)

Henry **Acland**, *Health in the Village*, 1884; *Health, Work and Play*, 1856.

Maurice B. **Adams**, *Modern Cottage Architecture*, London, 1904.

Malcolm **Airs**, "Good & Not Expensive...: Lord Harcourt's Nuneham Courtenay", *Architectural History*, vol. 44, 2001.

Gordon **Allen**, *The Cheap Cottage and Small House*, London, 1919.

W.H.G. **Armytage**, *Heavens Below*, London, 1961.

W. **Ashworth**, *The Genesis of Modern British Town Planning*, London, 1954; "British Industrial Villages in the 19th century", The *Economic History Review*, 2nd series, Vol. 3.

M.W. **Barley**, *The English Farmhouse and Cottage*, London, 1961; *The House and Home*, London, 1963.

Mavis **Batey**, "Nuneham Courtenay", reprinted from *Oxoniensia*, 33, 1968.

Jonathan **Beecher**, *Charles Fourier: the Visionary and his World*, Berkeley & Los Angeles, 1986.

Colin and Rose **Bell**, *City Fathers*, London, 1969.

Leonardo **Benevolo**, *The Origins of Modern Town Planning*, London, 1967.

Maurice **Beresford**, *History on the Ground*, London, 1957; (ed)., *Deserted Medieval Villages*, London, 1971.

John **Birch**, *Country Architecture*, 1874.

Alan **Brown**, *The Whiteley Homes Trust*, Chichester, 1992.

G. **Camblin**, *The Town in Ulster*, London, 1951.

R.H. **Campbell** and J.B.A. **Dow** (eds)., *Sourcebook of Scottish Economic and Social History*, Oxford, 1968.

Cardiff National Museum of Wales. J.B. Lowe, *Welsh Industrial Workers Housing* 1775–1875, Cardiff, 1977.

F. **Choay**, *Modern City Planning in the 19th Century*, London, 1969.

Chris **Coates**, *Utopia Britannica*, London, 2001.

Kate **Colquhuon**, *A Thing in Disguise? the Visionary Life of Joseph*

Paxton, London, 2003.

Howard **Colvin**, *Biographical Dictionary of English Architects 1660–1840*, London, 1995.

Nicholas **Cooper**, "The Myth of Cottage Life", *Country Life*, 25 May 1967; "The Design of Estate Cottages", *Country Life*, 8 June 1967.

Maurice **Craig** and the Knight of Glin, *Ireland Observed*, Cork, 1970.

Walter **Creese**, *The Search for Environment*, New Haven/ London, 1966.

E.W. **Culpin**, *The Garden City Movement up-to-date*, London, 1913.

Gillian **Darley** *The Idea of the Village,* exhibition catalogue, Arts Council of Great Britain, 1976.

G. **Darley**, P. **Hall** & D. **Lock**, *Tomorrow's New Communities*, Joseph Rowntree Foundation, York, 1991.

J.G. **Dunbar**, *The Historic Architecture of Scotland*, London, 1966.

Enid **Gauldie**, *Cruel Habitations*, London, 1974.

Mark **Girouard**, *The Victorian Country House*, Oxford, 1971.

Ruth **Glass**, "Anti-Urbanism", *Current Sociology*, No. 4, 1955.

J. **Griscom**, *A Year in Europe*, 1823.

Carla Federica **Gutermann**, *Leumann: Storia di un imprenditore e del suo villaggio modello,* Turin, 2006.

A.M. **Hadfield**, *The Chartist Land Company*, London, 1970.

Mr and Mrs S.C. **Hall**, *Ireland, Its Scenery and Character*, 3 vols., 1846.

Dennis **Hardy**, *Alternative Communities in Nineteenth Century England*, London, 1979.

Dennis **Hardy** and Colin **Ward**, *Arcadia for All: the legacy of a makeshift landscape*, London, 1984, Nottingham, 2004

Eileen **Harris**, with Nicholas **Savage**, *British Architectural Books and their Writers,* Cambridge, 1991.

John **Harris** & Michael **Snodin**, *Sir William Chambers: Architect to George III,* exhibition catalogue, London 1996.

J.F.C. **Harrison**, *Robert Owen and the Owenites in Britain and America*, London, 1969.

M.A. **Havinden**, *Estate Villages* (Ardington and Lockinge), London, 1966.

Dolores **Hayden**, *Seven American Utopias*, Cambridge, Mass. and London, 1976.

H.R. **Hitchcock**, *Architecture in the 19th & 20th centuries*, London, 1958.

James **Hole**, *Homes of the Working Classes with Suggestions for their Improvement*, published under sanction of the Society of Arts, 1866.

M. **Holloway**, *Heavens on Earth*, London, 1951.

W.G. **Hoskins**, *The Making of the English Landscape*, London, 1955.

J.M. **Houston**, "Village Planning in Scotland 1745–1845", *Advancement of Science*, V, 1948.

Ebenezer **Howard**, *Garden Cities of Tomorrow*, 1899, this title edition of 1902.

Christopher **Hussey**, *The Picturesque*, London, 1926; "The Picturesque Village", *Country Life Annual*, 1950.

Tobias **Jones**, *Utopian Dreams*, London, 2007 (includes an account of the Joseph Rowntree Community, Hartrigg Oaks).

F. **Klingender**, *Art and the Industrial Revolution*, London, 1947.

R. Payne **Knight**, *An Analytical Inquiry into the Principles of Taste*, 1805.

S. **Lewis**, *Topographical Dictionary of England, Scotland, Wales and Ireland*, 1837–49.

J.C. **Loudon**, *Encyclopaedia of Cottage Architecture*, 1836, edition with Supplement, 1842.

Brian **Lukacher**, *Joseph Gandy: An Architectural Visionary in Georgian England,* London, 2006.

Thomas A. **Markus**, *Buildings and Power*, London, 1993.

David **Matless**, *Landscape and Englishness,* London, 1998.

J.E. Budgett **Meakin**, *Model Factories and Villages; Ideal Conditions of Labour and Housing*, London, 1905.

Mervyn **Miller**, *Letchworth the First Garden City,* Chichester, 1989

Mervyn **Miller**, *Hampstead Garden Suburb*, Stroud 1995.

Charles **Nordhoff**, *The Communistic Societies of the United States*, 1875, new edition Schocken, New York, 1965

D. **Owen**, *English Philanthropy*, London/Cambridge, Mass., 1965.

Robert **Owen**, *Report to the County of Lanark and A New View of Society*: 1821 and 1813/14 respectively.

Nikolaus **Pevsner** (ed)., *Buildings of England* series; *Studies in Art, Architecture and Design*, 2 vols., 1968.

S. **Pollard**, "The Factory Village in the Industrial Revolution", *English Historical Review*, 79 1964.

Uvedale **Price**, *Essay on the Picturesque*, 1794.

Prince **Pueckler-Muskau**, *Tour in England*, 1832.

J.M. **Richards**, *Castles on the Ground*, London, 1973.

Christopher **Ridgway** & Robert **Williams** (eds), *Sir John Vanbrugh and Landscape Architecture in Baroque England 1690–1730,* Stroud, 2000.

Henry **Roberts**, *Dwellings of the Labouring Classes*, 1850; *Improvement of the Dwellings of the Labouring Classes*, 1859.

Helen **Rosenau**, *The Ideal City*, London, 1969; *Social Purpose in Architecture*, London, 1970.

Royal Commission on the Historical Monuments of England (Lucy Caffyn), *Workers' Housing in West Yorkshire, 1750–1920,* London, 1986.

Thomas **Sharp**, *The Anatomy of the Village*, London, 1946.

Samuel **Smiles**, *Thrift*, 1875.

T.C. **Smout**, "The Landowner and the Planned Village", in Phillipson and Mitchison (eds)., *Scotland in the Age of Improvement*, Edinburgh, 1970.

A. **Somerville**, *The Whistler at the Plough*, 1852.

J.N. **Tarn**, "Some Pioneer Suburban Housing Estates", *The Architectural Review*, May 1968.

J.N. **Tarn** *Five Per Cent Philanthropy*, Cambridge, 1973.

Nicholas **Taylor**, *The Village in the City*, London, 1973.

Nigel **Temple**, *John Nash & the Village Picturesque,* Gloucester, 1979.

Alan Edward **Teulon**, *Victorian Thorney,* Northampton, 2000.

Joy **Thacker**, *Whiteway Colony: the Social History of a Tolstoyan Community,* Stroud, 1993.

W.M. **Thackeray** (pseu. Titmarsh), *Irish Sketchbook*, 1843.

Ulster Architectural Heritage Society, *Illustrated List of Buildings*, 1968-

Raymond **Unwin**, *Town Planning In Practice,* London, 1909.

Colin **Ward**, *Utopia,* London, 1974.

Lawrence **Weaver**, *Country Life Book of Cottages*, 1915 onwards.

Raymond **Williams**, *The Country and the City*, London, 1973.

Tom **Williamson**, *Polite Landscapes: Gardens & Society in Eighteenth-century England*, Stroud, 1995.

John **Woodforde**, *The Truth about Cottages*, London, 1969.

There are also many useful websites, offering detailed and up to date information, especially for those communities still under development; see, for example, those for Euroville (S. India), Findhorn, Poundbury, Joseph Rowntree Foundation and Bournville Village Trust. See also: *Bata-ville: we are not afraid of the future*, written and directed by Karen Guthrie and Nina Pope which links East Tilbury and Zlin, via a journey between the two. www.bata-ville.com.

Index

329

330

335

338

Also available from Five Leaves

Arcadia for All:
the Legacy of a Makeshift Landscape
By Dennis Hardy and Colin Ward
320 pages, 0907123597, £14.99

An exploration of how thousands of people from South-East England and the London hinterland built their own place in the sun, without benefit of local authority planners and building societies.

   Arcadia for All includes dozens of photographs of the "plotlands", and interviews with those whose lives were changed by building their own homes.

"...the authors venture some fresh, practical and civilised answers... with consummate delicacy, skill and fairness"

TIMES LITERARY SUPPLEMENT

"Arcadia for All *presents a powerful basis for a fresh analysis of town planning and building..."*

NEW STATESMAN

"Arcadia for All *affords a mix of fascinating information not easily available elsewhere"*

SUNDAY TELEGRAPH

"Arcadia for All: *(Ward) is the most distinguished British anarchist alive. Ward has spent long decades cheerfully advocating benign and peaceful ways to ignore both state and market. I recommend* Arcadia for All. *We need more books like this..."*

THE INDEPENDENT

Copies are available post free from:

Five Leaves,
PO Box 8786,
Nottingham NG1 9AW

or by credit card on www.inpress.co.uk.

Also available from Five Leaves

Cotters and Squatters: the hidden history of housing
by Colin Ward, 196 pages, ISBN: 0 907123 198, £9.99

Squatters were the original householders, and this book explores the story of squatter settlements in England and Wales, from our cave-dwelling ancestors to the squeezing out of cottagers in the enclosure of the commons.

There is a widespread folk belief that if a house could be erected between sundown and sunset the occupants had the right to tenure and could not be evicted. Often enquiry into the manorial court rolls shows this to be the case. Unofficial roadside settlements or encroachments onto the 'wastes' between parishes provided space for the new miners, furnacemen and artisans who made the industrial revolution, while cultivating a patch of ground and keeping a pig and some chickens. Colin Ward's book, full of local anecdote and glimpses of surviving evidence, links the hidden history of unofficial settlements with the issues raised by 20th century squatters and the 21st century claims that 'The Land is Ours'.

"...presents a wealth of fascinating anecdote, analysis and polemic highlighting the sheer variety of ways individuals have created sustainable homes and livelihoods in nooks and crannies at the margins of society."
REGENERATION AND RENEWAL

"A word of warning. Ward's deadpan style when writing about municipal bureaucracy is as scathing as his sense of humanity is strong. Planning and housing careerists should read it at home, not at work."
ROOF

"Rural squatters are now only a footnote in social history. Their families built themselves a house on some unregarded patch of land... For years, the environmental humanist Colin Ward has tried to rescue such people from the mythology of heritage museums, the indulgences of romantic novelists and the dust of local archives; and to draw lessons from them for today. Cotters and Squatters *is the latest vivid instalment of his campaign."*
THE INDEPENDENT

Copies are available post free from Five Leaves, PO Box 8786, Nottingham NG1 9AW or by credit card on www.inpress.co.uk.